SO-BXZ-072

For John, Dona, +
Karen
with best New
Year's wishes
— Pat
Jan. 1995

FORESTS OF SYMBOLS

PATRICK A. McCARTHY

FORESTS OF

WORLD, TEXT & SELF IN MALCOLM LOWRY'S FICTION

SYMBOLS

The University

of Georgia Press

Athens and

London

© 1994 by the University of Georgia Press

Athens, Georgia 30602

All rights reserved

Designed by Erin Kirk

Set in Linotype Walbaum by Tseng Information Systems, Inc.

Printed and bound by Thomson-Shore, Inc.

The paper in this book meets the guidelines for permanence
and durability of the Committee on Production Guidelines
for Book Longevity of the Council on Library Resources.

Printed in the United States of America

98 97 96 95 94   C   5 4 3 2 1

Library of Congress Cataloging in Publication Data

McCarthy, Patrick A., 1945–

Forests of symbols : world, text, and self in

Malcolm Lowry's fiction / Patrick A. McCarthy.

p.   cm.

Includes bibliographical references (p.) and index.

ISBN 0-8203-1609-1 (alk. paper)

1. Lowry, Malcolm, 1909–1957—Criticism and interpretation.

2. Symbolism in literature.   3. Self in literature.   I. Title.

PR6023.096Z727   1994

813'.54—dc20   93-5337

British Library Cataloging in Publication Data available

To my father,

and to

the memory of

my mother

Contents

Acknowledgments

My work on this book was made possible by the generous financial support of the University of Miami, including a semester on sabbatical leave, two summer fellowships, and travel grants that enabled me to work with the manuscripts and other materials at the Malcolm Lowry Archive. I am indebted to the Special Collections staff at the Main Library, University of British Columbia, where the Lowry Archive is housed, for their assistance. In particular, I want to thank Anne Yandle and George Brandak, whose encouragement and cooperation proved crucial to this project. I would also like to acknowledge the professional assistance of the staff at the University of Miami's Otto G. Richter Library for their help in locating a number of sources.

For permission to quote unpublished materials in the Malcolm Lowry Archive, I am grateful to the estate of Malcolm Lowry and to the University of British Columbia. Quoted by permission of Sterling Lord Literistic, Inc. Copyright by the estate of Malcolm Lowry.

Chapter 4 was published in *Studies in Canadian Literature/ Études en littérature canadienne* (1992) as "Wrider/Espider: The Consul as Artist in *Under the Volcano*," and a version of chapter 3, entitled "Lowry's Forest of Symbols: Reading in *Under the Volcano*," is forthcoming in the *Journal of Modern Literature*. I am grateful to the editors of these journals for permission to reuse this material. I also want to thank Zack Bowen, who read drafts of these two articles, as well as the readers for the journals, all of whom offered pertinent advice.

My interest in Lowry's fiction began in the 1960s, when I took a course from Douglas Day; more recently, as my citations of their work indicate, I have profited greatly from studies by other Lowry scholars. This book also benefited from my conversations or correspondence with Chris Ackerley, Frederick Asals, Sherrill Grace, Phillip F. Herring, Morton P. Levitt, Pierre Schaeffer, R. J. Schork, Paul Tiessen, and Sue Vice, as well as with numerous colleagues and students at the University of Miami, including Peter Bellis, Zack Bowen, Gordon Browning, Laurence Donovan, Ronald B. Newman, Frank Palmeri, and Laura Peterson. Special thanks go to Nancy Grayson Holmes for the confidence she showed in presenting this project to the University of Georgia Press, and to the readers for the Press, Frederick Asals and Paul Tiessen, for their generous assessment of the manuscript and their suggestions for revision.

Finally, I want to thank my wife, Kitty, and my children—Keely, Cailín, and Brendan—for their patience and love during the years I spent writing this study.

A Note on References

Sources are cited parenthetically within the text. For Lowry's published works, Douglas Day's biography, and Ackerley and Clipper's *Companion,* I have used the following abbreviations:

A&C   Chris Ackerley and Lawrence J. Clipper, *A Companion to "Under the Volcano"*

CA/ML   *The Letters of Conrad Aiken and Malcolm Lowry, 1929–1954*

CML   *The Cinema of Malcolm Lowry: A Scholarly Edition of Lowry's "Tender Is the Night"*

CP   *The Collected Poetry of Malcolm Lowry*

DG   *Dark as the Grave Wherein My Friend Is Laid*

GE   "Garden of Etla"

HL   *Hear Us O Lord from Heaven Thy Dwelling Place*

LCH   "Malcolm Lowry: Letter to Clemens ten Holder"

ML   Douglas Day, *Malcolm Lowry: A Biography*

ML/GN   *The Letters of Malcolm Lowry and Gerald Noxon, 1940–1952*

NS   *Notes on a Screenplay for F. Scott Fitzgerald's "Tender Is the Night"*

OF   *October Ferry to Gabriola*

PS   *Malcolm Lowry: Psalms and Songs*
SL   *Selected Letters*
SP   *Selected Poems*
U   *Ultramarine*
UV   *Under the Volcano*
UV/1940   *The 1940 "Under the Volcano"*
WP   "Work in Progress: *The Voyage That Never Ends*"

All other published sources are cited by the author's name, followed if necessary by a short title.

The abbreviation UBC precedes references to unpublished manuscripts and notes in the Malcolm Lowry Archive (Special Collections Division, Main Library, University of British Columbia). References are by box and folder number followed, where appropriate, by page numbers: for example, UBC 14:10, 1–34 for box 14, folder 10, pages 1–34. It should be noted that the box and folder numbers cited here sometimes differ from citations in earlier studies of Lowry, since some materials were shifted from one box to another in the mid-1980s in order to accommodate new acquisitions. I have silently corrected obvious typographical errors in citing Lowry's typescripts.

Gordon Bowker's *Pursued by Furies: A Life of Malcolm Lowry* (Toronto: Random House of Canada, 1993) was published too late to be cited in this study. It should be consulted for further information about Lowry's life generally and his relationship to such people as Conrad Aiken, Paul Fitte, Nordahl Grieg, and Burton Rascoe.

FORESTS OF SYMBOLS

And I would find myself and not an image.
W. B. Yeats, "Ego Dominus Tuus"

Introduction

Richard Ellmann once wrote
that "if we must suffer, it is better to create the world in which
we suffer, and this is what heroes do spontaneously, artists do
consciously, and all men do in their degree" (Ellmann xxiv).[1]
Ellmann was writing about William Butler Yeats, but his words
apply with equal force to Malcolm Lowry, who shared Yeats's
interest in the occult and kept a copy of *A Vision* by his bed,
often reading it aloud (Hadfield 40–41, 70); more significantly,
Lowry resembled Yeats in his concern with the complex ways
in which poems and fictions both reflect, and in turn shape,
their creators' identities. To a large extent, Lowry's works are
essays in self-representation, attempts to create for himself an
identity that generally involves a romantic, if ironic, portrait
of the artist as sufferer (even though cheerfulness, as Lowry
liked to say, is always breaking in). Comparable to Yeats in this
respect—in his effort to forge an identity that is not all image
but contains and expresses his uniqueness—Lowry also shares
the Irish poet's tendency to see himself in relation to a cosmic
web of symbols and circumstances. Douglas Day observes that
"Lowry, seeking to understand the outside world, knew only
to look at himself" (ML 69), but the reverse is also true: if

Lowry understood the cosmos in terms of his inner self, he also understood himself in relation to the patterns and meanings that confronted him when he looked out at the world. What he saw in that world—in particular, his complex entanglement with the texts and symbols that he encountered, and in part created, as he struggled to achieve an authentic vision of his own identity—is the subject of this book.

Lowry is best known as the author of *Under the Volcano* (1947), now widely regarded as one of the twentieth century's most important novels. Most critics, I suspect, would agree with his biographer's description of Lowry as "a great author who happens to have written only one great book" (ML 471). Indeed, the disparity between *Under the Volcano* and Lowry's other works is one of the most striking features of his writing. The only other long work he published during his lifetime was a somewhat derivative apprentice novel, *Ultramarine* (1933), while the bulk of his writings were still in various stages of composition when he died in 1957. Two novels (*Dark as the Grave Wherein My Friend Is Laid* and *October Ferry to Gabriola*) have been published posthumously, along with a collection of stories and sketches (*Hear Us O Lord from Heaven Thy Dwelling Place*). In addition, various pieces—most notably the novella *Lunar Caustic*, which had earlier been published separately—have appeared in a miscellaneous volume (*Malcolm Lowry: Psalms and Songs*). More recent publications include Lowry's screenplay for a cinematic version of Fitzgerald's *Tender Is the Night* and his *Collected Poetry*. Among several works still unpublished are the drafts for yet another unfinished novel, *La Mordida*.

Lowry's failure to complete most of his post-*Volcano* work, and his unwillingness to send it out into the world, provided the starting-point for this investigation. Why would such a talented and dedicated novelist, author of one of the masterpieces of modern fiction, be incapable of duplicating his achievement? We might conjecture that Lowry found the subject of *Under the Volcano* particularly amenable to his treatment, and that he never discovered another such subject; alternately, we might suppose that the long and difficult composition of *Under the Volcano*, which occupied Lowry for a decade, drained him of his creative energies and left him unable to complete another project of the same magnitude. Other explanations could easily be found in Lowry's personal circumstances or in his alcoholism, although it might be observed that he led a frequently unsettled and alcoholic life during the writing of *Under the Volcano* and that his drinking was at least as much a result of his problems with his writing as it was their cause.

Closer to my own position are those critics who have connected the problem Lowry faced to the sort of fiction he was attempting and to his aesthetic theories. William Empson thought Lowry's "life was ruined by a mistaken critical theory" (quoted by Kilgallin, *Lowry* 19), and Matthew Corrigan has attributed Lowry's failure to complete his projected sequence of works, *The Voyage That Never Ends*, to "his congenital inability to understand . . . aesthetic rest or hiatus"—that is, to his lack of "negative capability" (Corrigan 438). Sherrill E. Grace, who regards Lowry's adaptation of expressionistic techniques as a means of reconciling the visionary and solipsistic features of his writing, suggests that the problem with the Consul—the protagonist of *Under the Volcano*—is partly due "to his Expressionist vision and limitations," and she questions "whether Lowry himself managed to control and outgrow his enthusiasm for Expressionism" ("Expressionist Vision" 109). Charles Baxter maintains an analogous position, viewing the Consul's attempt to base meaning on a world divorced from material reality as the source of his dilemma. Lowry too falls into this "idealization process" in his later works, according to Baxter (126), but in *Under the Volcano* the author's recourse to a reality exterior to the Consul (mainly his brother, Hugh) protects Lowry.

Two other critics who have dealt with these issues are Ronald

Binns and Barry Wood. Binns has called attention to "the strains involved in the writing of 'anti-novels,'" noting that Lowry suffered "a crucial underlying anxiety about the merits of the mode" ("Anti-Novel" 95). In a later study, Binns considers Lowry's belief that "an organic work of art, having been conceived, must grow in the creator's mind, or proceed to perish" (DG 154) and argues that this theory contributed to the formlessness of Lowry's manuscripts by making it impossible for him to find a logical stopping-point (*Malcolm Lowry* 72). Wood, who has treated the problems of the later fiction in his essay "Malcolm Lowry's Metafiction: The Biography of a Genre," regards the long composition of *Under the Volcano* as the beginning of Lowry's progressive entanglement with his work, an involvement that led to (and was exacerbated by) Lowry's turn toward metafictional techniques and themes.

Although these explanations are all undoubtedly valid insofar as they help us to understand why Lowry found it so difficult to write, they do not account for Lowry's almost pathological fear of success as a writer—a fear expressed memorably in *La Mordida*, where Lowry refers bitterly to "the bitch-goddess, success" (UBC 14:4, 352),[2] as well as in a poem that begins, "Success is like some horrible disastar [sic] / Worse than your house burning" (CP 214).[3] For Lowry, writing was both his life and a threat to his life: although he seems to have assumed that he could discover or define his identity only through writing, he also feared that the process of composition would leave him without any identity apart from the work. It is for this reason that the profound identification of the writer and the work, combined with the belief that the "organic work of art" must continue growing or "perish," represents such a dilemma: to stop writing and publish a work in its "final" form means to limit one's possibilities, to turn the work over to others who will read it (and the author) in their own limited terms; and if the work "perishes," so, in a sense, does the writer. It is also true that the author who keeps writing does not risk failure:

if Lowry (or his alter ego, Sigbjørn Wilderness) never mails off the final manuscript, it cannot be rejected by a publisher or subjected to a hostile review.[4] Yet the drive toward completion is equally important, for this attempt to create the finished work of art, which ideally would incorporate the author's totalizing vision of himself[5] and of the world, is in large part what prompts the act of writing. It is perhaps significant that in his 1951 "Work in Progress" statement Lowry associated death with an "accepted" manuscript, while in "Through the Panama," which was written at about the same time, death resembles "a rejected manuscript" (WP 74, HL 93). The conflicting desires to continue and to finish—to keep open the infinite play of meanings and yet to create a coherent and balanced work/self that can have significance for others—are present, in various forms, throughout Lowry's work.

Again and again, Lowry's central characters are writers or artist figures who are endangered by writing—their own or that of other people. For instance, Sigbjørn Wilderness, the autobiographical protagonist of *Dark as the Grave* and of several stories, shares Lowry's writer's block and his fear of being exposed as a plagiarist. The entanglement of author and work becomes most complex in "Through the Panama," in which Sigbjørn is writing a novel about a novelist, Martin Trumbaugh, who is returning to Mexico, the scene of his earlier novel (obviously *Under the Volcano*), to write a new book entitled *Dark as the Grave Wherein My Friend Is Laid.* The novel Sigbjørn is *now* writing, he notes, "is about a character who has become enmeshed in the plot of the novel he has written, as I [Sigbjørn/Lowry] did in Mexico" (HL 27). In a later passage from the same story, Sigbjørn wonders if an author can be not merely "enmeshed by, but *killed* by his own book and the malign forces it arouses" (HL 36).

The situation in which Sigbjørn Wilderness finds himself is typical of Lowry's protagonists. In the notes for an unfinished short story, "Ghostkeeper," Lowry imagines his character "standing *within the possibilities* of his own story and of his own life—something like Sigbjørn in relation to the Volcano" (PS 223). More intriguing, perhaps, is Lowry's yet unpublished fragment of a novel entitled *The Ordeal of Sigbjørn Wilderness*, in which the protagonist, during a stay at the hospital, has a psychic experience or dream-vision that eventually would have incorporated all of Lowry's fiction. Sigbjørn is thus both a character in the story and its author—but so, in a sense, is Malcolm Lowry. The fear of being entrapped by a work of fiction runs throughout *Dark as the Grave*, recording Lowry's growing feeling, during his 1945–46 visit to Mexico, that he was constantly reliving events that he had described in *Under the Volcano*. The same fear emerges in a passage from the manuscript novel *La Mordida:* "it was as if *he* were the character, being moved about for the purposes of some other novelist and by him, in an unimaginable novel, not of this world" (UBC 13:18, 59). Lowry's novel *In Ballast to the White Sea*, whose only manuscript was lost in a fire, also dealt with the same basic dilemma, according to a letter from Lowry to David Markson: Lowry wrote that the narrative concerned a young author who reads a novel by a Scandinavian author and is so influenced by the novel that it begins to take over his life and the novel he is trying to write, so that he and his main character become indistinguishable from the protagonist of the earlier novel (SL 255–57). Here, Lowry is dealing with his real (if exaggerated) fear of being exposed as a plagiarist—a fear based principally on similarities between *Ultramarine* and Nordahl Grieg's *The Ship Sails On*—but he also reveals a fundamental existential dilemma in his attitude toward reading and writing.

Although the pattern described here assumes its most sinister proportions in the later, unfinished, works, it is related to aspects of *Under the Volcano*. The Consul is not a transparently autobiographical figure (his politics, for example, are based more on Conrad Aiken's views than on Lowry's), but he resembles, and perhaps caricatures, Lowry in his inability to see anything as having only a literal meaning or as being unrelated to his own situation. In a passage deleted from the final text of the novel, the Consul recalls Baudelaire's description of life as a forest of symbols, adding that the symbols were more fundamental, more *real*, than life itself; in fact, "Life was indeed what you made of the symbols and, the less you made of life the more symbols you got. And the more you tried to comprehend them . . . the more they multiplied" (UV/1940 322). Throughout *Under the Volcano*, the symbols multiply for the Consul and for the reader. For that matter, the reader is, in a very real sense, the Consul's other self, an alternative interpreter of the symbolic text that is the Consul's world of experience. Appropriately enough, the book abounds in other texts that the Consul reads, and misreads, in ways that make them peculiarly relevant to his own situation—for instance, a sign in a public garden, written in Spanish, which really asks that people keep their children from destroying the garden but which the Consul mistranslates as a threat of eviction. Given his penchant for elaborate symbolic interpretations of even the smallest incident, it is unsurprising to find the Consul declaring that "everything is to be found in Peter Rabbit" (UV 175). For the Consul, and at times for Lowry, everything is to be found everywhere, and nothing is devoid of personal and cosmic significance.

The rich, tapestrylike symbolic patterning of *Under the Volcano* is certainly one of the novel's strengths, another being its vivid and compelling portrayal of the Consul's inner experience. The book's elaborate symbolism, including its proliferation of analogies to the Consul's situation, requires that the reader interpret the world much as the Consul does, but at the same time we need to recognize that Geoffrey Firmin's obsessive private readings of events are a major cause of his destruction. Clearly, such a reading of the world is paranoid and solipsistic, for it insists that everything centers on the Consul and that, in a sense, the world is an extension of his identity; yet it proves surprisingly accurate. Binns observes that Lowry's "poetic balancing" of elements in *Under the Volcano* "lends credence to the Consul's perception of an irrational, magical world, since the narrative itself proceeds analogically" ("Materialism and Magic" 179). Frederick Asals even argues that *Under the Volcano* forces Lowry's reader to "suffer" in a fictional world where "serial solipsism is the inescapable condition" ("Revision and Illusion" 105–6). Whatever the implications of this paradox for readers, Lowry himself appears to have found it difficult to maintain his own identity apart from the increasingly convoluted fictions that he attempted to write after *Under the Volcano*. This complex and tortured involvement with his fictions, I believe, further undermined Lowry's sense of his individual identity and contributed to his inability to complete and revise his later works.[6]

In the chapters that follow, I plan to explore the relationship between world (especially the world of written language) and self in Lowry's works, considering not only the way in which acts of reading, writing, and interpretation define a character but also the threat that they pose to his sense of a coherent identity. Chapter 1 focuses on the search for an authentic identity in works written before *Under the Volcano*, particularly *Ultramarine, In Ballast to the White Sea*, and *Lunar Caustic*. Since both *Ultramarine* and *In Ballast* feature autobiographical protagonists who must come to terms with the influence of other writers on their work, this chapter includes consideration of Lowry's obsession with plagiarism. Always insecure about his talent as a writer, Lowry feared in later years that if *Ultramarine* were reissued in its original form, scholars might discover how closely it resembled Grieg's *The Ship Sails On*— a book that indeed influenced Lowry's first book, although certainly not to the extent that he later claimed, and perhaps even believed. Plagiarism involves an intimate relationship between at least two texts, and the theme of plagiarism raises the general question of the extent to which originality is possible:

whether or not a modern writer can really "make it new," to cite Ezra Pound's famous dictum. In Lowry's novels, the plagiarism motif provides us with material for examining questions of literary influence and intertextuality, issues that had a very real and personal meaning for Malcolm Lowry. More generally, the early fiction shows that while a sympathetic identification with another person is essential for the artist's development, the character who sees others as extensions of himself finds his own identity dissolving into incoherence.

The next three chapters focus on *Under the Volcano*, Lowry's one undoubted success, where all of the issues raised in his other works are developed. In chapter 2, I consider the implications of Geoffrey Firmin's (the Consul's) projection of himself onto his world. I see Geoffrey's solipsistic reading of the world in personal terms—for instance, his belief that he is being watched by a range of spies and enemies, including a sunflower—as part of the web of correspondences, or forest of symbols, that ultimately undermines his sense of individual identity. Chapter 3 builds upon this analysis by looking into acts of reading in the novel, ranging from Jacques Laruelle's appropriation of the *sortes Shakespeareanae* technique to the Consul's incessantly personal and symbolic readings of signs, newspaper headlines, and other texts. In chapter 4, the analysis of *Under the Volcano* concludes with an examination of the Consul's role as a figure of the artist, someone who produces texts that bear a curious and ironic relationship to Malcolm Lowry's. Here, I argue that Lowry's portrayal of Geoffrey is significant, in part, because his characterization represents both a serious and complex exploration of Lowry's own situation and an ironic perspective on the dilemma of the self-involved artist.

The remaining works examined here were written in the last decade of Lowry's life, following the publication of *Under the Volcano*. Apart from some short stories, these writings, which include posthumously edited and published works as well as others that remain in manuscript, are unfinished. By this time,

Lowry had conceived an ambitious scheme for incorporating all of his fiction (and even his poetry) into a series of works called *The Voyage That Never Ends*. Chapter 5 outlines that sequence (paying particular attention to *The Ordeal of Sigbjørn Wilderness,* which Lowry planned as the narrative frame for the *Voyage*) and explores its implications for the later fiction. The chapter concludes with an examination of the relationship between Lowry's writer's block and the attempt to assimilate his works into the cyclic vision of *The Voyage That Never Ends*. Chapter 6 examines, first, Lowry's two later Mexican novels, *Dark as the Grave* and *La Mordida*, in which he recorded his sensation of being trapped within the world he had created in *Under the Volcano,* and then *October Ferry to Gabriola,* Lowry's Canadian novel. Day finds in *October Ferry* "Lowry's earnest attempt not, for once, to write about an artist" (ML 438), but as I hope to show, by this time Lowry found it all but impossible to avoid the themes and situations that had dominated his post-*Volcano* fiction.

In chapter 7, I look at Lowry's posthumously published volume *Hear Us O Lord from Heaven Thy Dwelling Place.* This series of stories, which Sherrill Grace identifies as parallel to *The Voyage That Never Ends* (*Voyage* 139), recapitulates the themes of the larger sequence, but Lowry also intended it to serve as a counterpoint to the obsessive self-involvement of the *Voyage* sequence: although "Through the Panama," "Elephant and Colosseum," and some other stories again involve the dilemmas of writers, Lowry described the volume as "a kind of . . . *Volcano* in reverse, with a triumphant ending" (SL 338). Nonetheless, Lowry's visions of paradise are rarer than those of the abyss, and his attempt to achieve a final transforming vision of simplicity and love is far less successful than his earlier work in which, as he wrote his publisher, Lowry told us "something new about hell fire" (SL 80).

The conclusion provides an overview of Lowry's work—in particular, his concept of the artist and his attempt to produce a totalizing vision—in the context of literary modernism. Inadvertently, Lowry's fiction becomes a critique of the modernist enterprise, demonstrating how the modernists' emphasis on organic form and intricate design, as well as their expansion of linguistic and symbolic meaning, poses a serious problem for writers who, like Lowry, have difficulty in maintaining a safe distance from their works. Lowry attained that distance only rarely, and through great sacrifice. Even so, as I hope to demonstrate, his work as a whole testifies movingly to one man's lifelong struggle to portray the visionary artist's complex relationship to the world that he both perceives and half creates.

ONE

The Search for Authenticity:
*Ultramarine, In Ballast to
the White Sea,* and *Lunar Caustic*

In "China," one of Malcolm Lowry's early stories (PS 49–54), the anonymous narrator sets forth one version of a theme that recurs throughout Lowry's fiction: the almost solipsistic rejection of any reality other than one's own. The story's narrator, a retired ship's fireman, has sailed to China during a "terrible war" (presumably the Chinese civil war of the 1920s), but he says that he doesn't "believe in China," which remains for him "like a muddle . . . just like a dream, mostly a queer dream." Despite having been within earshot of the war, he recalls nothing of it apart from what he read in English-language papers, but he can recount in some detail a cricket game played by his crew against men from another British ship. Aware of his limitations and somewhat apologetic about them, he nonetheless states that "the nearer we got [to China] the less I believed in it," since he always regards wherever he is located as *here* rather than *there:* unable to cope with difference, his imagination either domesticates or ignores everything that cannot be readily assimilated within his experience, seeing it only in terms of the values he brings with him. The war's unreality continues even after the game, when he watches stevedores unloading war materiel from the ship. Nor can the narrator imagine that it could be otherwise, as he declares in his concluding address to the reader:

> And here's what I want to ask you again. Haven't you felt this too, that you know yourself so well that the ground you tread on is your ground: it is never China or Siberia or England or anywhere else . . . It is always you. It is always the earth of you, the wood, the iron of you, the asphalt you step on is the asphalt of you whether it's on Broadway or the Chien Mon.
> And you carry your horizon in your pocket wherever you are. (PS 54)

Read for its political content, "China" seems primarily to attack Western (and especially British) narrow-mindedness and insularity with respect to other peoples, including those threatened by the arms exported by capitalist economies. The narrator implies that the feeling that one is "always 'here'" is a particularly British problem (PS 50), and the fact that he is a product of an elite English public school lends credibility to the interpretation of the story as an indictment of British upper-class indifference to the world outside its social circuit. Even so, the narrator has shown his independence of his social class by signing on aboard the *Arcturion* as a fireman and, after some initial resentment by his fellow firemen, winning their approval, so on one occasion at least he has expanded his horizons. The problem is that he has only exchanged one set of prejudices for another: now, like the other firemen, he regards the sailors with contempt, even admitting that "they all looked the same to me, those sailors: they were all sons of bitches and now after so long I can only see them at all through the kind of mist there was then" (PS 53). Perhaps more important than the story's overt political and social theme is Lowry's recognition that the narrator, refusing to confront China as anything except a projection of his own values and experience, never really comes to terms with himself.

Almost precisely the opposite situation develops in another early story, "June the 30th, 1934," which centers on the Reverend Bill Goodyear's train journey from Paris to London. His companion on the train, a disabled war veteran named Firmin, has little in common with his namesake in *Under the Volcano* except that both men smoke pipes. Rather, it is Goodyear who resembles the Consul: in his reflections on "a sort of determinism about the fate of nations" (PS 43; cf. UV 309), in the ease with which he sees events in cosmic terms, and perhaps above all in his involuntary assumption of a fabricated identity, when he tells Firmin that he too served in the First World War and that his brother was killed in the war. Ironically, however, the connection with Firmin that Goodyear creates for himself eventually comes to have real meaning, in part because he discovers that seven years earlier he saw a play produced by Firmin, but mainly because of a series of hallucinatory experiences in which he first imagines that he sees a boy running alongside the train, then sees the boy as his own son, and later envisions him as Firmin in the years before the war. Finally, he realizes, "for a moment [Goodyear] *was* Firmin, the Firmin who had returned from the war, wounded, to discover only that he had to become someone else" (PS 47). By the end of the story, the bare-legged boy running outside the train takes on a universal meaning as innocent youth sacrificed to war: to the First World War, like Firmin, and to its inevitable sequel, foreshadowed by the "Hitler Atrocities" (the "Blood Purge" of Hitler's SA followers on 30 June 1934) and the plans for German rearmament that Goodyear reads about in a newspaper.

One difference between Bill Goodyear and the narrator of "China" is that Goodyear's vision of himself is not narrow, static, and simplistic. On the contrary, it evolves throughout the story, reflecting his sympathetic identification with Firmin and all he comes to represent. For Goodyear, Firmin—who is engaged in mining metals for a German company—is both a victim of war and someone actively involved in making the next war possible. While passing through customs (always a frightening experience for Lowry), Goodyear even doubts his own authenticity, imagining himself as "a dutiable metal" smuggled into England (PS 46–47), but his very uncertainty is an aspect of his growing insight into his relationship to the events and forces around him. At the end, he seems to foresee the next war and to recognize that "man makes his cross," but his inability to act on that insight—and, perhaps, humanity's passive response to avoidable disaster—is symbolized by his falling asleep in the train "as the express screamed on like a shell, through a metal world" (PS 48).

Both "China" and "June the 30th, 1934" are slight pieces, but they show that even at this stage in his career Lowry was intrigued by the way questions of identity hinge on a character's response to external reality. Lowry's more ambitious early works—*Ultramarine, In Ballast to the White Sea,* and *Lunar Caustic*—all focus on artist figures whose attempts to come to terms with their identity depend on their sympathetic identification with other people. In these works, the quest for authenticity succeeds only to the extent that the protagonist is able to face his limitations and recognize how much of his identity is shaped by his expectations and experiences.

In May 1927, two months before his eighteenth birthday, Malcolm Lowry signed on as a deckhand aboard the Blue Funnel liner SS *Pyrrhus,* which spent the next few months sailing from Liverpool to the Orient and back. Aside from youthful wanderlust and a desire to postpone his entry into Cambridge University, one of Lowry's primary motives for the trip was to

establish his independence from his family. The attempt, however, was undermined by Lowry's reliance on his father's help
to secure the position; even worse, his affluent family drove
him to the docks, where his admiring mother told a reporter
that her son was "bent on a literary career" and hoped "to
compose some more Charlestons during the voyage." On his
return, Lowry described the voyage in unromantic terms and
said that he intended "to go on to a university and compose
some more fox-trots and write fiction" (ML 90–91).

Lowry soon began transforming his own experiences into
those of Eugene Dana Hilliot in his first novel, *Ultramarine*
(1933), which he managed to use also as his Cambridge thesis.
Like his creator, Dana goes to sea aboard a freighter in order
to gain the experience he needs to become a writer, but bar-
riers of age, social class, and education stand between him
and the other men. By the end of the novel, however, he has
earned some measure of respect from the crew, and his as-
signment to the stokehold, along with the firemen, marks an
important stage in his initiation into manhood. That process
of initiation, which involves Dana's willingness to accept the
chaotic reality around (and within) him and his immersion
in what Conrad calls the "destructive element," is inseparable
from his discovery or creation of his identity, both as a person
and as a writer. Paradoxically, however, the most important
discovery that he makes in the course of his voyage is that he
cannot write—or, at least, that anything he might write would
be inferior to the life around him.

Ultramarine anticipates several themes and narrative strategies that reappear in Lowry's subsequent works. The direct
introduction of signs, notices, headlines, and other writing into
the narrative prefigures the more elaborate incorporation of
these materials in *Under the Volcano, Dark as the Grave,* and
October Ferry to Gabriola; the alternation between the protagonist's mind and the reality around him recurs in later fic-

tion, as does the use of simultaneous conversations; and as a rather obsessed (and potentially alcoholic) writer who cannot write, Dana is the precursor of all of Lowry's artist figures. Coincidence also plays a significant role in this novel, especially through the reappearance of another ship, the *Oxenstjerna*, onto which Dana projects his own ideals and anxieties. Like several of Lowry's other protagonists, too, Dana is in effect trapped within a fiction at least partly of his own making. Having spent his life living within "inverted, or introverted, commas" (U 17), Dana carries his romantic vision of a sailor's life to sea with him, but is soon forced to question his preconceptions. In chapter 2, for example, Dana switches to the third person to describe his life aboard ship:

> *Seaman*, with bucket on his arm, with singlet on his back, with sweat rag round his neck, Dana Hilliot, nineteen, enters the messroom. In the bucket is a mixture of soda and hot water. To this he adds three drops of lime juice, Board of Trade bottle, price 15s. He then gets his scrubber—Star Brush Company— and his wad—one of the second steward's cast-off singlets—and goes down upon his knees under the messroom table. In this hieratic position he scrubs so energetically that sweat trickles down him and drops now on to the deck, now into the bucket; sweat appears in beads on the metacarpi of Eugene Dana Hilliot. While he scrubs he thinks of Janet . . . (U 53)

The mundane details and self-mockery in this description undermine the romantic image of the sailor-writer, but irony is itself an alternative aesthetic pose that insulates Dana from a direct encounter with the life around him. Throughout much of *Ultramarine*, as Elizabeth Rankin observes, Dana's "tendency to withdraw from present reality often takes the form of withdrawal into art" as he adopts one aesthetic pose after another ("Beyond Autobiography" 59). Dana initially seeks "ready-made myths and structures to explain and excuse his experience," but eventually comes to realize that basing his life on aesthetic models separates him from the real (if unromantic and unliterary) life of the ship ("Beyond Autobiography" 61). He alternately desires acceptance as one of the crew and a special status as an aesthete among hooligans, but never really fits either role. Trying to be heroic, he is shoved aside when he offers to save a pigeon stranded on a topmast and held back, later, when he says he will dive into the bay to save the pigeon from drowning;[1] when he challenges the ship's cook, Andy, to a fight, he learns that Andy has a metal plate in his chin and could be killed by being hit, so that Dana's attempt to assert himself only makes him look like a bully. Nor can he be a writer without overcoming his obsession with his own mind and problems, for in his present state he could produce nothing more than what he calls "that usual self-conscious first novel . . . of which the principal character would be no more and no less . . . than the abominable author himself" (U 96).

What Dana must do, instead, is to recognize and accept his limitations by seeing himself in terms of a larger reality. By the last chapter, he does make significant progress in this direction, even achieving a sort of epiphany in a letter to Janet, where he imagines himself as both connected with and distinct from Andy; there, too, he dismisses his writing with the statement that "you or any woman can do that for me. I don't know a damn thing yet" (U 186). Throughout most of the novel, however, Dana has trouble finding that he has anything in common with the ship's crew, while his constant stream of allusions shows that he conceives of himself in terms that are almost entirely dependent upon myth, literature, and Western culture generally, even when the terms of the comparison are contradictory—as when he sees himself first as Narcissus and then as Christ (U 98–99). Likewise, his largely imagined literary career seems to be mainly a series of appropriations from other authors. His first two names recall Eugene O'Neill and Richard Henry Dana, two writers associated with the sea, while in one extravagant monologue he aligns himself with Masefield, Whitman, Chatterton, and Shakespeare; elsewhere, in addition to epigraphs from Chaucer and Richardson, there are references to a wide range of works, including the Book of Job, Wordsworth's Preface to *Lyrical Ballads*, and Eliot's *The Waste Land*. [2]

Although the self-consciously literary nature of *Ultramarine* seems at times overdone, it is an integral element in Lowry's Künstlerroman, for Dana's mind is the primary means by which Lowry portrays the writer's struggle to find an authentic voice for himself without being overwhelmed by his literary predecessors. That struggle is Lowry's as well as Dana's, and *Ultramarine* makes it clear that its author was acutely aware of his precursors. What Lowry later called "borrowings, echoes, design-governing postures" (SL 115) appear in every chapter, contributing to the portrait of Dana as a young man whose identity is shaped more by what he has read than by the life he has lived. Even his desire to enter the community of sailors and use their language faithfully in a work of fiction is, we discover, largely attributable to the influence of Wordsworth's Preface: " '—a selection of the real language of men—' '—the language of these men—' '—I propose to myself to imitate and as far as possible to adopt the very language of these men—' " (U 66). As Mark Williams notes, "Dana's problem is that, while he wishes to effect a second romantic revolution in literary discourse by shucking off abstractness and reaching the point where language originates in the 'real' activities of ordinary men, his mind is cluttered with literary quotation" (Williams 75).

While Lowry drew upon many authors, however, the works that most directly influenced his own novel were not those by the writers named above but Conrad Aiken's *Blue Voyage* (1927) and Nordahl Grieg's *The Ship Sails On* (1924; English translation 1927), both of which he read while composing *Ultramarine*. Between Aiken's presentation of a fragmented consciousness and Grieg's realistic portrayal of life on

a freighter, Lowry discovered models for his depiction of inner
and outer worlds. He also incurred debts that would resurface
throughout his career.

❧

The general outlines of Lowry's relationship to Conrad Aiken
are clear enough, and the relationship has been discussed by
several critics.[3] Lowry admired Aiken, sought him out, and
arranged to spend summer 1929 with him in Massachusetts,
with Aiken receiving a stipend from Arthur Lowry for acting
as his son's guardian. Aiken resumed the role in 1933, when
Lowry accompanied him and his wife to Spain. During that
trip, however, Lowry's relationship with his literary father became strained, partly by sexual jealousy over Jan Gabrial, an
American woman whom they met in Granada (and who would
become Lowry's first wife) and partly by professional jealousy.
Their relations deteriorated further during a 1937 meeting in
Cuernavaca, where they quarreled over Lowry's drinking and
his openly Oedipal desire to "absorb" and overcome Aiken.
Nonetheless, the two men remained in touch at least sporadi-
cally over the next two decades, speaking of one another with
affection and admiration.

In a 1963 interview with Robert Hunter Wilbur, Aiken said
that "an interesting specimen of [Lowry's] deliberate attempt
to absorb me came to light because there was a page recount-
ing the dream of eating the father's skeleton which comes into
my own novel, *Great Circle*. He was going to put this in his
book and it didn't seem to matter at all that *I'd* had the dream
and written it out" (Aiken, "The Father Surrogate" 39). In
his fictionalized autobiography *Ushant* (1952), where Lowry
is called Hambo, Aiken describes the issue in greater detail,
recalling that Hambo "avowed his intention of absorbing all
he jolly well could of D. [Aiken], in that curious and ambivalent relationship of theirs, as of father and son, on the one
hand, and teacher and disciple on the other, absorbing him

even to the point of annihilation" (*Ushant* 294). When Hambo and D. quarrel over Nita (Jan Gabrial), Hambo declares, "You had eaten your father's skeleton—why then shouldn't I eat yours? Not symbolically only, either, my dear fellow. No, by no means." Comparing himself to a starfish digesting an oyster or a nation invading and annexing another country, Hambo says that he will absorb D. until the older man "will only appear to be echoing me, imitating me, parodying me—you will no longer have a personality of your own" (*Ushant* 352–56).

Lowry's imitation/absorption of Aiken began with his first letter to Aiken, whose closing signature—"te-thrum te-thrum / te-thrum te-thrum / Malcolm Lowry" (SL 4, CA/ML 7)— echoes the sound of the boat's engine in *Blue Voyage*. (A little over two decades later, when Lowry announced that his own use of "Frère Jacques" derived from "twenty years' search for an onomatopoeia for a ship's engine" [NS 44], he indirectly signaled that he had found a replacement for Aiken's "te-thrum.") In fact, Aiken probably influenced Lowry in more significant ways than any other writer. Aiken was to some extent the model for Abraham Taskerson, in *Under the Volcano*; in the same novel, Lowry also mined Aiken's *Blue Voyage* for the Consul's cat puns and his phrase *sortes Shakespeareanae* (*Collected Novels* 83, 86), derived the Consul's theories about historical determinism at least partly from Aiken's discussions of Spengler (A&C 155–56), and re-created a story Aiken told him about an insect—originally a dragonfly, according to Aiken—escaping from the mouth of a cat (A&C 203). A more substantial appropriation was William Blackstone, a seventeenth-century English settler in Massachusetts who "went to live among the Indians," as the Consul puts it (UV 51). Aiken, who had come upon the Blackstone saga in the course of researching Massachusetts history, told the story to Lowry, who quickly claimed Blackstone as his own property (*Ushant* 294). Eventually, Aiken appears to have been willing to relinquish sole ownership of the Blackstone legend (which, coincidentally, he developed in his poem "The Kid," published in the same year as *Under the Volcano*). In *Ushant* he acknowledges the connection between Blackstone and Lowry, calling Hambo the doppelgänger both of Blackstone and of Aiken and referring to Blackstone as "the prototypical Hambo" (*Ushant* 297, 337).[4]

Lowry's technique as a writer was also affected by his admiration for Aiken, whose work involved styles and themes that Lowry found congenial. Richard Costa traces Lowry's use of interior monologue and simultaneous conversations to Aiken, although he notes that earlier examples of these narrative strategies occur in the works of such writers as Flaubert and Joyce (Costa 30–32). The modernist emphasis on consciousness, almost to the exclusion of physical action, could be found in any number of writers, but Lowry had only to look to Aiken to find an example of the inwardness he sought in his own narratives. (When they met for the last time, in 1954, Lowry told Aiken that in *October Ferry to Gabriola*, which he was then writing, "nothing happens. Nothing should, in a novel," to which Aiken responded, "No. No *incidents*" [Markson 224].) It is also striking that in *Ushant* Aiken employs the same complex doubling effect, the same metafictional alternation between the writer's life and his art, that figures so prominently in *Dark as the Grave, La Mordida, The Ordeal of Sigbjørn Wilderness,* "Through the Panama," and other works that Lowry was composing about the same time. In *Dark as the Grave,* for example, Lowry appears as Sigbjørn Wilderness, author of a manuscript called *The Valley of the Shadow of Death* (i.e., *Under the Volcano*), who is currently engaged in writing a book entitled *Dark as the Grave Wherein My Friend Is Laid.* Similarly, in *Ushant,* Aiken is presented as D., author of such books as *Purple Passage* (*Blue Voyage*) and *A Heart for the Barranca* (*A Heart for the Gods of Mexico*), who is currently writing a book named *Ushant,* where D.'s father-son relationship to Hambo is represented through the characterization of the Narrator and Hans (with Elspeth playing the part of Nita, who in turn is Jan

Gabrial). Although Lowry began working on these ideas before the publication of *Ushant,* it seems likely that Aiken influenced his development through earlier conversations in which he and Lowry expounded on their ideas of art's relationship to life.[5]

Douglas Day says that after publishing *Under the Volcano* Lowry was "literally terrified that some reviewer might check his first novel *Ultramarine* out of a library and discover that it contained material stolen from Conrad Aiken and Nordahl Grieg (which it did not) and expose Lowry as a fraud" (ML 26–27). In a similar vein, Tony Kilgallin writes, "The debts to *Blue Voyage* and *The Ship Sails On* plagued Lowry unnecessarily with fears of plagiarism for the rest of his life" (Lowry 92). Neither Day nor Kilgallin cites a specific source for this claim, and while Lowry's letters and Aiken's reminiscences both assert Aiken's powerful influence on Lowry, there is little evidence that he feared being exposed for his appropriation of material from the man who once acted as his guardian—at least not until comparisons of *Under the Volcano* with Charles Jackson's *The Lost Weekend* and other works made Lowry overly sensitive to charges that his work was derivative. It is also difficult to reconcile the claim that Lowry feared being exposed for stealing from Aiken with his own ironic claim actually to have written *Blue Voyage* (but not Aiken's other works) in a previous life (Markson 230; cf. SL 249, 252).

Nonetheless, it is striking that in one of his earliest letters to Aiken, Lowry asked "Do you think I have any individual style of my own or am I unconsciously imitating someone's work?" (CA/ML 12). In 1933, Lowry felt compelled to defend *Ultramarine* against the charge of being overly dependent on *Blue Voyage* by citing the works of Joyce and Eliot as examples of the "greater freedom" of allusion available to the modern writer (CA/ML 41–42). Concerning Lowry's use of Aiken, we might cite not only Eliot's poetic practice but also his observation, in his essay on Philip Massinger, that "immature poets imitate; mature poets steal; bad poets deface what they take, and good poets make it into something better, or at least something different" (Eliot 153). Or, adopting the terms in which Harold Bloom develops his Freudian model of creativity and influence, we could regard Lowry as an "ephebe" struggling to overcome his precursor and thereby to become the father/creator.[6] (In *Ultramarine*, Dana Hilliot seems to imply a similar theory of creation when he says that as a writer he would become both his father and his mother, creating—and thereby controlling—his own creators.[7]) In any event, what is most striking about Lowry's relationship with Aiken is that, almost from the beginning, Lowry felt himself in control, so that by insisting on Aiken's influence on his works he was in effect able to create his literary father. Whether or not "Lowry chose to exaggerate his debt to Conrad Aiken in order to conceal his more essential one to Joyce," as Williams maintains (Williams 81), it is certainly true that Lowry sought out Aiken at least partly because he believed he could dominate their literary relationship by using Aiken's techniques in the service of his own more complex art.

The situation with respect to Nordahl Grieg is quite different. M. C. Bradbrook says that "in general, *Ultramarine* is indebted to Aiken for verbal patterns, whilst the larger structural pattern is indebted to Grieg" (Bradbrook 45), a statement that remains fundamentally sound even though Hallvard Dahlie has demonstrated that *Ultramarine* contains over a dozen passages directly traceable to *The Ship Sails On* ("Lowry's Debt" 43–44). Dahlie argues persuasively that Lowry's borrowings from Grieg are incorporated into "a careful and respectful pastiche rather than mere plagiarism," which shows that Lowry was intent on going beyond "the straight-forward realism that characterizes Grieg's novel" ("Lowry's Debt" 41). Similar situations and themes appear in the two novels, and while many parallels might be explained by the fact that Grieg and Lowry were working in the same genre, it is apparent that Lowry depended on Grieg for at least some of the material that he then transformed in the process of composing his more ironic and experimental Künstlerroman.

We might exonerate Lowry on the charge of plagiarizing from Grieg by noting that many apprentice novels are derivative and that his transformation of Grieg's material in *Ultramarine* justifies his borrowings. Lowry's own judgment, however, was more severe. In 1931 [8] he traveled to Norway to meet Grieg, later claiming somehow to have obtained Grieg's permission to adapt *The Ship Sails On* for the stage; then apparently he lost touch with Grieg for some years. When he wrote to Grieg in 1938, Lowry referred to his sense of identification with Benjamin Hall, the protagonist of Grieg's book, which he said "eventually led me into mental trouble"; he added, "Much of *Ultramarine* is paraphrase, plagiarism, or pastiche from you" (SL 15–16). What he did not mention was that he was well into the writing of *In Ballast to the White Sea*, a novel based on Lowry's conviction of his belatedness with respect to Grieg and intended, it would seem, to resolve the "mental trouble" caused by his identification with Grieg's protagonist.

In later years, however, the relationship only became more troubling. In December 1943 Grieg was killed when the British plane in which he was riding as an observer for the Norwegian resistance movement was shot down over Berlin; six months later, Lowry's shack in Dollarton, British Columbia, burned down, taking with it all of Lowry's single manuscript for *In Ballast to the White Sea*, apart from the few pages now on deposit at the University of British Columbia (UBC 12:14–15). After the fire, Malcolm and Margerie Lowry traveled to Oakville, Ontario, to stay with Gerald Noxon, Lowry's college friend, who worked for the Canadian Broadcasting Corporation. One day Noxon, who had no idea of Lowry's connection with Grieg, happened to mention Grieg's death to Lowry, who had not yet heard the news. Noxon says that Lowry was stunned at the report, which he regarded as part of the "terrible concatenation of events which . . . was starting to spell out doom" (Noxon 20).[9]

The coincidence must have seemed like divine retribution: Grieg had died before Lowry was able to complete the novel that explored his indebtedness to Grieg, and now the novel was gone too. Originally, of course, the possibility of writing a novel based on Grieg's influence on Lowry might well have been one reason for Lowry's insistence on that influence: that is, Lowry could have fostered the idea that he was a plagiarist in order to create a new work out of his anxiety. With Lowry, however, the myth always threatened to become real (as he learned in 1945–46 when he returned to Mexico and found himself constantly involved in situations that seemed to derive from *Under the Volcano*), and it was difficult for him to write about plagiarism and excessive influence without becoming entrapped by his own theme. Moreover, Jackson's *The Lost Weekend*, published in 1944 and soon made into a popular movie, seemed at the time to expose Lowry to the wholly unfounded charge that he stole the idea for *Under the Volcano* from that book, even though (as Lowry explained to Jonathan Cape) he had begun *Under the Volcano* long before *The Lost Weekend* appeared (SL 62). Over the years, Lowry's myth of his plagiarism (mainly from Grieg) assumed larger and larger proportions, contributing to the charge of plagiarism lodged against Hugh Firmin by the music publisher Bolowski in *Under the Volcano* (UV 172) and appearing more directly in the newspaper headlines Sigbjørn Wilderness imagines in *Dark as the Grave*: "Wilderness's Works Written by Erikson [Grieg], or Writer Confesses Old Murder, or Wilderness Admitted Liar" (DG 13).

There are several reasons for the prominence of the plagiarism motif in Lowry's work. His concept of authorship was shaped both by the romantic age's insistence on originality and spontaneity and by the modernist awareness of literary tradition, often in the form of direct allusions to earlier works.[10] Together, these precepts bring pressure to bear on a highly self-conscious author like Lowry, who realizes that since all language is to a large extent dependent on previous language, every writer is in some degree a plagiarist. For Lowry, the pressure was increased by the fact that, as Tony Bareham has observed, he regarded other writers as "authorities" ("The Great Figure" 63–65), and by Lowry's identification of author and work, which means that questions of literary influence are central to the writer's sense of identity.

Lowry's anxiety about potential charges of plagiarism is evident throughout his career. In a series of letters written in 1926 to Carol Brown, a young woman who had aroused his romantic interest, Lowry first claimed to be the true author of a story that had been published by the American author Richard Connell; then, guilt-stricken, he retracted the claim (Grace, "Respecting Plagiarism" 463–64). A 1940 letter from Lowry to Aiken refers to *Ultramarine* as his "first early plagiaristic paen to puberty" (CA/ML 117), and in June 1946 he told his editor, Albert Erskine, that he had considered adding a set of notes to *Under the Volcano*, partly to help explicate the book and partly "to acknowledge in these notes any borrowings, echoes, design-governing postures, and so on," a strategy that appears intended to forestall possible charges of plagiarism (SL 115).

Even more striking is a May 1953 letter to Arabel Porter of *New World Writing*, which was publishing "Strange Comfort Afforded by the Profession." In the letter, Lowry called attention to similarities between his story and an article by Howard Griffin, published in *Twelfth Street* in 1949, but denied that he had read Griffin's article before writing his story (UBC 3:5; cf. Grace, "Respecting Plagiarism" 467). In the course of an unnecessarily elaborate defense, Lowry suggested that the copy of *Twelfth Street* in which he eventually read Griffin's article had been left in the Lowrys' house by Earle Birney, who had a poem published in the same issue; to complicate things further, Lowry claimed that Birney's poem contained a passage borrowed from Lowry. Birney, who became the editor of Lowry's *Selected Poems*, later read the letter to Porter and inserted an angry note, dated 29 May 1969, in the file (UBC 3:15). In his note Birney denies having plagiarized anything from Lowry in either of the two poems he published in *Twelfth Street*, both of which were composed before he met Lowry, and he suggests that any connections between Lowry's work and his own probably involve plagiarism on Lowry's part.

The most dramatic illustration of Lowry's anxiety, however, is what appears to have been his panicked response to a patently false allegation of plagiarism lodged against him in 1935 by Burton Rascoe, an American critic who was then working as an editor for Doubleday. According to an unpublished note by Rascoe,[11] Lowry's agent, Harold Matson, sent Rascoe the manuscript of a novel by Lowry (apparently the ill-fated *In Ballast to the White Sea*), which he hoped to interest Doubleday in publishing, and enclosed a copy of *Ultramarine*. Rascoe immediately charged Lowry with having plagiarized virtually everything in *Ultramarine* from his own story "What Is Love?", a fragment from his unpublished (and eventually abandoned) novel, *Gustibus*, subsequently adding for good measure that *In Ballast*, of which he apparently read very little, was plagiarized from Charles Morgan's 1932 novel *The Fountain*. Rascoe further claimed that Lowry told him that he had considered committing suicide as a result of the accusation and that he admitted having plagiarized *Ultramarine*, recording the confession in a letter (now lost) that was witnessed by Matson.

Rascoe's charges were discovered by Victor Doyen, who discussed them in his 1973 dissertation. Doyen calls the allegation of plagiarism "preposterous" and notes that Lowry's indebtedness to Rascoe was apparently limited to "two [pairs of] quotations—a Latin and an English one—which appear on the same page of Lowry's story" ("Fighting the Albatross" 46).[12] Rascoe was prone to making such charges: in a 1918 essay he had accused Stuart Pratt Sherman of having plagiarized from Jules Lemaître (Hensley 58–59; Rascoe, *Before I Forget* 408), and in his eccentric volume *Titans of Literature* he called *Paradise Lost* "one of the baldest plagiarisms in the history of literature"

(*Titans* 281). Lowry mentioned the accusation against Milton in a conciliatory letter that he sent to Rascoe in May 1940, in which he said he felt somewhat "absolved" by Milton and repeated that *Ultramarine* had not involved "deliberate plagiarism," although the "whole book was hopelessly derivative." With respect to Rascoe's work, however, Lowry maintained that the derivation was limited to the "Latin Quotations" (he forgot about the English ones).

Lowry's purpose in writing the letter, obviously, was to placate Rascoe in case he was still angry over the "plagiarism," the absurdity and falsehood of the charge being less important to Lowry than the fact that even a groundless accusation by a man of Rascoe's stature could do irreparable damage to his career. Moreover, as he neared completion of the 1940 version of *Under the Volcano*, which he mentioned (although not by title) in the letter to Rascoe, Lowry obviously feared that if the book were accepted Rascoe would arise from his past and denounce him as a plagiarist. An even more important factor, however, was that Rascoe had made precisely the accusation that Lowry most deeply feared: the charge that he was not a writer with his own identity but only an appropriator of others' work. In writing *In Ballast to the White Sea*, Lowry had, essentially, already accused himself of plagiarizing from Grieg, and there is a good deal to say for Joe Nordgren's belief that when Lowry wrote *Lunar Caustic* he was trying to stake out his own territory to avoid being overwhelmed by Aiken's influence (Nordgren 130–31). A charge of plagiarism just at that time was apparently more than Lowry could handle rationally.

Throughout the later works, plagiarism recurs as a significant and even intrusive theme. In *La Mordida*, for example, Sigbjørn sees a man who looks like Riley, a fine swimmer whose style Sigbjørn copied so well that he once actually outswam Riley. Sigbjørn's musings lead directly to his conviction that he is only an imitator of another author's writing style (UBC 13:19, 88–89). Later he thinks, "Frankly I think I have no gift for writing. I started by being a plagiarist. Then I became a hard worker, as one might say, a novelist. Now I am a drunkard again. But what I always wanted to be was a poet" (UBC 13:23, 180). Sigbjørn's obsession with his lack of originality also emerges in a line that Lowry considered using at the end of a chapter: "all night long he was attacked by swarms of clichés" (UBC 14:5, 267). Likewise, in the notes for *The Ordeal of Sigbjørn Wilderness*, the protagonist, awakening in a hospital, recalls dreaming about a murder trial that involved the murderer's "identification with a character in a book" as well as his plagiarism of a detective story whose manuscript reveals how he committed a locked room murder (UBC 22:19, 16). Later he overhears a man accusing him of stealing his novel about an alcoholic from *Drunkard's Rigadoon*, the name Lowry assigned to *The Lost Weekend* in his post-*Volcano* fiction (UBC 22:19, 65).

The plagiarism motif also plays a part in some of Lowry's notes concerning the revision of *Lunar Caustic*. He describes a character called the Earl of Thurstaston, a patient at the psychiatric hospital, whose profound sense of identification with a novel by a Scandinavian writer leads him to believe "that he is condemned for the rest of his life to be a character rather than a human being or even a writer," making it impossible for him to "write anything original at all" (UBC 15:12, "Lunar Caustic" ts. 5, 12). Lowry's adaptation of the theme and situation of *In Ballast to the White Sea* underscores the similarities between that work and *Lunar Caustic*, both of which, as David Benham has noted, involve a crisis of identity that leads first to paralysis and withdrawal, and then to a tentative move toward acceptance of the value to be found "in fulfilling the self through interaction with others" (Benham 64–65). In the published version of *Lunar Caustic*, however, the Earl of Thurstaston appears as the sailor Bill Plantagenet, who is a musician rather than a writer, and there is no obsession with a Scandinavian writer (although Plantagenet has a fixation on Melville). For Lowry's treatment of his relationship to Grieg, therefore, we need to turn to whatever evidence remains concerning *In Ballast to the White Sea.*

In one of the rare surviving manuscript pages of *In Ballast to the White Sea*, an undergraduate named Sigbjørn tells his brother, Tor, that instead of a thesis he has been granted permission to write a novel based on his experiences at sea. Unfortunately, he says, "Some other blighter by name of Erikson had my experience before me & has written about it so well I can't ever hope to write my bleeding little masterpiece" (UBC 12:15, ch. 2). The manuscript stops a few pages later, so for a more detailed outline we must rely on a 1951 letter to David Markson in which Lowry summarized the book's complex plot, referring to the main characters by letters (SL 255–57, 261–65). The book's autobiographical hero, A, is a Cambridge student and would-be writer whose sense of "kinship" with Y, the protagonist of a book by a Scandinavian writer whom Lowry calls X, leads him to question his own identity—for "how can A be A when he's Y?" (SL 256). At first, A tries to work out his problems by writing letters to X, but he fails to send them, much as Geoffrey Firmin, in *Under the Volcano*, writes to his ex-wife, Yvonne, but never mails the letter. Eventually, however, A makes a trip to Norway, where he visits his mother's grave, falls in love with a girl who becomes instrumental in his salvation, finds X through an improbable series of coincidences that Lowry claimed were based on his own experience, and discovers even more connections with X. All of this results in a kind of spiritual and artistic rebirth, not only for A but also for X. Lowry added that he had come to regard the recognition of such relationships as a creative force, noting that "Aiken once told me that he considered it primarily an operation of genius. Genius knows what it wants and goes after it" (SL 264). Lowry originally planned for *In Ballast to the White Sea* to be the third, "paradisal," part of a trilogy entitled *The Voyage That Never Ends*, with *Under the Volcano* as the inferno and *Lunar Caustic* as the purgatorio (SL 63, 113–14, 255). After the fire destroyed *In Ballast*, he revised the plan for the *Voyage* sequence, making it a longer and more complexly related series of works that would include a completely rewritten version of *Ultramarine*, incorporating "what can be salved in memory, where it fits in," of *In Ballast* (WP 73). Lowry found it difficult to write anything without conceiving of it as part of a larger scheme, and from the beginning he seems to have intended *In Ballast to the White Sea* as an extension and justification of *Ultramarine*. In this sense, Dana Hilliot's isolation from the rest of the crew and their qualified acceptance of his presence at the end of *Ultramarine* sets forth the pattern that will recur in the life of *In Ballast*'s protagonist, who in turn is the fictionalized author of *Ultramarine* (a role that Sigbjørn Wilderness will fulfill with respect to *Under the Volcano*). In his letter to Markson, Lowry implies another comparison with Dana when he says of A that his "longing for the sea emerges into a longing for the fire of the stokehold, for the actual torment—masochistic, though it somehow isn't, but above all for the fire . . . the fire in which he sees himself purged and emerging as the reborn man" (SL 261). Moreover, by novel's end, A and X are both "realigned on the side of life":

> A's action has also resulted in his salvation by his girl; in effect both the life of the imagination and life itself has been saved by A's having listened finally to the promptings of his own spirit, and acted upon those promptings, rather than the analytical reductions of reason, though it is reason too—by virtue of harmony with the great forces within the soul—that has been saved, and on this note the story and the trilogy closes. (SL 263)

In Ballast shows Lowry for the first time explicitly developing his motif of the writer who believes that he is "being written." This idea reappears often in the post-*Volcano* fiction, but in those works the struggle between life and art is one that Lowry found increasingly difficult to resolve, in part because more and more he found the claims of imagination and experience antithetical to one another. Although it presented itself to Lowry in somewhat exaggerated form, the dilemma he faced is one that has confronted any number of writers ever since the romantics decreed that artistic expression should be based on personal experience. Distinguishing between two romantic and post-romantic myths of the artist as hero—the Ivory Tower myth and the Sacred Fount myth—Maurice Beebe notes that while the Sacred Fount tradition presumes "a close relation between art and experience" and implies "that life and art are interchangeable," this intimate connection may pose a danger for the artist: "The inference of the Sacred Fount myth is that life and art are so closely related that one can exhaust or destroy the other. Because there is only so much life to be lived, that which is turned into art is made unavailable for living" (Beebe 16–17). Lowry's later works provide a perfect example of this theme, even suggesting that for Lowry and his protagonists it is art, not life, that really counts: in *La Mordida*, Sigbjørn's wife, Primrose, finds it necessary to remind him that "we're living this. You're not writing it," to which he replies, "But my god, what earthly point would there be in living it if I didn't write it?" (UBC 13:21, 141). To cite the line from Yeats's "The Choice" which Bradbrook chose for the title of the prologue to her book, Lowry's posthumous fiction seems to show that the writer must choose between "perfection of the life, or of the work."

In Ballast, on the other hand, implies something rather different. There, the young artist eventually works through the web of coincidences and influences that seem to ensnare him, discovering that he can become a writer precisely by realizing his relationship to X, and by extension to all other people. Moreover, while he initially fears the uncertainty and chaos that appear all around him, he ultimately embraces it. A's trip to Norway to meet X is the equivalent of Dana Hilliot's journey from insularity to acceptance, or—as in Rankin's interpretation of *Ultramarine*—from "the aesthetic impulse" to "the creative impulse, the life impulse, which is chaos itself" ("Beyond Autobiography" 61). It might also be related to the journey in Lowry's poem "The Plagiarist," where his persona can make sense of his life only through "certain pamphlets" that he finds as he crawls on his "pilgrimage" to the grave (SP 76, CP 204–5). Ideally, such a discovery would lend order and significance to an apparently chaotic and meaningless existence, and indeed one of the functions of art is precisely to provide a context in which experience can be understood. Yet in claiming the pamphlets as his own, the plagiarist in the poem cedes authority over his identity, aligning it with an arbitrarily discovered pattern rather than entering into a creative relationship with the text.[13] The poem's dark treatment of its theme is far more typical of Lowry than the triumphant conclusion he planned for *In Ballast to the White Sea*, and the loss of the one novel in which he apparently believed that he had discovered a means of resolving the conflict between influence and identity looms as one of the great catastrophes in his life.

In Lowry's work, people are often identified with, or shaped by, texts—those they read and those they create—so there is typically an underlying struggle between life and art. That struggle, in *Ultramarine*, leads to Dana's realization that his aestheticism, including his imitation of authors who do not know "how to swarm up a rope with passion" (U 171), has separated him from the ship's life, and therefore from his own development as a person and as an author. The novel's conclusion is ambiguous, and Dana's future is far from certain, but at least he has largely outgrown the facile literary identities that he once adopted as a substitute for experience and has seen the possibility of entering directly into the life around him. *In Ballast to the White Sea*, on the other hand, places the competing demands of life and art on a more dialectical basis, so that they feed creatively on one another. From this perspective, the apparent resolution of *Ultramarine* is only an early stage of the writer's development into artistic maturity. *In Ballast* would also, ideally, have served as the "paradisal" volume of the *Voyage* sequence that Lowry originally intended as a trilogy, and its successful resolution of the crisis of identity would have been contrasted with the infernal ending of *Under the Volcano* and the purgatorial vision of *Lunar Caustic*. In those works, and in Lowry's fiction generally, the protagonists' status as interpreters of a world that is intricately involved with their own identity is a sign of the difficulty Lowry faced in distinguishing between self and world.

In June 1936,[14] Lowry—"a drunkard recovering from delirium tremens," to cite his own description of Bill Plantagenet (WP 75)—was admitted to New York's Bellevue Hospital for psychiatric observation. Upon his release he first went on a binge, then began writing a story based on his experiences at Bellevue (ML 197). Originally entitled "The Last Address" and later revised as "Swinging the Maelstrom," the story remained unpublished, apart from a 1956 French translation, until 1963, when Earle Birney and Margerie Lowry published a composite of the two earlier versions as *Lunar Caustic*, using the title Lowry settled on in the 1940s. There we find another, more frightening, treatment of the conflict between life and art, world and self, that runs throughout Lowry's oeuvre.

Bill Plantagenet might, in fact, be regarded as a somewhat older and more world-weary incarnation of Dana Hilliot. Plantagenet is an alcoholic sailor who is prone to assume false identities (the opening paragraph implies that he sees himself as a ship, and when he arrives at the hospital he initially gives his name as "the s.s. Lawhill"); he is also an artist figure, although his art is jazz music rather than literature; and he is a well-read man whose experiences often seem inseparable from his reading. While Dana Hilliot's insecurity about his identity is largely a matter of immaturity, however, Plantagenet's alcohol-inspired paranoia makes it difficult for him to have any stable sense either of his own identity or of the real existence of the world around him. Like the Consul in *Under the Volcano*, he is simultaneously too involved in the world and too deeply alienated from it; moreover, his extreme sensitivity to the pain he sees in the world often makes him withdraw from it into alcoholic oblivion. At the end, the asylum appears to have done him little good, for his decision to "strike his blow for the right" leads him only to the washroom of a bar, where he flings his empty whiskey bottle at an obscene wall drawing that symbolizes "all the indecency, the cruelty, the hideousness, the filth and injustice in the world"; then he returns to the bar and curls up in a fetal position in a corner where "he could not be seen at all" (PS 306).

On the level of narrative, *Lunar Caustic* moves from the outside (the streets) to the inside (the asylum) and back outside again, with the final movement into the bar signaling Bill Plantagenet's retreat once more into the confines of his imagination. On another level, however, the story begins with Plantagenet seeing everything as an extension or projection of himself, continues with his gradual acceptance of some other people (even though Dr. Claggart suggests that Plantagenet is still projecting himself onto Garry and Mr. Kalowsky), and concludes with his inability to sustain the more lucid vision that he had in the asylum. Thus, in the beginning, as he moves from one bar to another, he sees an old woman trying to mail a letter which he decides must be for him; he imagines himself "like Ahab stumbling from side to side on the careening bridge" (although his own lack of balance results from drunkenness rather than from high waves); and he enters the hospital screaming "I want to hear the song of the Negroes. . . . Veut-on que je disparaisse, que je plonge, à la recherche de l'anneau [15] . . . I am sent to save my father, to find my son, to heal the eternal horror of three, to resolve the immedicable horror of opposites!" (PS 260–61). His search for his father and son leads him to adopt surrogates: Mr. Kalowsky, who calls himself the Wandering Jew, and Garry, who reminds Plantagenet of the young Rimbaud. Ultimately discharged from the hospital on the grounds that he is not an American citizen and cannot be treated at the taxpayers' expense, Plantagenet maintains his sense of kinship with his adopted family just long enough to send them some oranges and a packet of foreign stamps. Soon, however, the outside world—the "mysterious world over which merely more subtle lunatics exerted almost supreme hegemony" (PS 279)—once again turns surreal: he imagines seeing the other patients, his ex-wife, his parents, and numerous Immigration officials; in a church, he envisions Christ being offered a drink of whiskey (and furtively takes one himself, wondering, "When so much suffering existed, what else could a man do?"); he is "mocked at" by signs, haunted by the sound of the subway. As he withdraws into the bar's womblike security, his regression into an infantile state seems complete.

At the hospital, Plantagenet confronts the benign authority of Dr. Claggart, a friendly but overworked staff doctor who has resigned himself to accepting the meager results allowed by his resources. In "Swinging the Maelstrom," the doctor is Plantagenet's American cousin, Philip, and the fundamentally sympathetic portrayal of this character continues in *Lunar Caustic*, where he is not related to his patient. For that matter, the portrayal of the hospital generally bears little resemblance to the totalitarian environments of the asylums in such works as Ken Kesey's *One Flew over the Cuckoo's Nest* or Marge Piercy's *Woman on the Edge of Time*: there are, for example, no threats of lobotomies or other mind-control operations in *Lunar Caustic*, and apart from an overbearing head nurse who denies Plantagenet his dinner because he washed without asking permission, the staff members are hardly menacing. To the

extent that *Lunar Caustic* is a critique of a political and social
system, its emphasis primarily falls on society's neglect, rather
than its active abuse, of the mentally ill: while other authors
give us stories of involuntary commitment, Lowry's protagonist
seeks out the hospital, postponing his entry until he is sufficiently drunk, but eventually he is expelled, against his will,
for economic reasons. The story's principal focus, however, is
not on the political and economic system but on the alcoholic's
vision of himself, the world, and others.[16]

That vision, as in *Under the Volcano*, involves constantly proliferating symbolic meanings and numerous unstable correspondences between self and world. For Plantagenet, as for the
Consul, virtually everything seems to have a personal meaning. Looking at the sky at night, he sees the stars as "wounds
opening in his being, multiple duplications of that agony, of
that eye. The constellations might have been monstrosities in
the delirium of God. Disaster seemed smeared over the whole
universe" (PS 267). Later, watching Claggart's response to a
puppet show, he sees the doctor as a god watching man go
wrong, and he imagines himself as having "voyaged downward
to the foul core of his world," to the asylum, where he finds
"the true meaning underneath all the loud inflamed words, the
squealing headlines, the arrogant years" (PS 279). Plantagenet's mind is filled with terrifying and obsessive visions drawn
in large part from Melville, Poe, Rimbaud, James Thomson,
and other writers who have dealt with the descent into the
abyss; yet despite his Blakean insistence that "the road of ex-
cess leads to the Palace of Wisdom" (PS 295), his overwrought
imagination achieves only brief, grotesque glimpses of the
truth. Moreover, his understanding is severely limited by his
tendency to project his own situation onto other people and
onto the universe as a whole, so that—again, like the Consul—
he often fails to recognize any clear distinction between what
he sees when he looks inside and outside himself.

What makes life momentarily "tolerable" for Plantagenet,

he realizes, is the "comradeship of his two friends" (PS 269): Garry, a delusional boy who was committed to the asylum after slitting a little girl's throat with a broken bottle, and Mr. Kalowsky, an elderly Jew committed by his brother for "threatening people's lives and turning on the gas" (PS 292). Although he eventually recognizes Garry as "a part of himself" and Mr. Kalowsky as "a part of the shadowy meaning of his destiny" (PS 299), Plantagenet's sympathy is not merely self-projection but stems at least partly from a real concern for other people who have difficulty in dealing with the world. Particularly interesting is his involvement with Garry, whom Lowry called "Plantagenet turned inside out" in his *Lunar Caustic* notes (UBC 15:12, "Lunar Caustic" ts. 2). Both are types of the artist, and Garry holds a particular interest as the one person in the story who seems to believe firmly in the healing powers of language. (When he first meets Plantagenet, Garry tells him, "I'll tell you stories, then you'll get better" [PS 263], and later, when he teaches semaphore code to another patient, Garry seems to have therapy in mind again.) Both Garry's stories, which almost inevitably conclude in a vision of structural collapse, and Plantagenet's interpretations of the stories are desperate—and for the most part unsuccessful—attempts to convert chaos into order, to discover meaning within the absurdity of their existence. Chaos, however, is everywhere: physically, in such repeated images as the broken barge; socially and politically, in newspaper headlines ("Thousands Collapse in Heat Wave. Hundreds Dead. Roosevelt Raps Warmongers. Civil War in Spain" [PS 260]) and New York signs ("Business as usual during alterations: Broken Blossoms: Dead End: No cover at any time. World's loveliest girls. Larger, more modern" [PS 305]); psychologically, in the patients' tormented visions. Ultimately, there seems to be little hope of genuine recovery for any of the patients.

As Beverly Rasporich has noted, "in his purgatorial quest, [Plantagenet] is not only searching for an honest identification of this world, he is also seeking to decipher the relation between man and his god" (Rasporich 59). That quest is embodied in another aesthetic motif: Plantagenet's "hysterical identification with Melville" (SL 24–25). From the fact that the doctor's name is Claggart, we might expect him to resemble the false witness of *Billy Budd*, but far from envying Bill Plantagenet (much less framing him for mutiny), Dr. Claggart tries his best, within his limited resources, to help Plantagenet recognize his problems and gain some control over his life. The story's one direct reference to *Billy Budd* is a note scribbled by Plantagenet while the doctor talks with one of the nurses:

> Maison de Pendu. For Billy Budd.
> a house where a man has housed himself.
> a house where a man has hanged himself.
> (PS 295)[17]

Bradbrook observes that in this note, Plantagenet "casts the doctor for the role of villain" (Bradbrook 51). He also, of course, portrays himself as both a suicide and a martyr, confirming his identification with a former member of his band whom he earlier imagined seeing hanged outside the hospital (PS 267). The fact that Plantagenet sees Dr. Claggart and himself in such complex terms is a measure not merely of his paranoia but also of Melville's deep impress on his imagination. Again, as in *Ultramarine*, the point is that too great a reliance on literary models of experience makes it difficult to see events in their true light. Since Plantagenet resembles Billy Budd no more closely than Dr. Claggart does his Melvillean namesake, Plantagenet's attempt to forge a parallel between the story and his experience shows how far he is from accepting responsibility for his own life.[18]

Moby-Dick may exert an even more powerful hold on Plantagenet's imagination. From his early vision of himself as "Ahab stumbling from side to side on the careening bridge" (PS 260), his identification with the novel and its author is apparent. Significantly, he is eager to reshape experience to fit it into a Melvillean pattern. When Garry tells a story about a black whale, Plantagenet asks, hopefully, "Are you sure it wasn't a white whale"; then, despite Garry's insistence that the whale was black, he plays "four jagged chords," including "one for the Pequod [and] one for the whale, white or black it didn't matter which" (PS 284–85). Once again, Lowry's protagonist tends to substitute art for life, literature for personal experience.

Plantagenet's fascination with Melville began at Cambridge, was sufficiently strong to bring him to America (PS 266–67), and intensified when he and Ruth, his wife, took a cruise from New York to New Bedford on the *Providence*—a cruise also taken by Lowry and Jan Gabrial. On that trip, "every beat of the engine which took them nearer to New Bedford, nearer to Herman Melville, was also taking them nearer to their own white whale, their own destruction" (PS 301). In comparing the breakup of his marriage to Ahab's doomed quest for the whale, Plantagenet romanticizes and exaggerates the "tragedy" of his life, just as he romanticizes Garry's pathetic stories by comparing their images to the tormented symbolism of Rimbaud's poems (PS 293–94). The allure of Melville and Rimbaud, and perhaps of such jazz musicians as Bix Beiderbecke, stems partly from their status as misunderstood, neglected artists in conflict with their societies, visionaries whose true value can be seen only after their deaths. Yet when he identifies himself and Garry with the romantic (or post-romantic) figure of the alienated artist, Plantagenet only reinforces his own estrangement from everything outside his circle of vision. Neither his Rimbaud-like sensory derangement nor his Melvillean obsession is enough to turn Plantagenet into a true artist: for one thing, his numerous allusions reveal how derivative his concept of the artist is, and for another, his tendency to see the world largely as an extension of himself makes him unable to sustain the human sympathy that Lowry, at least, found inseparable from artistic creation. Significantly, when Plantagenet attributes his failure as a pianist to his small hands, which are not big enough to stretch over an octave, Dr. Claggart shifts the focus to the real problem: "You didn't leave Ruth because your hands couldn't stretch an octave," he observes, adding, "Perhaps it was your heart you couldn't make stretch an octave" (PS 266).

It is interesting to speculate about what Lowry might eventually have done with *Lunar Caustic*, had he lived to complete the grand design of *The Voyage That Never Ends*. His "Work in Progress" statement reveals that he hoped to integrate the novella more fully into the *Voyage* sequence, making it complementary both to *Ultramarine* and to *The Ordeal of Sigbjørn Wilderness;* moreover, Lowry claimed, the revised *Lunar Caustic* "will be seen to lead up inevitably to Under the Volcano" (WP 73, 76). Other notes indicate that this version, which would have been 100 to 150 pages longer than the current text, would also have been more complexly related to the rest of the series: the Earl of Thurstaston, for example, could be regarded as the author of *Ultramarine*, and perhaps of some other works in the *Voyage*. At the same time, the revision would have incorporated more details from Lowry's life, including his fear of having contracted a venereal disease from a drunken encounter with a homosexual (ML 194), his half-serious conception of himself as "a character rather than a human being or even a writer," and his guilt over the suicide of his college friend Paul Fitte (UBC 15:12, "Lunar Caustic" ts. 1, 3, 5, 10–11).[19]

It seems doubtful that all of this would have resulted in a substantial artistic advance over the text that we now have, especially since the progressive entanglement of life and art was precisely the problem that Lowry came to find most difficult to resolve. Moreover, in the process of making Bill Plantagenet into the more patently autobiographical Earl of Thurstaston, Lowry risked upsetting the story's precarious balance between sympathy and judgment. Finally, in the process of incorporating the story into the *Voyage* scheme, Lowry appears to have planned on expanding the story's meaning without directly confronting its real weakness: its inadequately developed narrative line. Yet in some respects *Lunar Caustic* is the most significant work Lowry wrote before *Under the Volcano*, the work in which he most clearly confronted his demons and showed, through the alcoholic's blurred vision, the fearful world of symbols that Bill Plantagenet substitutes for human contacts. When he returns to his subject in *Under the Volcano*, the vision is both more intense and more frightening.

TWO

The Law of Series: Correspondence
and Identity in *Under the Volcano*

In a passage deleted from the final draft of *Under the Volcano*, the Consul stands in the Farolito—the cantina where he will be killed—considering, as Douglas Day puts it, "the antithetical natures of real life and symbolic life" (ML 273):

> Life was a forest of symbols, was it, Baudelaire had said? But, it occurred to him, even before the forest, if there were such a thing as "before," were not there still the symbols? Yes, before! Before you knew anything about life, you had the symbols. It was with symbols that you started. From them you progressed to something else. Life was indeed what you made of the symbols and, the less you made of life the more symbols you got. And the more you tried to comprehend them, confusing what life was, with the necessity for this comprehension, the more they multiplied. (UV/ 1940 322) [1]

The Consul's reference, of course, is to the first quatrain of Charles Baudelaire's sonnet "Correspondances":

> La nature est un temple où de vivants piliers
> Laissent parfois sortir de confuses paroles;
> L'homme y passe à travers des forêts de symboles
> Qui l'observent avec des regards familiers. [2]

For Baudelaire, as Stanley Burnshaw has noted, the existence of "vertical correspondences between the event visible to human beings and its corresponding event in the invisible world" was a source of power: "no longer just a maker of rimes," the poet "is an explorer and a wielder of vast, unsuspected powers, whose discoveries can literally bring heaven down to earth" (Burnshaw xxi). In Lowry's works, however, this magical power is also a fearful, potentially destructive, uncontrollable force. Lowry's analysis of the relationship between life and art, self and world, is nowhere more complex than in *Under the Volcano*, where the world often seems to be a great book whose symbols take precedence over life itself. At the same time, the Consul's acts of interpretation appear at least partially responsible for creating the cosmic web of meaning in which he finds himself entangled. Reading the symbols of the outside world, the Consul inevitably discovers some relationship to his own situation; but since he cannot control the multitude of meanings engendered, in part, by his readings, the correspondences that he finds between himself and the world ultimately undermine his sense of his own identity. If the three bullets fired into him by the Chief of Rostrums are the most obvious cause of the Consul's death, a contributing factor is the unstable, ambiguous, pluralistic nature of the language through which he attempts to come to terms with the correspondences between self and world.

One of the most striking elements of *Under the Volcano* is its reliance on coincidences and correspondences less suggestive of random occurrence than of the operations of a partly self-imposed fate. Of course, there is no reason why Yvonne's postcard, written nearly a year earlier, should not go astray and finally reach Geoffrey Firmin on the day of Yvonne's unexpected return (UV 192–93),[3] or why the volume of Elizabethan plays that he borrowed from Geoffrey should not have been returned to Jacques Laruelle on the anniversary of the Consul's death (UV 27), or for that matter why the Peter Lorre version of *Las Manos de Orlac*, which was playing at the cinema exactly one year earlier, should not have returned on 2 November 1939 (UV 24). Even so, coincidences like these occur with startling frequency, and their effect is reinforced by the fact that the novel's opening chapter takes place exactly one year after the remainder of the book, making the prologue also an epilogue. The first chapter's many foreshadowings, or prefigurations, of "later" events are, from another perspective, memories; likewise, the reader who sees in a subsequent chapter a recollection of a phrase or image from chapter 1 must recognize that within the novel's fictional chronology what the reader "remembers" will not occur for another year. Betsy Martinez perceptively remarks that "having read the first chapter, the reader is propelled through the remaining chapters by familiar motifs leading toward terminal consequences already implied. The course of events has been established within the reader's memory, which causes later events to be seemingly recalled upon first perusal" (Martinez 151–52). What Martinez calls the book's "profound sense of closure" (Martinez 142) is equally suggestive of the network of symbolic correspondences surrounding the Consul.

Nor are these apparently coincidental entanglements altogether confined to the events of Lowry's fictional world. Take, for instance, Geoffrey's casual association with Leon Trotsky. Their short beards introduce a physical similarity between these two stateless men, each a former official of a European government who would suffer a violent death in Mexico. In chapter 12, someone at the Farolito calls out that Geoffrey's real name is Trotsky (UV 358), and although Trotsky's murder in Mexico City will not take place until August 1940, nearly two years later, the Trotsky connection is obviously an omen of the Consul's death—just as, on another level, the Consul's fate prefigures Trotsky's assassination. Moreover, in the passage in which he is identified as Trotsky, the Consul himself argues that his name is William Blackstone (a claim soon undermined by his possession of Hugh's telegram); recalling that Trotsky's real name was Bronstein and that he took his nom de guerre from a forged passport, we might see a connection between the Consul's drunken attempt at adopting another name and Trotsky's more successful one. Since Trotsky was Jewish and Geoffrey is subjected to anti-Jewish accusations and threats at the Farolito, the analogy with Trotsky might also foreshadow the persecution of Jews during World War II. In relation to the Spanish Civil War, to which *Under the Volcano* frequently refers, Trotsky's murder by a Stalinist agent parallels the communists' betrayal of their Trotskyite and anarchist allies—an association made all the more relevant by Hugh Firmin's involvement with the doomed Spanish Loyalist cause. Finally, if we remember that Jacques Laruelle's motive in borrowing Geoffrey's collection of Elizabethan plays was to take notes for "a modern film version of the Faustus story with some such character as Trotsky for its protagonist" (UV 28), we can see another connection between the Faust-like Consul and Trotsky.

Although Trotsky is mentioned directly only twice in *Under the Volcano*—once each in the first and last chapters—the Consul's entanglement with Trotsky is sufficiently complex to justify the assertion that Trotsky's murder "casts a shadow of tragic inevitability over the novel" (A&C 49). The numerous analogies and coincidences found throughout the work enrich its narrative texture, generating meanings which greatly expand the thematic significance of the novel's events. Lowry contended that "the book was so designed, counterdesigned and interwelded that it could be read an indefinite number of times and still not have yielded all its meanings or its drama or its poetry" (SL 88), and in fact new patterns, correspondences, and subtleties may appear with any reading. Lowry's revisions of *Under the Volcano* necessarily included many cuts and clarifications of passages, but the main thrust of the revision process involved an expansion and deepening of significance that depended on an increasingly elaborate range of analogies to the book's situation and characters. According to Day, Lowry "had in him that which prohibited him from stopping at the thing in itself; the thing had to mean, had to relate to another thing, and so on until order and symmetry were lost in a maze of arcane correspondences and brilliant conceits" (ML 274). Lowry's friend Gerald Noxon is even more emphatic: Lowry's world, he says, "was one of extraordinary superstition. Everything that happened was a portent, and a fearful one usually" (Noxon 19). Yet it should be emphasized that in *Under the Volcano* Lowry was largely in control of his own tendency to expand and complicate the novel's forest of symbols, and took care to treat his elaborate correspondences both seriously and ironically, both as an aspect of "reality" (whether that reality reflects causation, Paul Kammerer's Law of Series,[4] Jungian synchronicity, J. W. Dunne's concept of serial time, or some other system) and as a product of the Consul's overwrought imagination.

Neither of the book's references to Trotsky can be attributed directly to Geoffrey's mind, but they are among the numerous circumstances and analogies framing what Stephen Tifft calls the Consul's sense of his "pernicious interconnectedness." As Tifft points out, "When events ratify [the Consul's] tragic apprehensions, he is incapable of determining whether those events are self-fulfilling prophecies or confirmations of a transcendent necessity—in other words, whether he is governed by internal or external necessity" (Tifft 67–68). Much the same dilemma faces the reader whose inclination to discount Geoffrey's self-involved, and apparently paranoid, interpretations of the world is countered by evidence that these interpretations are often consistent with the book's fundamental logic. The "meaningless correspondences that might be labelled: 'favorite trick of the gods'" (UV 16), as Laruelle calls them, are an informing presence in *Under the Volcano*, although certainly the Consul's predisposition to read symbolic meanings into every occurrence both extends the range of correspondences and leaves their status open to debate.

The narrative and thematic structure of *Under the Volcano* relies heavily on repeated or interlocking elements that tend to confirm the Consul's habit of deriving meaning through analogy. A familiar example is Laruelle's burning of Geoffrey's letter at the end of the opening chapter. Lowry observed that this passage "is poetically balanced by the flight of vultures ('like burnt papers floating from a fire') at the end of III, and also by the burning of the Consul's MSS in Yvonne's dying dream in XI" (SL 70; see UV 93, 336). Christine Pagnoulle goes one step further, noting a connection with the Consul's dying vision of universal conflagration: "the world itself was bursting, bursting into black spouts of villages catapulted into space, with himself falling through it all, through the inconceivable pandemonium of a million tanks, through the blazing of ten million burning bodies, falling into a forest, falling—" (Pagnoulle 48; UV 375). In this final scene, the manuscript has become the world, and the Consul's vision, which links his death to the mass destruction of the impending world war, also implies a return to the primordial chaos from which his manuscript would ideally have extracted a principle of order. The pandemonium or infernal chaos into which Geoffrey rapidly descends, from his appearance at the Farolito to his fall into the barranca, works on several levels here, implying a lapse into a totally undifferentiated state that obliterates all sense of identity.

Another example of the way elements are balanced within the book's narrative scheme is the coincidental appearance of various characters at different points in the text. In chapter 1, Laruelle recalls Geoffrey's suspicion that he is being spied on by such characters as "a man in dark glasses" and "a bald boy with earrings swinging madly on a creaking hammock" (UV 30). It is perhaps too much to assume that the appearance in later chapters of a man in dark glasses (UV 51, 211, 273) constitutes proof that he is one of the "spiders" feared by the Consul—although, at the same time, there is no real evidence to the contrary. What is probably more relevant is that the man is one of the Consul's doubles: he first appears right after Geoffrey puts on his own dark glasses, and Yvonne confirms the association for us by almost taking the other man's arm instead of Geoffrey's. Arnt Jakobsen asks, "Are the Consul's supposed followers real, or are they merely figments of a paranoid brain?" (*Introduction and Notes* 10). The Consul might be paranoid about other matters, but as Lowry told Clemens ten Holder, these "supposed followers" are quite real; Lowry also noted that he reintroduced the bald boy with earrings in chapter 8 (UV 240) so that Hugh could see him out of the bus window, thereby not only proving the bald boy's reality but also confirming Hugh's role as "the doppelgänger of the Consul" (LCH 49–50). If there is no reliable evidence to support Geoffrey's conviction that these people are pursuing him, it is clear, at least, that he has not simply manufactured their existence.[5]

On the other hand, the reappearance of such characters tends to reinforce the Consul's belief that they are all there to watch him. The old woman from Tarasco who keeps a chicken on a cord—a character first seen playing dominoes in the Bella Vista bar at 7 A.M. and last glimpsed at the Farolito twelve hours later—is obviously a crucial presence in the novel. To Yvonne she seems "like an evil omen" (UV 51), yet she is not directly or intentionally menacing. On the contrary: in chapter 12 she warns Geoffrey against the various "chiefs" who threaten him, and stands by him "loyally," as he imagines (UV 367, 371)— although it might be added that her loyalty, if that is what it is, undoubtedly owes something to the tequila he buys her (UV 346) as well as to her sympathy for him. Even so, her presence at the beginning and end of Geoffrey's final day, always in the same darkened rooms where he has gone to drink in solitude, is ominous. (In this regard we might note Perle Epstein's supposition that the old woman is an occultist whose dominoes are used to read the future by gematria [Epstein 80].) Yvonne's premonition about the old Tarascan woman is reinforced in chapter 9, at the bullring, when she looks into her compact mirror, first seeing Popocatepetl behind her. It seems a particularly bad sign that she is unable to see the "female" volcano, her mirror confirming Geoffrey's tragic isolation, since he is associated with the "male" volcano. Suddenly, as she is about to shut the mirror, Yvonne imagines "that, not Popocatepetl, but the old woman with the dominoes that morning, was looking over her shoulder" (UV 256–57). The volcano is an inverted image of the inferno or abyss, which is reflected more directly in the Farolito's "numerous little rooms, each smaller and darker than the last" that recall the ever-narrowing circles of Dante's hell (UV 200). In one of those rooms, "one of the boxes in the Chinese puzzle" (UV 343), the Consul will find the old Tarascan woman, as if to confirm Yvonne's intuition that the woman represents the Consul's fate.

Also present both at the Bella Vista and at the Farolito is Weber, an American who claims to have been in the French Foreign Legion and is now involved in smuggling guns into Mexico, probably for the Union Militar. Hugh met Weber in El Paso, quarreled with him about politics, then traveled with him into Mexico, first by cattle truck and then by airplane. Dale Edmonds believes that in chapter 12, when Weber hears the name "Firmin," he realizes who Geoffrey is (as Edmonds notes, "Hugh must have told Weber about his half-brother"), but that Weber refuses to intervene, and thereby contributes to the Consul's death ("Immediate Level" 74). Even if we do not accept Edmonds's argument that the Consul is in fact an antifascist "spider" killed by "the *fascistas* [who] seize upon a number of pretexts to hasten the death of one detrimental to their interests" ("Immediate Level" 81), he is undoubtedly right to stress that on the "immediate level" Weber is closely linked with the Consul's murderers. In another sense, however, Weber is also one of the Consul's many doubles (a role underscored by his association with Hugh), and his failure to act to protect the Consul mirrors the Consul's own unwillingness to save himself.

The scene at the Bella Vista bar in chapter 2, where we first hear the Consul's actual voice (as opposed to his words in the letter to Yvonne that Laruelle reads in chapter 1), sets up his relationship to Weber by first presenting both men as voices: Yvonne, outside the bar, first hears the Consul speaking to the bartender, Fernando, and then "yet another voice" speaking to someone about "—just a bunch of Alladamnbama farmers!" (UV 43). Weber's speech, which alternates with the Consul's at various points in the chapter (UV 47, 48, 51)— emerging as if from nowhere, like the voices of Geoffrey's familiars—is loud, arrogant, and often violent. Lowry called Weber's voice "a contrapuntal device . . . that at the same time is a motif of fate," adding that "he almost seems to answer Yvonne's and the Consul's voice and make comment on their situation, though Weber is in the next room and they don't know him from Adam" (LCH 47). The voice's emphasis on death ("They plugged 'em too. They don't miss it. They shoot first and ask questions later. You're goddam right") echoes the Consul's own concern, in his opening words, with the corpse that "will be transported by express." Both the Consul's language and Weber's seem to foreshadow the Consul's violent end, and Weber, as one of the Consul's other voices, may well represent his more destructive side. In any case, it was probably Weber's symbolic role to which Lowry referred when he said that although Weber "is not very important, in one way . . . he has to be there, bracing something far down within the substructure of the whole" (LCH 46). That "something" is the web of destiny, woven out of correspondences, that surrounds the Consul.

That Hugh, the man in dark glasses, and Weber are all

doubles for the Consul is consistent with the narrative structure of *Under the Volcano*, which presents us with numerous
analogies to the Consul's situation. Lowry encouraged this sort
of interpretation, both in his letters and in the way in which he
structured the text. In his letter to Jonathan Cape in defense
of the book (SL 57–88), Lowry said that Geoffrey, Yvonne,
Hugh, and Laruelle are "aspects of the same man, or of the
human spirit." Among other figures associated with the Consul, Lowry pointed to the drunken rider of chapter 1, "the man
with bloody hands" on the poster for *Las Manos de Orlac*, the
infant Horus, "the madman futilely and endlessly throwing a
bicycle tire in front of him [and] the man stuck half way up the
slippery pole" in chapter 7, and the dying Indian of chapter 8.
Moreover, a premonition of the Indian's death, and therefore of
the Consul's, may be found in the dead man Geoffrey imagines
seeing in the pool.

Other doubles include the many animals that roam throughout the novel. The insect that escapes from the mouth of Mr.
Quincey's cat (UV 140) represents the possibility of Geoffrey's
salvation (but only if he "unceasingly strives upward," as the
epigraph from Goethe's *Faust* reminds us). On the other hand,
Hugh's warning about trying to stop an armadillo from bur-
rowing into the ground—"It'll not only never come back,
Yvonne, but if you try to stop it it will do its damndest to pull
you down the hole too" (UV 113)—refers obviously to the dangers inherent in trying to rescue a self-destructive man like
Geoffrey. The Consul's self-destructiveness is also represented
by the scorpion that stings itself to death (UV 187–88, 338),
while his entrapment by circumstances beyond his control is
reflected in the bull who, "drawn, lured into events of which he
has no real comprehension," becomes "hopelessly entangled"
in lassoes at the bullring (UV 258, 259). The Consul's declaration that "everything is to be found in Peter Rabbit" (UV 175)
sets up a parallel to Beatrix Potter's rabbit, whose eviction from
Mr. McGregor's garden mirrors the Consul's fall from grace

and the threat posed by godlike authorities. *Peter Rabbit* also contains a temperance lesson—Peter overeats, gets sick, and has to be put to bed—which connects the story both to the Consul's alcoholism and to the Aztecs' use of the rabbit to symbolize drunkenness (see A&C 416). The association of rabbits with intoxication is one reason why, in chapter 12, Geoffrey imagines that the rabbit in the Farolito is one of the many "phantoms of himself" that "correspond . . . to some faction of his being" (UV 362). The Consul is also projected onto the world through the horse that he releases (UV 373). As a representation of his soul's "destructive force" (SL 85), the horse stands in opposition to the eagle that Yvonne frees (UV 320): the eagle's upward flight suggests the transcendence of the material world that the Consul has desired but not achieved, his own situation being more precisely imaged by the horse's wild plunge back into the dark wood of error.

Among the other animals that represent aspects of his mind or situation is the bird Geoffrey identifies as a coppery-tailed trogon: the bird's "exact name," he adds pedantically, is "*Trogon ambiguus ambiguus . . .* the ambiguous bird!" (UV 74–75). Geoffrey implies one point of correspondence between the ambiguous bird and himself when he calls the bird "a solitary fellow." The bird's significance might also lie in its redundant and ambiguous name, which is paralleled by the uncertainty about the bird's real identity: it is possible, and even likely, that Geoffrey and Yvonne are not looking at *Trogon ambiguus ambiguus* at all, since Yvonne claims that the bird they see is a cardinal, and since the ambiguous bird's habitat normally does not extend to Mexico (A&C 116). Ironically, Geoffrey's attempt at precision (the bird's "exact name") results in ambiguity and confusion, a typical example of the book's tendency to merge one element into another and defy the possibility of a precise identification or interpretation.

The animals most commonly associated with the Consul, however, are the pariah dogs that follow him throughout much of the novel. They are the Consul's familiars, a role that, as critics have noted, is suggested by the terms used to describe them: one dog appears "familiarly at heel," and later a dog in the garden (perhaps the same one) seems "disturbingly familiar" (UV 66, 127). Derived from the Tamil word for "drummer," *pariah* refers first of all to one of the lower castes of southern India, although the term is also used more generally to signify members of other lower castes and even outcastes; a pariah-dog, according to the *OED*, is "a yellow vagabond dog of low breed which frequents towns and villages in India and the East," but in *Under the Volcano* the term refers simply to any ownerless mongrel. Geoffrey is aware of the etymology of *pariah:* he refers to it directly ("Pariah: that meant drums too" [UV 75]), and it probably influences his allusion, in his letter to Yvonne, to "the howling pariah dogs . . . [and] the drumming" that keep him awake at night (UV 35). The pariah dog's marginal status is one point of contact with the Consul, but the word also originates from India, Geoffrey's boyhood home, which might be why he slips into Anglo-Indian slang ("the garden's a rajah mess, I'm afraid" [UV 66]) when the dog makes an appearance.

The pariah dogs play a complex role in the novel, their relationship to the Consul changing according to circumstances. The "dark shapes of pariah dogs" that haunt the cinema in chapter 1 (UV 26), for instance, are one sign of Geoffrey's continuing spiritual presence in Quauhnahuac a year after his death. A more sinister meaning emerges at the end of chapter 2, where a "hideous pariah dog" follows Geoffrey and Yvonne home (UV 64). In Goethe's *Faust*, Part I, Mephistopheles gains entrance to Faust's home in the shape of a black poodle and then is unable to leave because of a pentagram on the windowsill that the dog fails to notice when he enters. While the dog in *Faust* is a demonic spirit, however, the one in *Under the Volcano* seems almost a projection of Geoffrey's own spirit onto the world. In chapter 12, the Consul looks forward apprehensively to what he imagines will be a night of delirium tremens, with his sleep "interrupted by voices which were really dogs barking, or by his own name being continually repeated by imaginary parties arriving" (UV 342). If the voices can be traced to dogs, however, the dogs might just as readily be traced to Geoffrey's mind. At the novel's end, Geoffrey's close relationship to the pariah dogs will be confirmed as a dead dog is thrown into the barranca after him, in fulfillment of the ancient Mexican custom of burying a dog alongside its master to help him cross the river of death (see Epstein 216 and DG 227).

❧

Lowry's interest in the symbolic correspondences and systems that underlie the novel's maze of analogies was encouraged by his reading in a wide range of arcane, occult, mythical, philosophical, religious, and psychological works. Among the books from his personal library that are now part of the University of British Columbia's Lowry Archive are Bergson's *Creative Evolution*, Boehme's *The Signature of All Things*, Bullfinch's *Mythology*, Frazer's *The Golden Bough, Transcendental Magic* by Alphonse Constant (Eliphas Levi), and an edition of *The Bhagavad-Gita* published by the United Lodge of Theosophists, as well as works by Aleister Crowley, Charles Fort, and Charles Stansfeld-Jones ("Frater Achad"). The Consul's own bookshelves contain "numerous cabbalistic and alchemical books" in addition to "a heterogeneous collection" of other volumes (UV 175, 185), while Lowry's letters and manuscripts point to still more sources, including Annie Besant, Baudelaire, Madame Blavatsky, Blake, Thomas Burnet, J. W. Dunne, the *I Ching*, Hermann Keyserling, Arthur O. Lovejoy (*The Great Chain of Being*), S. L. MacGregor Mathers, P. D. Ouspensky, Paracelsus, Emanuel Swedenborg, and of course Yeats's *A Vision*.

Lowry derived specific concepts and images from these books, but one general point that should be made here is that his interest in, and knowledge of, these authors seems to have varied greatly. In a 1940 letter to Margerie's mother, Lowry called Dunne's *An Experiment with Time* "rewarding" and Ouspensky's *A New Model of the Universe* "terrifically exciting," while reserving his greatest enthusiasm for Charles Fort's speculations on paranormal phenomena: "I look upon the day I first hit upon *Lo!* in a public library as a red-letter day in my life" (SL 26). The impact of Fort on Lowry's imagination may also be seen in *October Ferry to Gabriola*, where Lowry says, "Surely few writers were ever capable so swiftly and convincingly of disaffecting a reader from the regular bounds of his cosmos" (OF 139). On the other hand, in *La Mordida* Sigbjørn Wilderness seems to speak for Lowry when he contends that "William Blake had been crushed" by the "giant machinery" of occultism and confesses his inability, "in spite of repeated attempts in the past," to understand Yeats's system in *A Vision* (UBC 14:2, 323; 14:3, 325).[6] A second point is that these writers imply different, and often conflicting, perspectives on the nature of Lowry's coincidences and analogies, serving to counterpoint rather than reinforce one another, just as the Consul's numerous identifications are often contradictory. Lowry was a novelist and poet, not a scholar, and a reading of his work strictly within the limits of one system of ideas runs the risk of sacrificing artistic complexity in favor of rational consistency.

Even so, Lowry's sources would generally agree that, as Matthew Corrigan puts it, "truth is something already there in the universe," needing only to be provoked "through 'correspondence' into revealing itself" (Corrigan 431). A similar assumption lies beneath the Consul's belief that everything is symbolic. Superficially, at least, the Consul would seem to be employing the Hermetic doctrine of correspondences between the spiritual and material worlds ("as above, so below"), which

Lowry might have derived from Swedenborg (see A&C 30–31, 59).[7] This doctrine assumes the possibility of our rising above nature into a harmonious relationship with the spiritual universe. There are indications that this is what the Consul seeks through his mystic studies and even, to some extent, through his drinking. The result, however, is precisely the opposite, at least in part because he often reads correspondences backward, seeing the universe in terms of himself rather than assimilating his own situation to the larger patterns of the cosmos.

In *The World and the Book*, Gabriel Josipovici has commented on our loss of the medieval conception of history (the world) as revelation (the book). Josipovici observes that "with the disappearance of the medieval notion of analogy inner meaning and outer form no longer seem to reinforce one another, and as the world, instead of manifesting the 'invisible things of God', becomes an enigma without a key, there is the danger that art will be relegated to the status of a mere commodity, a luxury" (*World* 47). Josipovici's comments on modern literature in general are particularly relevant to Lowry: "In modern literature analogy has become demonic—'le demon de l'analogie,' Mallarmé called it. For to discover correspondences in the world around us does not lead to the sensation that we are inhabiting a meaningful universe; on the contrary, it leads to the feeling that what we have taken to be 'the world' is only the projection of our private compulsions: *analogy* becomes a sign of *dementia*" (*World* 299). Likewise, Charles Taylor has observed that while modern writers like Baudelaire and Yeats "conceive of a spiritual order of correspondences" in their works, these correspondences are made available to readers only "through an epiphany wrought by the creative imagination," and we cannot conceive of such an order "which would be somehow available unrefracted through the medium of someone's artistic creation" (Taylor 427–28).

Thus, as the universe increasingly comes to seem an "enigma without a key" rather than a revelation of ultimate truth, we are tempted to read analogy in private terms, seeing the universe as an extension of ourselves. The Consul's proper course would be to "throw away [his] mind," as Dr. Vigil puts it, thereby following the philosophy of *la vida impersonal* (UV 6, 12; cf. DG 239). This philosophy assumes that although we are morally responsible for our actions, we should understand that our lives take place in the context of larger patterns and thereby recognize the greater and more significant reality that lies outside us. In his essay "Garden of Etla," Lowry associates the need to see one's life as "impersonal" with the cyclic form of time and history (which of course is incorporated into the structure of *Under the Volcano*), and he notes that the conception of others as "spiritual manifestations of oneself," although "evil," is "not wholly an illusion" (GE 46). What is wrong is to regard oneself as central and all-important: Gladys Andersen connects *la vida impersonal* with "the Oriental view that the cause of suffering is action resulting from desire for a separate self" (Andersen 438). Like Bill Plantagenet, Geoffrey fails on at least two counts: he typically avoids facing his own responsibility (except, ironically, for the *Samaritan* affair, in which he almost certainly was *not* responsible for murdering the German submarine officers), yet he reads the external world almost exclusively in terms of his own situation. Unable to find any meaning in the outside world except that which he places on it, he is eventually unable to discover any significance in his own existence.

Lowry himself recognized that he needed to present Geoffrey both as the victim of forces outside himself and as the author of his own doom, just as the *La Mordida* draft contains Lowry's reminder to himself that it was necessary to balance Sigbjørn Wilderness's responsibility for his actions against the sense that he is being persecuted (UBC 13:24, 239). Significantly, in his letter to Jonathan Cape in defense of *Under the Volcano*, Lowry referred first to the novel's depiction of "the forces in man which cause him to be terrified of himself," then to other inter-

pretations that gradually shift the emphasis to forces outside
the Consul:

> It is also concerned with the guilt of man, with his remorse, with
> his ceaseless struggling toward the light under the weight of the
> past, and with his doom. The allegory is that of the Garden of
> Eden, the Garden representing the world. . . . The drunkenness
> of the Consul is used on one plane to symbolize the universal
> drunkenness of mankind during the war, or during the period
> immediately preceding it . . . and what profundity and final
> meaning there is in his fate should be seen also in its universal
> relationship to the ultimate fate of mankind. (SL 66)

The Consul, then, is self-destructive, but he is also doomed
by large historical and cosmic forces ("the weight of the past,"
"the ultimate fate of mankind"). Moreover, he is in some sense
the agent who brings those forces into play, his drunkenness
not merely reflecting but stimulating "the universal drunkenness of mankind" that resulted in a world war. His multiple symbolic identifications tend to reinforce the ambiguity
of his situation: if he is a *compañero* of the dying Indian, he is
also the Spanish-born *pelado* who robs him, and he therefore
represents both the victims and the aggressors, the Aztecs and
the conquistadors. Likewise, his conviction of his own guilt
in the *Samaritan* affair during World War I associates him
with the death camps of World War II, whose existence was
well known before Lowry wrote his final draft of *Under the Volcano*. That association lends additional force to Lowry's contention that "you can even see the German submarine officers
taking revenge on the Consul in the form of the *sinarquistas*
and semi-fascist *brutos* at the end" (SL 88); yet in chapter 12
the Consul is repeatedly called a Jew, a role that makes sense in
light of his immersion in cabbalistic studies and other "Jewish
knowledge" (UV 185), his marginal status in Mexican society,
and his murder by the fascist militia.[8]

The Consul's dual roles parallel the book's ambiguous presentation of the relationship between perception and reality. Frequently we are misled by the narrator's description of Geoffrey's impressions as if they were objectively true. Thus in chapter 10, at the Salón Ofélia, we are told that he speaks brilliantly of a wide range of learned subjects: "But there was a slight mistake. The Consul was not talking. Apparently not. The Consul had not uttered a single word. It was all an illusion, a whirling cerebral chaos" (UV 308). The same shift from a character's mistaken perception of reality to a corrected version also occurs when the narration follows another character's perspective: in chapter 1, for example, when Jacques Laruelle first misreads a passage from *Doctor Faustus* and then realizes his error (UV 34), or in chapter 2, where Yvonne's initial impressions about the number of people in the bar, and about whether or not the barman is listening to Geoffrey, prove incorrect (UV 45–51). But there are more chapters (five) narrated from the Consul's perspective than from the viewpoint of any other person, and he is the character who inadvertently challenges the idea that there is an objective reality recognized by everyone. Thomas Gilmore points to the "almost pervasive ambiguity in the novel between hallucinations and reality," observing that "the ambiguity seems to lie in the nature of things, sometimes appearing to be simply an aspect of an extraordinarily rich and animated metaphorical texture" (Gilmore 26).[9] There is a sense in which the Consul's vividly realized hallucinations are somehow more real, more penetrating, than the mundane reality perceived by other characters; on that level, they are perhaps closer to visionary poetry than to typical alcoholic hallucinations, which, as Gilmore notes, tend to be uninteresting (Gilmore 21). Even so, the Consul's incessant retreat into the private world of his hallucinations and personal symbolic readings proves fatal, at least in part because he can never find any stable reality upon which to base a secure sense of his own identity.

For Geoffrey Firmin, there are no simple issues: every experience, every attempt to deal with reality, involves him in unexpected complexities and ambiguities. Even an attempt to calculate the number of drinks he has had shows how highly subjective his reality can be:

> The drink situation was now this, was this: there had been one drink waiting for him and this drink of beer he had not yet quite drunk. On the other hand there had been until recently several drinks of mescal (why not?—the word did not intimidate him, eh?) waiting for him outside in a lemonade bottle and all these he both had and had not drunk: had drunk in fact, had not drunk so far as the others were concerned. And before that there had been two mescals that he both should and should not have drunk. Did they suspect? He had adjured Cervantes to silence; had the Tlaxcaltecan, unable to resist it, betrayed him? What had they really been talking about while he was outside? (UV 303)

The Consul's "double-entry drink-counting system," as Art Hill calls it (Hill 136), typifies the alcoholic's belief that he is somehow in control of reality, that he can outsmart the dull-witted people around him who will never suspect what he is up to. Alternately, there is the paranoid suspicion that people are spying on him: "What had they really been talking about while he was outside?" On the one hand, the Consul imagines himself superior, almost godlike, virtually invisible,[10] as when he puts on his dark glasses at the Farolito and, believing no one is watching him, contemplates making an escape—although of course the attempt must be delayed until he has had one last drink (UV 362). On the other hand, everything centers on him, and he is the object of attention not only of Hugh and Yvonne but of Dr. Vigil, Mr. Quincey, and Señor Bustamente, whose conversation he suspects "to be entirely about him; what could be done with him, they were asking, how many drinks had he put away at the Gran Baile last night?" (UV 230). Followed by pariah dogs and pursued by "spiders," watched by a sunflower (UV 144, 179) and subjected to "the polygonous proustian stare of imaginary scorpions" (UV 174), the Consul is always under observation, if only in his own imagination, and he seeks out cantinas and other dark places partly to hide himself from the scrutiny (and judgment) of others.

The Consul's effort both to evade and to control reality is represented by his dark glasses. The glasses are one means by which he attempts to hide from, or deceive, other people; at the same time, they protect him from the glare of reality, allowing him to retreat into his inner world. As part of his image of "complete respectability" (UV 188), the dark glasses are probably not very successful, although the alcoholic's capacity for self-deception helps to maintain his illusion that everyone sees him as he wants to be seen. Far from helping him see clearly, the glasses tend to obscure his vision, so that he must remove them to look at the murals in the square (UV 212) or, in a dark room of the Farolito, to read Yvonne's letters (UV 344). (The room itself is "framed in dull glass" [UV 343], providing a kind of insulation similar to that allowed by the glasses.) He puts the glasses back on as a transparent disguise (UV 362); now thoroughly separated from reality, he persuades himself that he can see Yvonne's letters more clearly with his dark glasses (UV 364).

Geoffrey's decision to wear the glasses at the end of the novel, and his delusion that he can see better with them, are two signs that he has lost a clear and coherent sense of his identity. Instead, he attempts to contrive an identity out of the symbols of the external world—or, rather, to read that world almost entirely in terms of his own dilemma. In chapter 7, at the carnival, the glasses are among the items that fall from the Consul's pockets while he is in the "infernal machine": "Everything was falling out of his pockets, was being wrested from him, torn away, a fresh article at each whirling, sickening, plunging, retreating, unspeakable circuit, his notecase, pipe, keys, his dark glasses he had taken off . . . he was being emptied out, returned empty, his stick, his passport" (UV 222). For a moment he is willing to let it all go—"everything particularly that provided means of ingress or egress, went bond for, gave meaning or character, or purpose or identity to that fright-ful bloody nightmare he was forced to carry around with him everywhere upon his back, that went by the name of Geoffrey Firmin" (UV 223). Here, the desire to release the glasses and other items represents Geoffrey's attempt to escape from the prison of selfhood that he has created. If he does not have to carry Geoffrey Firmin on his back, perhaps he can carry some-one else, like the "old lame Indian" at the end of chapter 9, who carries "another poor Indian, yet older and more decrepit than himself" (UV 280). When the children return the glasses and other items to the Consul (apart from the passport, which he only imagined having taken), he is once more left encum-bered with himself. Significantly, although he sees Yvonne and Hugh, he heads directly for a cantina that reminds him of Dante's dark woods: "The Terminal Cantina El Bosque . . . seemed so dark that even with his glasses off he had to stop dead . . . Mi ritrovai per una bosca oscura—or selva? No mat-ter" (UV 225). His purpose, once again, is to retreat into his private world, evading *la vida impersonal* and the awareness of others that it implies.

In his discussion of the Mexican Day of the Dead, Octavio Paz says that through the fiesta Mexicans escape from themselves and their situations: the fiesta dissolves boundaries of time and space, gender and social class, liberating society from "its gods, its principles, and its laws." "The fiesta," Paz contends, "is a return to a remote and undifferentiated state, prenatal or presocial. It is a return that is also a beginning, in accor-dance with the dialectic that is inherent in social processes." Through the fiesta, then, people "exceed" and renew them-selves by participating in its cyclic ritual of death and rebirth (Paz 50–53).[11]

Since *Under the Volcano* takes place on the Day of the Dead, we might expect to find the Consul eventually participating in these timeless rituals, emerging from himself into a sense of oneness with others and with the universe itself. Yet the renewal of which Paz speaks is possible only for those who can throw away their minds, as Dr. Vigil would put it. The Consul's failure is represented in the complex, dreamlike experience that he has shortly before his death. Hearing a waterfall, he imagines himself in a place that seems to be both India and Mexico, combining the beginning and end of his life. Since the book he has been planning to write is apparently an attempt to re-create a spiritually harmonious universe by establishing connections between the mythologies of India and Mexico, this final hallucination, which places Popocatepetl in Kashmir, would seem to signify universal oneness, while the Consul's imagined ascent of the volcanic mountain represents his striving toward spiritual perfection. Yet the vision becomes increasingly fragmented through the addition of incongruous details, and eventually, when he believes that he has reached the summit, he finds that he is mistaken: the ground crumbles beneath his feet, and he falls into a nightmarish conflagration.

The vision that seemed to be a kind of Dantean ascent to paradise becomes, instead, a descent into the inferno. Perhaps on one level the reversal occurs because the hope of attaining oneness with the universe was only an illusion—because the universe does not, after all, wear a human face but is an infernal machine like the loop-the-loop in which the Consul becomes trapped in chapter 7. But it is also true that the Consul fails because of his inability to follow the precepts of *la vida impersonal*, because of his obsessive emphasis on the importance of his problems and situation: in short, because he fails to recognize the impossibility of living without loving. The rest of the world literally dissolves in this final hallucinatory sequence because for the Consul it does not really exist to begin with. Unable to recognize and embrace the otherness of the world, seeing it only as a forest of symbols that reflects his own situation, he can find no solid ground on which to base his own identity. While Lowry has at times been described as a solipsistic writer, *Under the Volcano* provides ample evidence that he was also acutely aware of the dangers of solipsism and of our need to discover ourselves in relation to other people.

THREE

Sortes Shakespeareanae:
Reading in *Under the Volcano*

Lowry's emphasis on destiny and chance correspondences in *Under the Volcano* manifests itself clearly in the numerous acts of reading that we see throughout the novel, for when Geoffrey Firmin reads he inevitably finds his own circumstances inscribed in the text. This is in fact the point of the reading practice that the Consul calls *sortes Shakespeareanae* (UV 34, 209). More commonly termed *sortes Virgilianae* (Virgilian lots), the practice originated, according to Sidney's *Defense of Poesy*, in the Romans' belief that poets had prophetic powers. Opening a copy of the *Aeneid* at random and beginning to read, people hoped to discover their future (Sidney 7). St. Augustine describes an apparently more spontaneous use of the practice in his *Confessions* when he reports that the crucial event in his conversion from heresy and wickedness came when he thought he heard a child's voice saying "Take it and read, take it and read." Understanding this directive as "a divine command to open my book of Scripture and read the first passage on which my eyes should fall," Augustine opened a volume of St. Paul's Epistles to Romans 13:13:

"Not in revelling and drunkenness, not in lust and wanton-
ness, not in quarrels and rivalries. Rather, arm yourselves with
the Lord Jesus Christ; spend no more thought on nature and
nature's appetites" (Augustine 177–78 [VIII.12]). Augustine in-
terpreted the passage as a reference to his sinfulness, and all
of his religious doubts were dispelled at once.

Virtually all of the acts of reading in *Under the Volcano* resemble *sortes* readings in their apparent randomness and their
implicit understanding that the reader's situation is symbolized or referred to by the text. One fairly obvious example
occurs when the Consul opens the telephone book in search
of Dr. Guzmán's telephone number and finds other significant
names and numbers "starting out of the book at him" (UV
208). These include 666 (not only the number of the Beast in
the Book of Revelation but the number on an insecticide advertisement [UV 188], and therefore a threat to the Consul in
his role as the self-destructive scorpion); Cafeaspirina (a form
of aspirin with caffeine, perhaps effective against hangovers);
and above all Zuzugoitea and Sanabria, the names of two of
the three "chiefs" who will persecute him at the Farolito. The
sequence is clearly ominous, and Geoffrey's attempt to locate
Dr. Guzmán, who perhaps could restore his physical health,
fails in the face of this apparent confrontation with destiny.

The same principle applies when, moments after Yvonne's
return, Geoffrey offers her a cigarette and she is struck by the
brand name on the package: "Alas" (UV 47). The name means
"wings" in Spanish and therefore should be a sign of hope
rather than despair, but for Yvonne, who reads it first as an
English word, it is obviously a portent of doom. (Lowry pre-
pares his readers for this "misreading" by introducing the word
in Geoffrey's letter in chapter 1, where it is associated with the
division between husband and wife: "Alas, what has happened
to the love and understanding we once had!" [UV 40].) Ironically, Geoffrey's offer of a cigarette is prompted by the voice of
an unseen man seated elsewhere in the cantina:

". . . Oh Christ, it's a shame! The horses all go away kicking in the dust! I wouldn't have it. They plugged 'em too. They don't miss it. They shoot first and ask questions later. You're goddam right. And that's a nice thing to say. I take a bunch of goddamned farmers, then ask them no questions. Righto!—smoke a cool cigarette—" (UV 47)

The voice, we later discover, is that of Weber, who emerges as one of the Consul's "doubles." Geoffrey has heard of Weber from Hugh (UV 60) but has never met him, so he has no way of recognizing his voice. Nonetheless, on rereading the novel, we can see that Weber's comments about horses running away and men who shoot first and ask questions later foreshadow Geoffrey's release of the horse and his murder by the Chief of Rostrums. Since the horse that bolts and runs when Geoffrey is shot will trample Yvonne, Weber's remarks refer, in a sense, to Yvonne's death as well as Geoffrey's.

That Weber will be in the Farolito and will make no attempt to save Geoffrey adds to the ominous nature of his early morning words. Significantly, Yvonne's premonition about the cigarettes is echoed in chapter 12 shortly before Weber is seen: "The Consul produced his blue package of cigarettes with the wings on them: Alas! He raised his head again; no, he was where he was, there was nowhere to fly to. And it was as if a black dog had settled on his back, pressing him to his seat" (UV 362).[1] The downward pressure exerted by the imagined dog confirms not only the direction in which the Consul has been headed throughout the narrative, but also the reading of "Alas" as a sign of his fate (rather than the possibility of escaping that fate through flight). Since the black dog "constitutes a reference to Goethe's Mephistopheles, who first appeared to Faust in the guise of a black poodle" (A&C 436), the Consul's final reading of the cigarette pack implies a rebuttal of the line from Goethe's *Faust* that appears as the final epigraph to *Under the Volcano:* "Whosoever unceasingly strives upward . . . him can we save."

If a simple text like the cover of a cigarette pack appears so deeply implicated in a character's fate, we can expect a more complex involvement with a text like Marlowe's *Doctor Faustus*. Lowry used elements from other versions of the Faust story—most obviously Goethe's, which supplied several allusions as well as the epigraph just cited—but as Ackerley and Clipper note, "*Doctor Faustus* is Lowry's single most important source for *Under the Volcano*" (A&C 48). At the Salón Ofélia, ordering a small mescal and looking at the bartender's fighting cock, Geoffrey parodies what is probably the best-known line of Marlowe's play: "Was this the face that launched five hundred ships, and betrayed Christ into being in the Western Hemisphere?" (UV 286–87). Elsewhere, Hugh speculates that the Consul might be "a black magician" (UV 118), and for his part Geoffrey often associates himself with Faustus as a suffering soul who cannot ask for salvation, or as someone who even actively seeks damnation (UV 65, 314).

In his famous letter to Jonathan Cape in defense of his novel, Lowry noted that "in an obvious movie sense" the Ferris wheel seen at the end of the first chapter is "the wheel of time whirling backwards until we have reached the year before and Chapter II and in this sense, if we like, we can look at the rest of the book through Laruelle's eyes, as if it were his creation" (SL 71; see also WP 74). That is, we can regard the remainder of the book as, figuratively, a movie created by Laruelle.[2] It is significant, then, that despite the Consul's symbolic association with Faustus, his own copy of the play has been lent to Laruelle so that he can work on his "modern film version of the Faustus story with some such character as Trotsky for its protagonist" (UV 28). A year after Geoffrey's death, it remains for Laruelle, his alter ego, to open the book and read it as a prophetic set of references to Geoffrey and his death. That the play "contains" Geoffrey is underscored when Laruelle finds in the book a long, tortured letter from Geoffrey to Yvonne, its penmanship revealing its author's struggle against fate ("the hand, half crabbed, half generous, and wholly drunken . . . the words themselves slanting steeply downhill, though the individual characters seemed as if resisting the descent, braced, climbing the other way" [UV 35]). Geoffrey's identification with Faustus is once again foreshadowed/recollected at the chapter's end when Laruelle burns the letter and the bell outside chimes "*dolente . . . dolore!*" (UV 41–42), echoing words inscribed over hell's gate in Dante's *Inferno* (III.1–2).

It is in Laruelle's chance reading of passages from Marlowe's play, however, that we see most clearly the operation of coincidence that underlies Lowry's forest of symbols. The insertion of the Marlowe passages into the novel takes Lowry's reader by surprise, for we are not told that Laruelle has opened the book until we have suddenly been faced with a key passage. Lowry introduces the whole sequence—Laruelle's reading of parts of the play, then of Geoffrey's letter, followed by his ritualistic burning of the letter—by Laruelle's meditation on the *Samaritan* incident: during World War I, Geoffrey, then a young naval officer, was decorated for capturing a German submarine but was court-martialed (and acquitted) on charges that he was involved in murdering the submarine's officers by burning them in the ship's furnaces. Although no blame attached to Geoffrey, by 1938 he had begun to proclaim "not only his guilt in the matter but that he'd always suffered horribly on account of it"—an assertion that Laruelle discounted, regarding the Consul's life as "a quixotic oral fiction" and his proclamation of his guilt and suffering as "merely an excuse to buy another bottle of mescal" (UV 33). At this point, where the line between truth and fiction becomes uncommonly blurred, we are suddenly thrust into the text of Marlowe's play:

> *Then will I headlong fly into the earth:*
> *Earth, gape! it will not harbour me!*
M. Laruelle had opened the book of Elizabethan plays at random and for a moment he sat oblivious of his surroundings, gazing at

the words that seemed to have the power of carrying his own mind downward into a gulf, as if in fulfilment on his own spirit of the threat Marlowe's Faustus had cast at his despair. (UV 34)

As so often in *Under the Volcano,* a first impression—here, Laruelle's initial, unpremeditated reading of two lines from Faustus's last speech (Marlowe 49 [sc. xiv])—is subject to correction upon reexamination. For, as he quickly realizes, the passage in the play is not quite what he read: "He looked more closely at the passage. Faustus had said: 'Then will I headlong run into the earth,' and 'O, no, it will not—' That was not so bad. Under the circumstances to run was not so bad as to fly" (UV 34). Whether it is better to run than to fly into the earth is debatable, but in any case Laruelle's misreading, which takes place in an atmosphere of "elusive flickering candlelight," is a by-product of the ambiguities that plague the Consul himself and contribute to his death. As a sign of the threat to individual life inherent in a misread text, Laruelle's first reading of the passage is itself a dim echo of his earlier dissatisfaction with the present—the time just after the outbreak of World War II in Europe—when "individual life [has become] a mere misprint in a communiqué" (UV 5).

Although his misreading might have been produced by the dim and flickering light, Laruelle also imagines that a more sinister influence might be at work: "some correspondence, maybe, as Geoff liked to put it, between the subnormal world and the abnormally suspicious" (UV 34; cf. 355). The theme of running, in the correctly read quotation, is reinforced for Laruelle by the Promethean figure on the book's cover that identifies the volume as a Modern Library anthology, *Eight Famous Elizabethan Plays* (Markson 24). Within Marlowe's play, however, references to flight appear often enough so that Laruelle's misreading seems somehow appropriate. Kilgallin has observed that "the word 'fly' calls to mind the inscription on Faustus' arm, '*Homo fuge:* whither should I fly'" ("Faust and *Under the Volcano*" 27). The context of this passage is perhaps relevant to *Under the Volcano*, for it occurs just as Faustus signs a deed in his own blood, bequeathing his soul to Lucifer. At this point, the inscription first appears on Faustus's arm, then disappears, and then returns:

> But what is this inscription on mine arm?
> *Homo, fuge!* Whither should I fly?
> If unto God, he'll throw me down to hell.
> My senses are deceived; here's nothing writ—
> I see it plain; here in this place is writ
> *Homo, fuge!* Yet shall not Faustus fly.
> (Marlowe 18–19 [sc. v])

In misreading the Marlowe passage in the poorly lit room and then reading it correctly, Laruelle repeats the pattern of this earlier citation from the play, which questions not merely the source but the very existence of the words on Faustus's arm. It is noteworthy, too, that both in this excerpt and in Laruelle's initial version of the later passage from *Doctor Faustus*, flight is impossible.

Kilgallin points out that Laruelle's misreading is significant in another way: "This simple slip is intensified when, several pages later, we hear the line, 'where I come from they don't run.' The speaker is Weber, a witness to Geoffrey's murder, which, in Geoffrey's own way, was a literally physical attempt to enact Marlowe's quotation on his last night of life" ("Faust and *Under the Volcano*" 27). An earlier exclamation by Weber, "We come through with heels flying!" (UV 47), is equally relevant; significantly, it is also Weber whose mention of a cigarette prompts Geoffrey to offer Yvonne an Alas (Wings), which reinforces the image of flight. The point here is not merely that the *Doctor Faustus* passage and Laruelle's reading of it set up the run/fly motif that echoes throughout *Under the Volcano*, but that when Laruelle opens the play he is roughly analogous to the reader opening *Under the Volcano*, for he finds in *Doc-*

tor Faustus some of the key themes and images that we will discover in the novel. Literally, of course, Laruelle is reading *Doctor Faustus* a year after the Consul's death, so on one level the play seems merely to record and symbolize a fate that has already occurred; but the words actually on the page of *Eight Famous Elizabethan Plays* were the same when Laruelle borrowed the volume eighteen months earlier (six months before the events of chapters 2 through 12), so it could also be argued that the play indicates that Geoffrey's fate was inscribed long before he lent the book to Laruelle.

Laruelle reads four more passages from the same anthology, all of them chosen at random because he is now intentionally playing the Consul's "absurd game . . . sortes Shakespeareanae." The first, taken from Faustus's conversation with the scholars in Marlowe's final scene, is *"And what wonders I have done all Germany can witness"* (UV 34; Marlowe 47 [sc. xiv]). As Laruelle reads this line, it seems to lead directly into the stage direction *"Enter Wagner, solus,"* which actually comes from a much earlier scene in *Doctor Faustus* (Marlowe 27 [sc. vi]). We might associate Faustus's "wonders" with Geoffrey, and Wagner's entrance with Laruelle, who has felt alone ("solus") since Geoffrey's death, but neither passage has the ominous tone of the lines Laruelle read earlier. Next, Laruelle reads an even more innocuous excerpt from the second play in the volume, Thomas Dekker's *The Shoemaker's Holiday*. These *sortes* readings prove successful enough that Laruelle tempts fate by trying one more:

> M. Laruelle closed the book on Dekker's comedy, then, in the face of the barman who was watching him, stained dishcloth over his arm, with quiet amazement, shut his eyes, and opening the book again twirled one finger in the air, and brought it down firmly upon a passage he now held up to the light:
> > *Cut is the branch that might have grown full straight,*
> > *And burned is Apollo's laurel bough,*

That sometime grew within this learnèd man,
Faustus is gone: regard his hellish fall—

(UV 34)

Even without Lowry's declaration that in his novel he is saying "something new about hell fire" (SL 80), few readers could miss the Consul's identification with Faustus. For his part, Laruelle is "shaken" by the passage he has lit upon, with its obvious relevance to the death of another "learnèd man," Geoffrey Firmin. Ironically, when Laruelle sets the book down, he sees a paper, which turns out to be an unposted letter from Geoffrey to Yvonne, flutter out of it. The image of the paper emerging from the hellish text might well represent the soul's rescue from damnation, as Faust is ultimately saved in Goethe's play. The letter's escape also seems to parallel the insect's escape from the jaws of Mr. Quincey's cat in chapter 5: "the insect, whose wings had never ceased to beat, suddenly and marvellously flew out, as might indeed the human soul from the jaws of death" (UV 140). This unexpected flight to salvation fulfills the promise made by the third of the novel's epigraphs, from the final scene of *Faust*, Part II: "Whosoever unceasingly strives upward . . . him can we save."[3]

Despite its message of hope, the vision of the insect's escape does not elate Geoffrey, who catches a glimpse of Hugh and Yvonne and then passes out (UV 140–41). Ackerley and Clipper report that in "earlier drafts of this passage . . . the insect's miraculous escape gave the Consul curious speculations," one of those speculations being "Her lips suck forth my soul, see where it flies" (A&C 203). The last passage is a quotation from Marlowe's *Doctor Faustus* that records Faustus's response to Helen of Troy:[4]

Was this the face that launched a thousand ships
And burnt the topless towers of Ilium?
Sweet Helen, make me immortal with a kiss. [*Kisses her*]

> Her lips suck forth my soul; see where it flies!
> Come, Helen, come, give me my soul again.
>   (Marlowe 45 [sc. xiii])

For us, the insect's escape from the cat might suggest Goethe's more optimistic rendition of the Faust story, but the canceled passage implies that for Geoffrey it is always Marlowe's version, in which Faustus is *not* saved, that is most relevant. It is appropriate, then, that Geoffrey's letter to Yvonne is doomed, like its author and for that matter like Faustus himself. Thus the letter escapes from the book of plays long enough to be read, its words returning momentarily to life as Geoffrey will in the next eleven chapters; but after reading the letter, Laruelle consigns it to the flames. Few images could convey more dramatically the combination of significance and instability that Lowry finds in language than the Consul's posthumously discovered letter, which is resurrected and then burned with each reading of Lowry's cyclic narrative.

The characters of *Under the Volcano* lead a highly textual existence, for they are constantly portrayed as surrounded or confronted by written words, whether those words emanate from a poster, a movie marquee, a letter or telegram, a book, magazine, or newspaper, a tourist brochure, a menu, or one of the numerous signs that proliferate throughout the novel. These alternate texts, which are normally presented so as to make them typographically distinct from the narration that surrounds them, serve a variety of functions. Repetition of one text—an advertisement for *Las Manos de Orlac, con Peter Lorre* (UV 24, 46, 60, 109, 217, 231, 240) or the railroad station sign that identifies the town as Quauhnahuac (UV 7, 235), for example—contributes to the complexity and unity of the novel, unfolding meaning by associating the motif with a range of other images and situations. In his introduction to *Under*

the Volcano, Stephen Spender has compared the interpolation of such texts into the novel to the "kinetic" technique of the cinema (Spender xviii–xix), while Victor Doyen sees them as an aspect of the book's "spatial form," which militates against our straightforward progression through the narrative by requiring that we reinterpret earlier parts of a work in the light of later sections ("Elements" 69–70). Whether the comparison is with the film *I Am a Camera,* as Spender suggests, or with other novels that call attention to their status as printed books by using unusual typography (Sterne's *Tristram Shandy,* Joyce's *Ulysses,* Karel Čapek's *War with the Newts,* and John Dos Passos's *U.S.A.* trilogy come to mind), one effect is to emphasize the visual rather than the aural aspect of words, their existence as writing rather than as speech.

In a Bakhtinian analysis of *Under the Volcano,* Jonathan Arac has called attention to the way the book's "variety of styles and tones," including its use of letters, telegrams, and printed announcements, and the frequent citation of other literary works, challenges the hegemony of any single viewpoint in the novel (Arac 483).[5] Ronald Binns makes a similar point about the typographic variousness of the book, observing that its "general effect is of a breaking-down and blurring of any single homogeneous stable reality" (*Malcolm Lowry* 52). Whereas Lowry reinforces our sense of his novel's thematic unity by giving it a circular structure and establishing innumerable correspondences and associations within the narrative, he also introduces alternative discourses which impinge upon the Consul's (and the other characters') consciousness, emphasizing their separateness by typographic means. Marshall McLuhan has observed that the medium of print, with its appearance of regularity, fostered the development of a fixed or consistent narrative viewpoint that is not typical of oral and manuscript cultures (McLuhan 126–27, 135–36), but the converse is also true: that is, print may also underscore the sharp distinctions between different perspectives. In *Under the Vol-*

cano, the typography provides us with a visual reminder that despite their individual claims of linguistic (and, often, political) authority, the book's separate discourses are only partial and arbitrary representations of reality.

The dialogical or polyphonic nature of *Under the Volcano* is reinforced by the variety of voices that speak to us, silently, from outside the narrative itself: through the epigraphs at the beginning and the *Le gusta este jardín* sign with which the novel closes. Originating from four different countries and originally written in four different languages (although the Greek quotation is given to us only in English translation), the three epigraphs and the postscript reinforce the novel's international character. Moreover, these texts that lie outside the narration may be read against each other as well as in relation to the intervening narrative. The order of the epigraphs from Sophocles' *Antigone,* Bunyan's *Grace Abounding for the Chief of Sinners,*[6] and Goethe's *Faust* might be purely chronological, but it also sets up an alternation between the emphasis on salvation in the first and third citations and the spiritual desolation that Bunyan describes. The result, as Binns has noted, is a triad of epigraphs that "are contradictory and irreconcilable, pointing in opposite directions" (*Malcolm Lowry* 38). This ambiguity exists not only among, but within, the epigraphs, for each epigraph may easily be read in a way contrary to its apparently dominant meaning. The citation from Sophocles seems to emphasize the wondrousness of mankind, but it also insists on our mortality ("only against Death shall [man] call for aid in vain"); Bunyan describes his inability to "desire deliverance," yet the work's very title proclaims that he has found salvation; and Goethe's "Whosoever unceasingly strives upward . . . him can we save"—rendered first in German and then in English, almost as if to call attention to the two ways in which it could be read—also implies the angels' inability to save those who do *not* unceasingly strive upward. Likewise, the garden's sign, which will be discussed later in this chapter, delivers a message that is fundamentally ambiguous.

The intrusion of innumerable printed texts on the narration reinforces the Babel-like effect created by the many voices that speak in the novel, ranging from the voice of the unseen Weber in chapter 2 to "the Babel . . . the confusion of tongues" that will besiege the Consul at the Farolito (UV 366). Like the voices, the printed notices seem to emanate from nowhere, so that it becomes impossible to trace their origins, much less to assign them a single meaning. The political chaos and violence discernible both in the novel's background (the Spanish Civil War and the preparations for World War II) and in its foreground (Mexico in the late 1930s, with its numerous "chiefs" and contending militias vying for power) is underscored by a sort of semantic anarchy: the multiplication of linguistic meaning forces the characters to make arbitrary choices among the many possibilities that confront them. For Geoffrey (and, to a lesser extent, for Laruelle, Yvonne, and Hugh), the result is that his own private obsessions and his reading of the world as an extension of himself come to dominate his interpretation of the language he encounters.

This tendency is particularly evident in the novel's often comic encounters between English and other languages. These linguistic crossings frequently involve a meaningful confusion of words with similar sounds, as when the gnomelike postman informs the Consul that he has brought mail "for your horse" (UV 192). Perle Epstein notes that the substitution of "horse" for "house" is significant because "Geoffrey's occult power is embodied in the horse symbol" (Epstein 129). Geoffrey himself underscores an aspect of his relationship to the horse when he responds, "What?—nothing for Señor Calígula," referring to the Roman emperor Caligula's insane proposition that his horse be made a consul (see A&C 269–70). The mistake broadens in significance when it becomes apparent that the postman is bearing Yvonne's postcard, whose nearly year-long odyssey in search of the Consul has ended on the same day that Yvonne herself has returned, and only a few hours before she will be trampled to death by the horse that the Consul will be shot for releasing. In short, the postman's simple mistake opens up a sequence of meanings and associations that lead, with a kind of tragic inevitability, to the novel's conclusion, thereby reinforcing our sense that the book's events are following a predetermined path.

Among the many written texts that the characters read, this linguistic slippage habitually points to the most sinister meaning available. Thus, when the Consul plays *sortes Shakespeareanae* with a copy of Jean Cocteau's *La Machine infernale*—a version of the Oedipus myth that portrays human beings as the victims of an infernal mechanism called the universe—he immediately hits upon a passage, taken from near the play's end, that emphasizes the insignificance of our lives and values in comparison to the gods' designs (UV 209). Pressing his luck, the Consul opens the book again, this time to the epigraphs, where he finds a phrase that he mistranslates as "The gods exist, they are the devil," compounding his error by misattributing the quotation to Baudelaire. Geoffrey's misinterpretation of "Les dieux existent: c'est le diable" ("the gods exist; that's the devil of it") is clearly his own error rather than Lowry's, since in the 1940 draft the Consul announces to Laruelle, "I've just learned that the gods exist and that that is the devil" (UV/1940 190); Ackerley and Clipper might well be right in arguing that the error in authorship is also Geoffrey's mistake (A&C 290). The effect of the Consul's two errors is, first, to underscore his interpretation of the universe as a diabolical mechanism (the gods exist, but they are hostile devils, antagonistic to our hope of salvation), and, second, to align this vision of the universe with the Baudelairean view of the world as filled with symbolic correspondences.[7]

Shifting from a French text to a Spanish one, the Consul reads both a personal and a universal meaning into a newspaper headline: "Es inevitable la muerte del Papa. The Consul started; this time, an instant, he had thought the headlines referred to himself. But of course it was only the poor Pope whose death was inevitable. As if everyone else's death were not inevitable too!" (UV 213). Geoffrey attempts to shrug off his personal association with the inevitable death proclaimed by the newspaper (an association reinforced, for English-speaking readers, by the similarity between *muerte* and *murder*), but the headline remains a threat, as we can see from the fact that it reappears, ominously, at the end of the chapter (UV 230). Although Geoffrey is not literally a father in the final text of *Under the Volcano*, Hugh sometimes calls him Papa (UV 117, 257), and at times he is treated as Yvonne's symbolic father. In the 1940 typescript (in which the Consul *was* Yvonne's father), Lowry's pencil note in the margin next to the headline's second appearance, at the end of the chapter, reads "No inverted commas" (UBC 25:23, 37). The published text also gives us the headline without quotation marks or any other indication as to its source, so that the words seem to possess a kind of external authority akin to the repetition of the *Le gusta este jardín* sign at the novel's end.

Confusion arises often enough when Lowry's English speakers try their luck at Spanish (Yvonne recalls having missed the joke when someone told her that Lechería, "milk shop," meant a brothel [UV 55]), or when his Mexicans attempt to negotiate their way through English. The menu at the Salón Ofélia, written partly in English to accommodate the tourist trade, involves so many strange combinations that Lowry found it necessary to devote considerable space in a letter to his German translator to the significance of these items (UV 290–91; LCH 51–56). Lowry noted that virtually every dish listed on the menu has "an overtone of the fiendish (though expressed in a ridiculous manner) pertaining to the Consul's general situation, or the whole situation, largely sexual, once or twice even political" (LCH 52). He did not need to add that there is something particularly ominous about the choice of "spectral chicken of the house" by people who will soon be confronted by death.

It would be a mistake to overlook the comic element in Lowry's presentation of verbal errors, but we would be equally wrong to dismiss the book's semantic ambiguity as thematically insignificant. Often the errors contribute to Lowry's presentation of thematic correspondences, as when Señora Gregorio's "Where do you laugh now" (followed by her "Here's to your love") implies an association of life, laughter, and love—three elements that only Yvonne can supply for Geoffrey—or when Geoffrey's choice of oblivion over self-awareness is suggested by Señora Gregorio's substitution of "drink" for "think" (UV 226–28). At the same time, this tendency for one word to be transformed into another implies a view of language as inherently unstable and ambiguous. Nor is this semantic instability confined to attempts by Lowry's Mexican characters to speak English, for the same blurring of lines between one word and another can occur in writtten English. Thus Yvonne imagines herself "seeing, as might the Consul, the sign in the Town House window 'Informal Dancing in the Zebra Room' turn 'Infernal'—or 'Notice to Destroy Weeds' become 'Notice to Newlyweds'" (UV 264).[8] Language that is so volatile defies any attempt to restore order by fixing on a hierarchy of meanings. Ronald G. Walker and Leigh Holt observe that the Consul resembles Faustus in his attempt to evade "the world of human ambiguity" (Walker and Holt 114), and it might be added that one means of escaping ambiguity is to abandon hope and settle for the most sinister, the most personally devastating, meaning that presents itself. The Consul's abandonment of hope is signified by the bell that rings out in Dantean tones, "*dolente . . . dolore!*" (UV 42, 373), while his preference for damnation over uncertainty may be inferred from his persistent, almost will-

ful, misreading of *Le gusta este jardín* as a threat of his own
eviction from the Garden.

Under the Volcano abounds in signs and public notices: signs
that announce a boxing match, point the way to Parián, invite
us to buy Cafeaspirina or the latest clothing styles from Europe
and the United States, or recommend Dr. Vigil's clinic for the
treatment of venereal disease and sexual disorders. Perhaps
most memorable is the sign that confronts Geoffrey Firmin in
the public garden near his home, as he stumbles about with the
bottle of tequila that he providentially stashed behind a bush:

> ¿Le gusta este jardín? it asked . . .
> ¿LE GUSTA ESTE JARDÍN?
> ¿QUE ES SUYO?
> ¡EVITE QUE SUS HIJOS LO DESTRUYAN!
> The Consul stared back at the black words on the sign without
> moving. You like this garden? Why is it yours? We evict those who
> destroy! Simple words, simple and terrible words, words which
> one took to the very bottom of one's being, words which, perhaps
> a final judgement on one, were nevertheless unproductive of any
> emotion whatsoever, unless a kind of colourless, cold, a white
> agony, an agony chill as that iced mescal drunk in the Hotel
> Canada on the morning of Yvonne's departure. (UV 128–29)

The sign and its interpretation reverberate throughout *Under
the Volcano*, becoming, Lowry claimed, "the most important
theme of the book" (SL 74). Almost immediately after seeing it, Geoffrey has doubts about his translation: " 'Why is it
yours? . . . Do you like this garden? . . . We evict those who
destroy!' Perhaps the sign didn't mean quite that—for alcohol
sometimes affected the Consul's Spanish adversely (or perhaps
the sign itself, inscribed by some Aztec, was wrong)—but it
was near enough." Even in this state, Geoffrey is aware that
the sign "certainly seemed to have more question marks than it
should have" (UV 129)—an observation that suggests that the

defects might lie partly in the sign, unless the extra punctuation is one of the Consul's hallucinations—but he is unable to extricate himself from the sinister interpretation on which he has settled.

The sign will be invoked three more times, its implications becoming more threatening and all-embracing with each appearance. In chapter 7, Geoffrey imagines that Laruelle tells him "I can see the writing on the wall." Realizing that Laruelle has left and that he has been carrying on a conversation with himself, Geoffrey finds that "the writing was there, all right, if not on the wall. The man had nailed his board to the tree: ¿LE GUSTA ESTE JARDÍN?" (UV 219). Here, the sign's association with judgment and suffering is reinforced by the crucifixion image and by the reference to the mysterious writing on the wall at the feast of Belshazzar, on the day before Belshazzar was killed (Daniel 5).[9] The sign's reappearance in chapter 8 comes during the bus ride, just after Geoffrey sees an undertaker's sign that reads, ominously, *Quo Vadis?*—another connection with the crucifixion, since in the Latin Vulgate these words, meaning "where are you going," were addressed by Simon Peter to Jesus, who responded by saying that Peter could not follow where he was going and that Peter would deny him three times before the cock crows (John 13:36–38; see A&C 311).

This time, the correct translation is supplied: "¿Le gusta este jardín, que es suyo? ¡Evite que sus hijos lo destruyan! Do you like this garden, the notice said, that is yours? See to it that your children do not destroy it!" (UV 232). Since the chapter is generally linked to Hugh's viewpoint, this translation—presumably the "real translation" which, Lowry said, "can be in a certain sense even more horrifying" (SL 74)—could be seen as Hugh's reading of the sign, which in fact is what Lowry at one time intended (according to his notes to Albert Erskine, 22 June 1946 [UBC 2:5, 5]). The evidence of the published text is inconclusive on this score, but the corrected translation is clearly located outside Geoffrey's consciousness, and even its association with Hugh's viewpoint is tenuous. Certainly the sign's final and definitive appearance on the endpage, with the punctuation corrected, cannot be attributed to any of the characters, and seems even outside the narrator's purview. Rather, it emerges as the author's direct address to the reader, urging that the garden—that is, the world, which belongs to us—not be destroyed. In the context of a novel whose action takes place on the Day of the Dead 1938 and 1939, with European wars providing the background for the act of random and gratuitous violence in the book's conclusion, the plea not to destroy the garden takes on added significance.

In an unpublished letter to Albert Erskine (16 July 1946), Lowry said that when the sign makes its final appearance at the novel's end, "the two meanings should explode simultaneously" (UBC 2:6, 3). Ironically, the passage never would have accumulated so much thematic weight and complexity had Lowry not miscopied, and mistranslated, the sign when he was in Mexico in 1936–38, finally recognizing his mistake in early 1946, when he returned to Mexico with Margerie.[10] As it stands, however, the *Le gusta este jardín* sign contrasts strikingly with the writing on Jacques Laruelle's wall, *No se puede vivir sin amar* (UV 6, 195, 209, 375)—"One cannot live without loving." The unnamed "estupido" who Laruelle says wrote the words on the wall (UV 6) knew something that the book's more sophisticated characters need to learn, for as Dale Edmonds has observed, "the four main characters of the novel . . . are incapable of loving, incapable of the selfless giving that Lowry suggests is necessary for real love" (Edmonds, "Immediate Level" 93; see also Costa 73). The Consul betrays Yvonne by having intercourse with the prostitute María, as Yvonne betrayed him through her affairs with Hugh and Laruelle, but the failure of their love takes other, and perhaps more significant, forms as well. Christ's two key injunctions—to love God and to love our neighbors as ourselves—set standards that

Geoffrey is unable to meet, at least in part because of a deeper
and more fatal deficiency in what Dr. Vigil terms "that part
used to be call: soul" (UV 5). What Geoffrey lacks, fundamentally, is the ability to love himself, to will his own salvation.
In his preference for the bottle over Yvonne, and in his failure
to aid the dying Indian, Geoffrey reveals his affinity with the
spiritual condition described by the epigraph from Bunyan, a
state of despair bordering on self-hatred.

The meanings that the *no se puede* inscription has for us
(and, presumably, for Geoffrey as well) are somewhat at odds
with those it has in its source, *De los nombres de Cristo* (1583),
by Fray Luis Ponce de León. Fray Luis emphasizes not that
love is essential to life but that it is inevitable and its effects not
always beneficial: "all men love, both the good and the bad,
the happy and the unhappy, and . . . one cannot live without
loving," but "just as love for some men is the cause of their
good fortune, so for others it is the fountain of their misery,
and accordingly love has very different effects in one group
as opposed to the other" (quoted in A&C 274). Lowry probably never consulted the source of the quotation, deriving the
phrase instead from Somerset Maugham's *Don Fernando; or,
Variations on Some Spanish Themes* (1935), where, as Tony Kilgallin notes, the description of Fray Luis "fits Geoffrey as well"
(*Lowry* 151–52); indeed, a casual reading of Maugham's passage suggests a meaning closer to the one implied by Lowry
than to the original passage by Fray Luis (see Maugham 282).[11]
Yet even if Lowry knew of the crucial differences between his
adaptation of *No se puede vivir sin amar* and its earlier significance for Fray Luis, he would surely have focused, as he has,
on the importance of love and the disastrous result of failing to
love. The words that the characters read in *Under the Volcano*
become detached from their original contexts, and their significance in the novel is largely determined by the minds and
situations of the characters who respond to them. The same
principle is at work, of course, whenever the characters react to
a Spanish word as if it were a similar English word: when *evite*

comes to mean *evict* rather than *avoid*, or when *alas* inevitably suggests something other than *wings*.

The ending of *Under the Volcano* juxtaposes Geoffrey's imagined ascent of Popocatepetl against his actual fall into the barranca, requiring us to see his life as simultaneously great and petty, his death as tragic and farcical—"a dingy way to die," in his own last words (UV 373). Two words he hears as he lies dying are "Compañero" and "pelado" (UV 374), and these words also define the poles of his character, signifying his association both with the dying Indian whose own last word is "Compañero" (UV 247) and with the pelado with "smeared conquistador's hands" who stole the Indian's money (UV 250). In his vision of his climb up the volcano, Geoffrey imagines himself as the Indian, "dying by the wayside where no good Samaritan would halt." Suddenly, help is on the way:

> . . . ah, he was being rescued at last. He was in an ambulance shrieking through the jungle itself, racing uphill past the timberline toward the peak—and this was certainly one way to get there!—while those were friendly voices around him, Jacques' and Vigil's, they would make allowances, would set Hugh and Yvonne's minds at rest about him. "No se puede vivir sin amar," they would say, which would explain everything, and he repeated this aloud. How could he have thought so evil of the world when succor was at hand all the time? (UV 375)

In the 1940 typescript, this passage was substantially like the published version, but it was followed by the contrary vision of the other sign:

> And now he had reached the summit, strong hands were lifting him. He opened his eyes; why were they shut? Raising his head, he found he was looking straight at a lamplit notice: ?Le gusta esta jardin? ?Que es suyo? !Evite que Hijos los destruyen! (UV/ 1940 350)

Although the Consul's response is somewhat comic ("Odd— what was the point of one of these damned things on the top of old Beatrice, of old Popeye?"), the sign's appearance here clearly constitutes a final warning to him, one that cancels, or at least tempers, the message of charity that he reads in *No se puede vivir sin amar*. Or, to look at the matter from another perspective: the two signs give us, one final time, both the Consul's great potential and his inability to fulfill that potential, his recognition that one must love others and his failure to believe in his own capacity for love or salvation.

In the published text, Lowry achieves a similar but somewhat more complex effect by moving the garden sign to the endpage, where it stands apart from the Consul's reading of it, and by giving us the definitive text of the sign—arranged on three lines, as on page 128, but with the punctuation corrected, so that we are reminded both of the Consul's interpretation and of the correct translation. Almost inevitably, we are reminded as well of the end of *Candide*, with its injunction to cultivate our garden rather than engage in idle philosophical speculation. Miraculously, the garden is ours (but *why* is it ours, when we cannot deserve it?); it is up to us to save it from destruction by our *hijos*—our sons (but what if, like Geoffrey, we have no sons, despite our self-proclaimed association with el Papa?); if we do not act to save the garden, we will bring about our own eviction. If at the book's end the two meanings of the *le gusta* sign "explode simultaneously" for the reader, as Lowry hoped they would, that is partly because by freeing the words from the narrative, Lowry thrusts us abruptly into the position which the Consul, that earlier reader of the sign, occupied only a few hours before. Whereas the responsibility for reading the sign and acting on it was his before, it is now ours.

⚜

In a discussion of *Tristram Shandy*, Gabriel Josipovici has observed Sterne's refusal to say whether language shapes or merely describes reality, whether figures of speech create or reflect the novel's events (*Writing* 17–19). A similarly circular relationship exists between the Consul's apparently chance encounters with various texts and his sense of his own identity, for each appears to engender (and to be engendered by) the other: from one perspective, the Consul's readings appear perverse and paranoid, an extension of his own identity over the world, yet the texts that he reads also help to shape that identity. Like the Consul, Lowry was also simultaneously the creator of his novel and the creation of the events involved in its composition, a process which, Malcolm Bradbury notes, involved "the collation of seemingly random data which was then capable of being constructed—or rather, constructed itself—into significance" (Bradbury 166). The impression of his being at once inside and outside the novel would later become a highly complex problem for Lowry, but at this stage he managed to be simultaneously involved and detached, identifying himself both with the victimized (and yet self-victimizing) Consul and with the figure of authority who posts the commandment at the book's end.

Ironically, while the documents that people encounter by chance often serve to define and circumscribe their identity, other documents that should identify them prove unreliable. For example, in chapter 3 Geoffrey heads off for a "nameless cantina" in search of "a couple of necessary drinks," intending to return before Yvonne discovers that he is missing. Instead, he falls flat on his face in the Calle Nicaragua, where, after conducting a conversation with himself, he is found by a stereotypical Englishman who helps him up, gives him a drink of Burke's Irish whiskey, and then drives off (UV 77–81). Geoffrey's own anonymity is reflected in the namelessness of the cantina he is seeking and in his thoughts about Hugh's habit of traveling without his passport (as the Consul himself will spend the day without his own passport). When the Englishman picks him up, the Consul is quick to identify him by his school tie, but this sign proves misleading, for the man is wearing his cousin's tie.

If Geoffrey is skillful at identifying English school ties, he is less adept at maintaining a clear and consistent conception of his own identity. Just before the Englishman finds him, Geoffrey compares his mind to "Don Quixote avoiding a town invested with his abhorrence because of his excesses there," and upon his return to Yvonne he enters the room "innocently as a man who has committed a murder while dummy at bridge." Meanwhile, as he speaks to the Englishman, he finds "his own voice becoming involuntarily a little more 'English,'" as if the other man's tones are reshaping him. Finally, in an attempt to identify himself, Geoffrey pulls out a card that turns out not to be his own—nor, for that matter, Dr. Vigil's card, which he found earlier in his trousers pocket (UV 71)—but one from the Venezuelan government's department of foreign affairs. Throughout this scene, whether he imagines himself "sober as a judge" or "erect as Jim Taskerson," the Consul's descriptions of himself are fraudulent; even his language, like the card, often seems secondhand and absurdly inappropriate.

This comic scene has its tragic counterpart in chapter 12, when Hugh's telegram and card appear to identify Geoffrey as a member of the Iberian Anarchist Federation and belie his claim to yet another borrowed identity—as William Blackstone, the Puritan who went to live among the Indians. Earlier, at the Salón Ofélia, the Consul tried to imagine where, among the innumerable glasses and bottles of liquor he had drunk over the years, he might find "the solitary clue to his identity" (UV 293); now, at the Farolito, his sense of his own reality deteriorates further. The repeated question, "What's your names?" (UV 357, 358), seems relevant to a chapter in which names are confused or exchanged ("Mozart wrote the old testimony," but Moses wrote "the D minor quartet") and in which the Consul himself is accused of being a Bolshevik, a murderer, a Jew, a *cabrón* (cuckold), an "espider," Al Capone, and a *pelado*. For that matter, the Consul associates himself, by implication, with the scorpion that, "not wanting to be saved, had stung itself to death" (UV 338); with a "drowned Lithuanian" (UV 353); with the drunkards in Laruelle's picture, "Los Borrachones" (UV 361); and of course with the Indian who died by the wayside, unaided by any good Samaritan (UV 375). In the alcoholic haze and confusion of voices at the Farolito (including the voices of his own familiars, who return to persecute him despite his belief that he has managed to lose them), the Consul's identity becomes further blurred and fragmented. He is, in fact, intricately connected with everything and everyone around him: "he was surrounded in delirium by these phantoms of himself, the policeman, Fructuosa Sanabria, that other man who looked like a poet, the luminous skeletons, even the rabbit in the corner and the ash and sputum on the filthy floor—did not each correspond, in a way he couldn't understand yet obscurely recognized, to some faction of his being?" (UV 361–62).

In chapter 12, as Roger Bromley observes, the Consul "is trapped in a nightmare of bureaucracy, with figures like the chief of gardens, chief of rostrums etc., and where personal identity is rendered quite arbitrary and related solely to documents like passports or identity cards" (Bromley, "Boundaries" 289). A key element in this Kafkaesque sequence is Geoffrey's inability to prove his identity (much less to pass himself off as William Blackstone), a problem caused by his failure to take his passport with him. As an ex-consul, he should be alert to the importance of having the proper documents, especially in times of political turmoil. (Then again, Lowry, having written this episode, should have known better than to leave his papers and Margerie's in Cuernavaca while they traveled to Acapulco in 1946—a serious lapse in judgment that contributed to their ensuing troubles with corrupt officials.) Actually, in an earlier draft the Consul did have his passport; it fell out of his pocket while he rode the infernal loop-the-loop machine at the fair, and a little girl gave it back, so that in the last chapter, after telling him to pay for his whiskey, one of the chiefs can take the passport from him and read it aloud: " 'William Ames,' he spelled out aloud. 'Occupation, retired.'

He was scratching himself. 'What for you want to tell lies?' "
(UV/1940 344). On an annotated carbon copy of this draft, next
to "William Ames" (the Consul's name in this version of the
novel—a name, significantly, not given in its full form until
the chief reads the passport), Lowry wrote "Telegram" in the
left margin (UBC 27:5, 396), apparently signaling his intention
to delete the passport in favor of Hugh's telegram. The documents actually brought forth in the published text—the card
that Hugh left in the jacket pocket and Yvonne's letters, which
Geoffrey lost at the Farolito and Diosdado returned to him—
are contradictory and misleading, yet in some ways thematically appropriate: Hugh is not only Geoffrey's brother but one
of his doubles, and while the telegram certainly does not "say
you are Juden," as the Chief claims (UV 369), the connection
reinforces our sense that the Consul's murder by fascist police
foreshadows the Nazi persecution of the Jews.

David Markson has noted several parallels between this episode and *Alice's Adventures in Wonderland*, among them the
two works' hallucinatory atmospheres and claustrophobic loca-
tions, their persistent questioning of identity, the "perverse
notion of due process" expressed by the Queen of Hearts's
"Sentence first—verdict afterwards" and Weber's "They shoot
first and ask questions later," bottles which say (or might as
well say) "DRINK ME," and the presence in each work of a
white rabbit (Markson 183–84, 188).[12] Markson is less persua-
sive when he discovers another reference to Lewis Carroll in
Geoffrey's idea that he could write "obscure volumes of verse
entitled The Triumph of Humpty Dumpty" (UV 39)—Ackerley and Clipper point instead to a story by Sherwood Anderson
(A&C 69–70)—but the contrast between Geoffrey Firmin and
Humpty Dumpty, as interpreters of texts, nonetheless high-
lights the Consul's problems as a reader.[13] Humpty Dumpty's
claims that when he uses words they mean exactly what he
wants them to, and that he "can explain all the poems that ever
were invented—and a good many that haven't been invented

just yet," express his supreme confidence in his control over language, even though he admits that when he makes a word do an unusual amount of work, he pays it extra wages (*Through the Looking Glass*, ch. 6). For Humpty Dumpty, the ambiguity of language empowers the individual subject, lending him irrefutable authority over words, at least until he falls off the wall. The linguistic authority claimed by Humpty Dumpty is akin to the political language George Orwell decried in *1984* as well as in such essays as "Politics and the English Language" and "Reflections on the Spanish Civil War," works in which he pointed to the conscious manipulation of language for political ends. In *Under the Volcano*, the right-wing radio broadcast that repeatedly asks "Quiere usted la salvación de Méjico?" ("Do you want the salvation of Mexico?"—UV 365, 367, 368) and proclaims the wonderful benefits of civilization (UV 371) provides an example of this sort of dishonest manipulation of linguistic ambiguity, one consistent with Humpty Dumpty's attitude: when the broadcaster uses words like "salvation" and "civilization," they mean exactly what he wants them to mean.

If Humpty Dumpty and the radio broadcaster find it possible to limit the meanings of the words they use, the Consul finds himself swamped by the meanings that emerge from the words that he uses, reads, and hears, so the ambiguity of language becomes a threat to him. The language that seems to be *about* him ultimately *becomes* him, and the consequent blurring of linguistic boundaries is one sign that his own identity is dissolving into incoherence. Moreover, to the extent that he finds himself inseparable from the texts that he reads, the Consul's fate seems to be inscribed in the structure of the universe; to cite the metaphor that recurs in the later works, the Consul almost seems to be *written*. In one sense, of course, this results from his violation of *la vida impersonal* through his ascription of personal significance to external events, his refusal to take responsibility for his actions, and his selfish and self-centered attitude toward others. At the same time, it is hard to read *Under the Volcano* without developing the conviction that we are watching something predetermined and prefigured by the various writings, on the wall or elsewhere, that we read along with Geoffrey Firmin—writings that the Consul regards as part of the tangled forest of symbols whose meanings proliferate until he is left with no clear sense of identity apart from the symbols. From this terrifying correspondence between the proliferation of meaning in every text he reads and the progressive fragmentation and dissolution of his own identity, death proves the only escape.

FOUR

Wrider/Espider: The Consul as
Artist in *Under the Volcano*

In a letter to James Stern written in May 1940, Lowry described, among other things, his 1937 arrest in Mexico. According to Lowry, he was arrested because he was mistaken for a communist friend and was unable "to explain why I absolutely had to be drawing a map of the Sierra Madre in tequila on the bar counter." Once in jail, he was accused of being a spy: "Hissed they (as *Time* would say), 'You say you a wrider but we read all your wridings and dey don't make sense. You no wrider, you an espider and we shoota de espiders in Mejico'" (SL 29). Douglas Day believes Lowry was more apt to have been jailed because of his public drunkenness and "some difficulties over his passport (or lack of it)," and he is undoubtedly right to look skeptically upon Lowry's melodramatic account (ML 238). As to the allegation that Lowry was a spy rather than a writer, perhaps the charge was made in precisely those words, but it is also conceivable that Lowry's recitation of what he experienced a few years earlier was influenced by the draft of *Under the Volcano* that he completed about the time he wrote to Stern. In the last chapter of that draft, as in the published text (UV 371), the

Consul's declaration that his name is William Blackstone and that he is a writer is contradicted by one of the fascist chiefs, who threatens him: " 'You say your name Black. Is no Black.' He shoved him backwards a little. 'You say you a wrider. You are no wrider, you are de espider and we shoot de spiders in Mexico' " (UV/1940 345).[1]

Critics of *Under the Volcano* disagree about whether or not the Consul is really a spy, but few readers doubt that Geoffrey Firmin is indeed a writer. Unfortunately, he is an *artiste man-qué*, a failed (or at least inactive) writer who talks about fin-ishing his book but can barely manage to compose a letter; Yvonne even suggests, not altogether ironically, that he could have used the town's public scribe to answer her letters (UV 53). In view of Lowry's assertion that the book's "four main characters" may be regarded as "aspects of the same man, or of the human spirit" (SL 60), it is significant that the other three major characters are also failed or former artists: Jacques Laruelle is a former movie director, Yvonne an ex-actress, Hugh an unsuccessful song writer and more recently a jour-nalist who has filed his last story. The plight of the artist is central to most of Lowry's fiction, including *Under the Vol-cano*, which contains numerous references to artists and artist figures; even Hitler, according to Hugh, may be regarded as "another frustrated artist" (UV 156). Three supporting char-acters—Dr. Vigil, Mr. Quincey, and Cervantes—have names that echo or approximate those of well-known writers, and the narration often evokes a literary paradigm: "Darkness had fallen like the House of Usher" (UV 22). The powerful hold literary works have over Lowry's principal characters may be indicated by Hugh's experiences at sea, which were influenced by Jack London, of whom he had read "too much"; more sur-prisingly, those experiences also followed patterns suggested by Conrad and Melville, although at the time Hugh had read neither author (UV 157, 162, 165, 167). Similarly, Geoffrey's life has been profoundly shaped not only by the many authors he has read but, more directly, by the English poet Abraham Taskerson, with whose family he spent his adolescent years.

Lowry establishes the Consul's role as artist in several related ways. There is, first of all, his sense of identification either with writers, as when he imagines himself "a sort of Donne of the fairways" (UV 203), or with literary characters such as Don Quixote (UV 39, 79). Moreover, both his immersion in occult studies and his alienation from other people are consistent with the Consul's image of himself as a misunderstood visionary artist, an image reinforced by his reading of the world as a symbolic extension of his mind. In particular, the Consul's feeling that he is at once separate from the world and inseparable from it may be traced to the attitudes of the French symbolists. Maurice Beebe's comments on Baudelaire are pertinent here: "Merging with the crowd, yet remaining alone; in the midst of the world, yet hidden from it—such a paradox may be resolved only if we recognize that for Baudelaire what is outside the self is 'a forest of symbols which correspond to his various states of mind or feeling.'" Thus in "Correspondances," for example, "there is no separation, ideally, between self and cosmos" (Beebe 131). For the Consul, however, this simultaneous involvement with, and isolation from, the world tends to result not in coherence and significance but in the fragmentation and dissolution of the self.

Finally, there are the Consul's meager writings: the book he plans to write, his poem scribbled on the back of a bar tab, and his letter to Yvonne. In these enterprises Lowry portrays significant aspects of his own art but also shows, in painful detail, the danger that lies in wait for the artist whose obsessive self-involvement cuts him off from other people. The unwritten book, the unposted letter, and the unfinished poem all indicate that the Consul's solipsistic reading of the world in personal terms, and his refusal or inability to recognize any reality other than his own—in short, his failure to love another person as much as he loves his isolation and suffering—make him less a "wrider" than an "espider."

Writing to Yvonne in spring 1938, the Consul asks whether she imagines him at work on his book on "ultimate reality" or suspended between the cabbalistic sephiroth Chesed (Mercy) and Binah (Understanding), balanced precariously over a spiritual abyss. He considers himself inadequate for the task of writing the great book (instead, he believes, he "should have been producing obscure volumes of verse. . . . Or at best, like Clare, 'weaving fearful vision' "), but he observes wryly that the advantage in writing a book on "Secret Knowledge" is that the title explains why the book cannot be published (UV 39). By November, when Yvonne returns to him, he obviously has made no progress on the book. Even so, in a moment of repentence, he pledges to cut down on his drinking and then, perhaps, return to the book, which he now says (or thinks) will include "sensational new data on Atlantis" as well as "chapters on the alchemists" (UV 86). Yvonne later tells Hugh that Geoffrey has not worked on the book since she met him, which means that the book has been set aside for at least three years; furthermore, neither she nor Hugh knows whether or not Geoffrey is really informed about "all this alchemy and cabbala business," although his possession of a large number of books on the subject indicates a certain seriousness about it (UV 118). Nonetheless, advising Yvonne to take Geoffrey to an idyllic fishing village in British Columbia where he will have no distractions, Hugh says "perhaps he'll be able really to get down to his book" (UV 122), and at the bullring, Yvonne fantasizes about their house in Canada, where Geoffrey would write his book and she would type it (UV 271). Her vision of the Northern Paradise turns infernal in the dark woods that lead to Parián, however, and as Yvonne dies she envisions the Canadian house on fire, with the burning pages of the book manuscript scattered along the beach (UV 336).

The fire Yvonne sees in her dying moments is based on the one that destroyed the Lowrys' shack in June 1944, taking with it the manuscript of *In Ballast to the White Sea*. For that matter, Yvonne's vision of their life in British Columbia, in a shack between the forest and the beach, is clearly an idealized portrayal of the life Malcolm and Margerie Lowry led in Dollarton, where Malcolm wrote in longhand and Margerie transcribed "all his manuscripts from the slanting script with its queer familiar Greek e's and odd t's into neat clean pages" (UV 271).[2] As Yvonne imagines it, Geoffrey's book would be composed in an atmosphere of wholeness (they would work together on the book which would be, in effect, their child) and harmony with nature:

> and as she worked she would see a seal rise out of the water, peer round, and sink soundlessly. Or a heron, that seemed made of cardboard and string, would flap past heavily, to alight majestically on a rock and stand there, tall and motionless. Kingfishers and swallows flitted past the eaves or perched on their pier. Or a seagull would glide past. . . . (UV 271)

Yvonne's vision of "simplicity and love" stands in sharp contrast to the ambiguity, confusion, and alienation of the Consul's life. Significantly, she imagines the Consul outside (writing his book, chopping wood, fetching water from the well), but the settings where we more often see him are interiors, either the dark cantinas where he confronts his demons or mechanized enclosures (the bus and the "infernal machine"). While there is little doubt that on some level he and Yvonne desire much the same sort of life, Geoffrey's obsessive concern with symbolic correspondences, his solipsistic retreat into his own mind, and of course his drinking all ensure that he and Yvonne will never live to enjoy the Northern Paradise.

As Chris Ackerley has noted, the book the Consul plans

to write apparently involves "the re-assembling of Atlantis in terms of a secret knowledge which will lead to spiritual perfection" and is based upon "the identification of the magic and mysteries of Mexico with those of ancient India" ("The Consul's Book" 80, 82).[3] The parallels between Mexico and India that the Consul hopes to uncover or restore are imaginatively foreshadowed on the opening page of *Under the Volcano*, where the narrator places Quauhnahuac on the same latitude as "the town of Juggernaut, in India, on the Bay of Bengal" (UV 3). The Consul's subject matter generally resembles Lowry's in its encyclopedic nature, its emphasis on the interconnectedness of all things, both physical and spiritual, and its inquiry into the possibility of restoring the primordial harmony that the Consul imagines was represented by Atlantis. The Consul's book is in fact a kind of occult *Volcano*, a portrayal of what Lowry himself might have written (or left unwritten) had he given himself over wholly to mysticism.

The unwritten book is also a prime example of one of Lowry's recurrent themes in *Under the Volcano*: the failure of language as a means of salvation. Letters that remain unwritten or unmailed, Yvonne's postcard that wanders around the world before finally reaching Geoffrey, signs that the characters misread ("¿Le gusta este jardín que es suyo?") or whose implications they ignore ("No se puede vivir sin amar"), words that Geoffrey and Yvonne could speak to one another, but don't—in these instances and others we see precisely the sort of fragmentation, the fall into division, that the Consul's book, ideally, would reverse. Throughout the novel, that division is represented topographically by the abyss or barranca. In chapter 1, Laruelle stands on the bridge over the barranca, which he associates with "finality" and "cleavage," and recalls the legend that the earth split open throughout Mexico when Christ died (UV 15). On the same bridge, Geoffrey once advised him to "make a film about Atlantis" and talked "about the spirit of the abyss, the god of storm, 'huracán,' that 'testified so suggestively to intercourse between opposite sides of the Atlantic' " (UV 16). This sense of cleavage pursues the Consul through the book, affecting him politically through the severance of diplomatic relations between Britain and Mexico and personally through his divorce from Yvonne and his failure at intercourse when she returns; in his letter to Yvonne, he imagines himself "teetering over the awful unbridgeable void, the all-but-unretraceable path of God's lightning back to God" (UV 39), and his failure to bridge that abyss will be made explicit by his fall into the barranca at the end of the novel. Since the book he plans to write involves the rediscovery of lost spiritual truths, Geoffrey's psychic fragmentation, which gives birth to his "familiars," and his lack of "equilibrium" (UV 39) make it impossible for him to sustain his vision. Lowry's insistence on a complex relationship between author and work is particularly evident in the Consul's inability to write a book that is so obviously the antithesis of his own alienation and despair.

Obviously, one reason why the Consul cannot finish the book is that he does not write it: he talks about it, imagining the reviews that will compare his discoveries to those of Ignatius Donnelly (see A&C 132, 133), but instead of actually taking pen in hand and drafting a chapter he wallows in alcoholic self-pity. Lowry's many unfinished manuscripts make the analogy between the Consul and his creator almost irresistible, but there is at least one crucial difference between the two: Lowry was a dedicated writer who found it easy to start projects but hard to complete them, while the Consul only thinks and talks about writing his book. In his letter to Yvonne, the Consul's quip that the book's title, "Secret Knowledge," explains why it can never come out (UV 39) is meant both seriously and ironically, expressing his belief both that he is inadequate to the task and that there is no language that can convey "ultimate reality" directly and unambiguously. Immediately afterward, his reference to himself as Don Quixote ("the Knight of

Sorry Aspect") is equally significant: associating himself with the knight whose greatness was based on delusions, he reveals once again his recognition of his own absurdity, his commitment to the products of his imagination over material reality, and his inability to extricate himself from the identity that he has forged from models that mean as much to him as Amadis did to Cervantes' famous knight.

There is another failure underlying, or at least contributing to, Geoffrey's inability to write his book. That is his violation of the philosophy of the impersonal life—*la vida impersonal*—which is encapsulated in Dr. Vigil's advice to Laruelle, "Come, amigo, throw away your mind" (UV 6, 12; cf. DG 239). Both in his vision of himself as terribly, irrevocably alone and in his solipsistic vision of the world as a projection of his mind—the two poles of his relationship to external reality that lead his sense of his own identity to become increasingly blurred and fragmented—he violates the principles of harmony and equilibrium in the vision of "ultimate truth" that he would present through his book.

The letter he writes to Yvonne, but never mails, is one of Geoffrey Firmin's most eloquent and moving statements in the entire novel—and perhaps his most honest assessment of his situation, as well. Even so, the letter is replete with ironies whose significance emerges only in the aftermath of the Consul's death. Inserted in the anthology of Elizabethan plays that the Consul lent to Jacques Laruelle in spring 1938, lost when Laruelle misplaced it some months later, the letter resurfaces in chapter 1, a year after the Consul's death, when Sr. Bustamente finds the volume of plays and gives it to Laruelle. Since the letter falls out of the book just after Laruelle reads passages from Marlowe's *Doctor Faustus*, Walker and Holt observe that Geoffrey's "first words come as if straight from the pages of *Faustus* and are suited to it: 'Night: and once again the nightly grapple with death, the room shaking with daemonic orchestras' " (Walker and Holt 112). His statements that "the name of this land is hell" and "this is what it is to live in hell" (UV 36, 38) recall Mephistophilis' line, "Why this is hell, nor am I out of it" (Marlowe 12 [sc. iii]), a declaration which, although quite true, lures Faustus into a false sense of security. A final irony in the Consul's letter is contained in the line at which Laruelle stops reading: "come back to me, Yvonne, if only for a day" (UV 41). This letter, coincidentally resurfacing on the anniversary of its author's death, is so clearly an omen of that death that Laruelle can only burn it, thereby inadvertently confirming, once again, the identification of the doomed author with his text.

The most thorough analysis of the letter and its place within the novel has been carried out by Charles Baxter, who argues that Laruelle's burning of the letter represents "the simultaneously reverent and murderous attitude held toward language, particularly the language of art, in Lowry's novel" (Baxter 115). Baxter defines those attitudes as those of "the symbolist and the ironist," two aesthetic types represented by the Consul; in burning the letter, Laruelle gives us a momentary glimpse of the nineteenth-century symbolist's belief that literary language can allow "the object to burn with significance and light" before reverting to the modern ironist's recognition of the arbitrary and unstable relationship between language and whatever it purports to represent. It might be added that the most obvious problem with the letter is that even as he writes it, Geoffrey knows—and says in the letter (UV 40)—that he will never send it, just as he will not finish writing his book. The act of writing is therefore inherently ironic, for it is only by mere chance that the letter falls out of the volume of plays and gains an audience: Laruelle, and through him, us. Our reading is apparently incomplete, for the letter's text begins and ends with ellipses, and by destroying the letter Laruelle tries to ensure that it will have no subsequent

readers. Nonetheless, Lowry emphasized that the novel's shape
is "essentially trochal" (SL 88), and as we begin another revolution of his luminous wheel the letter will exist briefly before
being destroyed once again.

Baxter has linked the Consul's failure as visionary artist to
that of the Poet in Shelley's *Alastor*.[4] In that poem the imagination, divorced from the objects of natural affection, enters
into a deadly solipsism that eventually destroys the Poet (Baxter 118–19). Toward the end of chapter 5, Geoffrey refers to
Alastor, telling Dr. Vigil, "Ah, that the dream of dark magician in his visioned cave, even while his hand—that's the bit I
like—shakes in its last decay, were the true end of this so lovely
world" (UV 147). He repeats the lines to Laruelle in chapter 7, this time changing "this so lovely world" to "this so lousy
world" (UV 202). The Consul's reference is to lines 681–88 of
Alastor, where Shelley laments the Poet's death. Both Kilgallin
and Pagnoulle have noted that the Consul changes Shelley's
"the true *law* / Of this so lovely world" to "the true *end* of this
so lovely world," converting the passage into an eschatological
vision that foreshadows the Consul's own death in chapter 12
(Kilgallin, "Faust and *Under the Volcano*" 31–32; Pagnoulle
79). *Alastor*'s connection with the Consul's fate is reinforced,
ironically, by the statement Geoffrey makes to Dr. Vigil immediately after citing the lines from Shelley: "Jesus. Do you
know, compañero, I sometimes have the feeling that it's actually sinking, like Atlantis, beneath my feet" (UV 147). Like
Shelley (UV 204), the Consul will sink and drown rather than
admit he cannot swim; his allusion to the sinking of Atlantis connects his own isolation to the spiritual crisis that his
book supposedly would resolve; and the rare use of *compañero*
(comrade), a word associated both with the Indian's death and
with his own death (UV 247, 374), provides us with yet another
omen of the Consul's doom.

Since Lowry associates *Alastor* with the Consul's role as the
introverted visionary artist obsessed with the products of his

own imagination, it is interesting that in the 1940 typescript
of *Under the Volcano* the lines quoted here are actually written
by the Consul on the title page of *Doctor Faustus,* as Laruelle
discovers in the process of playing *sortes Shakespeareanae:*

> Too astonished to heed what he might have amusingly con-
> strued as a warning to himself, Laruelle tried opening the book
> with his left hand and, scarcely giving time to whatever knowl-
> edgeable coalitions there might be to do their work, he brought
> his finger down, to his relief, on the title page of the play. But
> looking again, Laruelle saw that the page was not blank at all,
> something was faintly pencilled upon it, as though an attempt
> had been made to rub it out. Looking still closer, and holding
> the book even closer up to the dismal light he read:
>> O, that God
>> Profuse of poisons which. . . .
>>> a star that feels
>> No proud exemption in the blighting curse
>> He bears, over the world wanders for ever
>> Love as incarnate death! Oh, that the dream
>> Of dark magician in his visioned cave
>> Raking the cinders of a crucible
>> For life and power, even when his feeble hand
>> Shakes in its last decay, were the true end
>> Of this so lovely world.
>>> University of Tortu, Lithuania, 19—
> And under this, over and over again had been written and
> erased, and rewritten as if by a man obsessed by a single thought,
> yet continually rejecting that thought even as another will within
> him endlessly jostled round it, the one word: Priscilla. (UV/1940
> 25–26; ellipsis in typescript)[5]

In this typescript, the letter's ambiguous status as a text that
is simultaneously present and absent, written to someone else
yet not meant to be read, is mirrored by the words written in
the book and then erased, which suggest both the instability
of language and the Consul's inability to believe in language

as a means of redemption.[6] The words the Consul inscribes in the book alternate not only between presence and absence but also between Shelley's solipsistic image of the "dark magician in his visioned cave" and the Consul's tentative reaching out to Priscilla (as the wife was called at this stage of composition). His wife's name, obsessively written, erased, and rewritten, represents the Consul's attempt to find love in another person, while the *Alastor* passage, celebrating the Poet's inner vision (even at the cost of life), implies that eventually the Consul will regard his own inner reality as more important than the life around him.

In the 1940 draft, the Consul writes the lines from *Alastor* on the title page of *Doctor Faustus* rather than in his letter, yet what he inscribes in the book resembles what he writes in his letter. In the novel's final form, the description of Geoffrey's handwriting in the letter dramatizes the conflict between life and death that he is experiencing: "But there was no mistaking, even in the uncertain light, the hand, half crabbed, half generous, and wholly drunken, of the Consul himself, the Greek e's, flying buttresses of d's, the t's like lonely wayside crosses save where they crucified an entire word, the words themselves slanting steeply downhill, though the individual characters seemed as if resisting the descent, braced, climbing the other way" (UV 35). Although this is presented to us through Laruelle's eyes, it undoubtedly reflects the Consul's own vision of himself, one that is highly romanticized and yet ironic. The general pattern of the handwriting represents Geoffrey's descent into the abyss, a descent interrupted by numerous instances of heroic resistance that imply his struggle against an implacable fate. Ackerley and Clipper note that the Consul's "t's foreshadow the encounter at the lonely wayside cross with the dying Indian" (A&C 60), but the crucifixion imagery here is ambiguous: the isolated crosses might suggest the Consul's role as sacrificial victim, but the t's that crucify entire words may also reveal his capacity to drag others to destruction along with him.

The Consul's isolation is a recurrent theme in his letter, as in the novel generally. Aware that at least some of the "reality" he experiences is hallucinatory, like the scornful repetition of his name by "imaginary parties" (UV 35), he is nonetheless unable to escape the feeling that his own reality is somehow deeper or more significant than that of others. Like Marlowe's Faustus, he is a doomed explorer of forbidden realms: "And this is how I sometimes think of myself, as a great explorer who has discovered some extraordinary land from which he can never return to give his knowledge to the world: but the name of this land is hell" (UV 36).[7] He also associates himself with Blake, who knew that "right through hell there is a path" (UV 36), and in his vision of the Northern Paradise he imagines that he and Yvonne are like Swedenborg's eastward-facing angels (UV 37), even though his own tendency is always to look away from the sun. Writing his letter in the Farolito, which comes to represent his imprisonment in his own mind, the Consul laments that no one else can tell him about Yvonne, and even finds that she cannot possibly understand him: "You cannot know the sadness of my life" (UV 40). Geoffrey's conviction of his difference from others derives in large part from his alcoholism, the drinking which he carries out "as if I were taking an eternal sacrament" (UV 40). His drinking reinforces the inwardness and preoccupation with the self that characterize his meditations, perhaps allowing him to see brilliantly, as when he alone understands "the beauty of an old woman from Tarasco who plays dominoes at seven o'clock in the morning" (UV 50), but at the same time making it all but impossible to tell anyone what he has envisioned; it is also what renders him incapable of understanding "more than the governing design" of Yvonne's letters (UV 38).

Virtually every aspect of Geoffrey's life—his decision to remain in Quauhnahuac after Britain severs diplomatic relations with Mexico, his involvement in occult mysteries, his failure to mail the letter to Yvonne, his drinking—seems calculated to prevent him from having to give up his isolation. Since, as Walter Ong has noted, "Writing and reading are solitary activities that throw the psyche back on itself" (Ong 69), the Consul's immersion in these processes both reflects and stimulates his radical separation from other people. Ideally, the letter he writes to Yvonne would lead to her return and end his suffering, but while he includes a brief vision of their Northern Paradise (UV 36–38) and recognizes that "love is the only thing which gives meaning to our poor ways on earth" (UV 40), he is principally intent on cultivating his image as sufferer. In terms of *la vida impersonal*, the Consul's "excessive remorse," which attributes "formidable value" to himself (GE 46), is a fatal flaw that inevitably results in his eviction from the garden of his soul. While the obsession with his suffering and his private visions provides him with the material for his writing, it also makes it very difficult for him to construct a coherent vision of reality in his book, or even to communicate his suffering to Yvonne by mailing the letter.

✦

The Consul's representation of himself as a tormented soul recurs memorably in the unfinished poem he writes below his bar tab on the back of a menu at the Restaurant El Popo, where Yvonne and Hugh find it when they stop for a drink on the way to the Farolito. The bill is headed "Recknung" (UV 330), the Consul's inadvertent pun on English "reckoning" underscoring the portentous implications of German *Rechnung* (bill, reckoning).[8] The boundaries of the text below the chit are undefined, as Lowry is concerned with revealing the remnants of the composition process rather than a finished product. On the left are various rhyming words and phrases the Consul tried out, while the poem on the right is described as "an attempt at some kind of sonnet perhaps, but of a wavering and collapsed design, and so crossed out and scrawled over and stained, defaced, and surrounded with scratchy drawings—of a club, a wheel, even a long black box like a coffin—as to be almost undecipherable" (UV 330).

Even so, enough remains of the text to make it clear that the Consul identifies himself with the "poor foundered soul / Who once fled north" (UV 331). The poem concludes ambiguously: throughout *Under the Volcano*, the north has been associated with rationality, civilization, and redemption, and the south with dissolution, as in the description of the highway on the book's opening page or the numerous visions of British Columbia as the Northern Paradise. Here, however, the tormented flight northward seems to reverse the dominant pattern of the book's geographical symbolism by associating the north with the infernal regions. The phrase "who once fled north" haunts Yvonne, echoing in her mind five times as she and Hugh leave the restaurant to plunge into the dark woods (UV 331–32). Yvonne soon comes to understand the poem much as we do, as evidence that the Consul has rejected the possibility of salvation: " 'Who once fled north.' But they were not going north, they were going to the Farolito. Nor had the Consul fled north then, he'd probably gone of course, just as to-night, to the Farolito" (UV 332). Once again, then, the Consul's isolation, his self-involvement, and his flight from redemption are reflected in his role as artist.

Even more than his letter or his book, the Consul's unfinished poem is intimately and complexly related to Lowry's own writing. In *Dark as the Grave*, Sigbjørn Wilderness recalls having written this same poem on the back of a Mexican menu, then rediscovering the menu and poem while he was writing *The Valley of the Shadow of Death* (as *Under the Volcano* is called in the later works) and inserting it into the manuscript as something written by the Consul (DG 84–85). What Sigbjørn describes is what Lowry actually did—his original poem, written on the back of a menu that advertises the Mexican national lottery, is now included in the William Loftus Templeton Collection at the University of British Columbia— so that Lowry manages to attribute his own composition to two of his characters, one of whom assigns it, in turn, to the other. While the strategy enables us to see Geoffrey and Sigbjørn as variations on their creator, it also distances Lowry from the Consul by placing his romanticized poem within the frame of Sigbjørn's fiction. Written out of his despair at the breakup of his first marriage, Lowry's poem signals his conviction of his own worthlessness and his inability to seek salvation: Ackerley and Clipper note that the poem resembles Francis Thompson's "The Hound of Heaven" (A&C 410), but while Thompson's persona finds salvation despite himself, the Consul's persona seems inevitably headed toward destruction.[9] By projecting his poem's language onto the Consul, Lowry relives the hopelessness he felt when his first marriage broke up, but he also exorcises the ghost of his own past by placing the poem within the context of *Under the Volcano* and then framing that book with *Dark as the Grave*, where the poem takes on new meaning as a harbinger of the Consul's death.

Already in *Under the Volcano*, the Consul's unfinished poem reflects Lowry's ambiguous attitude toward the relationship between writing and death. Richard Kearney's description of Samuel Beckett might apply to Lowry as well:

> Beckett's obsession with the suffering of being springs from his awareness that language—and more particularly writing— is a process of dying. Language brings us face to face with our own mortality by making us aware that we can never escape from time so as to become fully present to ourselves. We are finite, temporal, decentred beings who, as the structuralists declare, are spoken by language before we choose to speak it. (Kearney 70)

Thus, in Beckett's trilogy (*Molloy, Malone Dies,* and *The Unnamable*), despite their desire to lapse into silence and die, the narrators are kept alive by the words they write, speak, or imagine themselves speaking. Malone, for example, resolves to tell himself stories to pass the time while he waits to die, and when he finishes, presumably he is dead. For Beckett, being is inseparable from perception or consciousness, which requires articulation: as the Unnamable says, although he cannot believe in the "facts" of which he speaks, "I am obliged to speak. I shall never be silent. Never" (Beckett 291).

The awareness of death inherent in Beckett's language makes explicit one of the conditions that Maurice Blanchot finds in modern literature generally (Blanchot 87–107). Considering Kafka's belief that his best writing established a "relation with death," Gide's statement that he wrote "to shelter something from death," and Proust's conception of art as a personal triumph over death, Blanchot suggests that these writers recognize a fundamental kinship between writing and death. In writing, Blanchot argues, all three authors "want death to be possible: [Kafka] in order to grasp it, [Gide and Proust] in order to hold it at a distance" (Blanchot 95). Likewise, in his essay "Language to Infinity," Michel Foucault has pointed to "an essential affinity between death, endless striving, and the self-representation of language," an affinity particularly evident in alphabetical language, whose phonetic representation of spoken language begins the process by which language comes to dwell upon itself (Foucault 55–56).[10] Walter Ong, too, has noted the long-established relationship, in Western culture, between writing and death, beginning with Plato's attacks on writing in the *Phaedrus* and St. Paul's declaration that "the letter killeth, but the spirit giveth life" (2 Cor. 3:6). Paradoxically, the "dead" text preserves language, so that "its removal from the living human lifeworld, its rigid visual fixity, assures its endurance and its potential for being resurrected into limitless living contexts by a potentially infinite number of living readers" (Ong 81).

The association of writing with death or entrapment within

the work is a recurrent theme in Lowry's later fiction, culminating in his conception of "death as the accepted manuscript of one's life" (WP 74). In *Under the Volcano*, the Consul's writing is associated with death from the first words that Laruelle reads when he picks up the unposted letter to Yvonne: "Night: and once again, the nightly grapple with death" (UV 35). Between the margins of his sheets of paper, Geoffrey attempts to carve out his own space, create his own reality, forge his identity. The unfinished book or poem, the unmailed letter, is for this reason preferable to its completed counterpart, because it remains within the realm of the Consul's imagination, under his control. The many examples of Geoffrey's own readings indicate that a completed and published text comes to signify not what its author might have intended but what the individual reader sees in it. Similarly, in his poem "In Memory of W. B. Yeats," Auden observes that when poets die, their words are "modified" by every reading and become continuous with their readers' lives.

Lowry establishes the point another way. As Baxter notes, when the Consul's writings are exposed to the gaze of others, the "products of his imagination suddenly become commodities, *things*" (Baxter 116). The potential status of his writings as objects subject to manipulation by others is underscored by the emphasis on their physical appearance, much as the novel's typography tends to emphasize the existence of other written language—on signs and in the Tlaxcaltecan tourist brochure, for instance—as commodities. When Laruelle picks up the letter to Yvonne or when Yvonne imagines typing the Consul's manuscripts, the description of the Consul's handwriting emphasizes the document's physical appearance (UV 35, 271), while their susceptibility to fire removes the letter and manuscript from the realm of imagination and places them solidly within the temporal world of consumable objects.

Even more clearly, the poem that Hugh and Yvonne discover is circumscribed by the menu on whose reverse side it is written. Yvonne first reads the printed side, seeing the typed list of prices, the wheel-within-wheel logo of the national lottery, and the picture of "a smiling young woman" holding up lottery tickets which in turn portray a cowgirl who reminds Yvonne of her career as an actress in western movies (UV 329). Within the context of the *Volcano*, these images take on new and unforeseen meanings. Not only the cowgirl but the "happy mother caressing her child" in the lottery logo are ironically connected to Yvonne's past (her child died of meningitis at the age of six months); the woman with the lottery tickets who is seen "beckoning roguishly" has her counterpart in María, the prostitute with whom Geoffrey would be having intercourse around the time when Yvonne looks at the menu; the wheel suggests the book's circular structure as well as the pattern of fate that controls the Consul's destiny; and the image within an image— the woman contained within two wheels, the cowgirls on lottery tickets held by another woman—is related to the Farolito, whose increasingly smaller rooms are in turn a model of the universe (UV 200, 343, 347). The illustrations on the menu provide the context for the Consul's poem and, perhaps, influence the Consul's own drawings that surround the poem: the wheel and coffin, in particular, echo the images of entrapment on the other side of the menu, and the poem's references to escape, death, and a "cold cell" continue the theme.

In his poem the Consul describes himself (or his persona) as being unaware that "his pursuers gave up hope / Of seeing him (dance) at the end of a rope." The ironic connection between the persecutors and their victim, both of whom have abandoned all hope, is one of the finer touches in the poem, which, like his letter to Yvonne, shows that the Consul possesses real insight into his situation. Even so, the two works inevitably seem exaggerated, melodramatic, inescapably focused on his private world to the exclusion of other realities. Like his tendency to undertake ambitious projects (his book on "ultimate reality," no less) and leave them unfinished, the Consul's emphasis on his internal vision is typical of one strain of romantic artist—one that Shelley found sufficiently strong in his own character to write *Alastor* as, in effect, a warning to himself to resist the allure of imaginative partheno-genesis. (Mary Shelley's *Frankenstein* is based on much the same principle, albeit with the twist that Frankenstein fails not only to consider other people but to love his own creation as well.) Another aesthetic type that seems to be represented by the Consul is the expressionist: Sherrill Grace connects ex-pressionism to Geoffrey's "projection of inner confusion upon external reality" and his inability "to distinguish between self and not self . . . to act or to love" ("Expressionist Vision" 99, 109). Both the Poet of *Alastor* and the expressionist envision the world in terms of self, thereby violating Lowry's precept of *la vida impersonal.*

There is perhaps one more prototype for the Consul's role as artist, one that suggests why his work seems deficient, why he is unable to bridge the gap between writer and audience (and, indeed, is unwilling even to seek an audience). That prototype may be implied, ironically, by the Chief of Rostrums' decla-ration that the Consul is not a "wrider" but an "espider" (UV 371). The spider, or spy, resembles the plagiarist in merely ap-propriating what rightfully belongs to someone else, but the Consul as artist is less a plagiarist than a solipsist or egotist. In this regard he resembles the spider who, in Swift's *The Battle of the Books*, spins its web out of the materials of its own body, scorning everything that it does not produce. For Swift, who favored the Ancients (the bee) over the Moderns (the spider), the bee is an example of liberal and humanistic thought; in Lowry's terms, it might exemplify *la vida impersonal.* The spi-der, however, represents an art founded on narrowness and conceit. Cutting himself off from others, the spider proclaims his own superiority and self-sufficiency, but the results are un-satisfying: if his webs survive, that is only because they are hidden in a corner where they will not be put to use.

If the plagiarist represents one type of failed artist in Lowry's fiction, his converse is the egotist who, like Swift's spider, regards his imagination as both original and self-sufficient. Both types fail to create an authentic art because they misjudge or misconstrue the relationship of the self to exterior reality: the plagiarist assimilates another's text, thereby declaring hegemony over all written language, while the spider blindly asserts his superiority to both nature and culture. A crucial difference between the Consul and Lowry, in this respect, is indicated by *Under the Volcano* itself, for the novel incorporates the products of the Consul's imagination, written and otherwise, into a larger vision that includes other distinct viewpoints, discourses, and frames of reference.[11] Whereas the Consul can discover no way out of the labyrinth of his mind, we are permitted to glimpse the paths he has missed on his way through the dark woods to the Farolito, as he progressively excludes every reality but that of his tormented imagination. And the reality he most clearly evades, denies, and excludes is that of Yvonne, the intended recipient of his unposted letter, his would-be collaborator on the unwritten book, and the instrument of salvation from whom he flees to the Farolito. If, as Lowry tells us over and over, one cannot live without loving, then the failure of the Consul as artist tells us that in Lowry's view, at least, any art not founded on the capacity to love is also doomed to fail.

FIVE

The Grand Scheme:
The Voyage That Never Ends

Lowry's notes for his screen adaptation of *Tender Is the Night* include a detailed commentary on the meaning of Fitzgerald's title, with its allusion to Keats's "Ode to a Nightingale" (NS 60–68). As perceptive as these remarks are, Lowry's speculations about Fitzgerald's "affinity" with Keats are even more revealing, at least for critics of Malcolm Lowry's fiction. Both writers, Lowry maintains, were "perfectionists at bottom" whose work nonetheless contains more promise than fulfillment. For that reason, he argues that Fitzgerald would have associated himself with Keats, whose poems range from the "absolute perfection" of "The Eve of St. Agnes" to what Lowry describes as "the incomplete, the fragmentary, the juvenile, the damned, the marvelously promising, and finally the posthumous and the half-finished." Between Fitzgerald and Keats, Lowry discerns "a sad and shared story of great capabilities that were not to be realized" (NS 70).

What is most intriguing about this assessment of Keats and Fitzgerald is how readily the same terms apply to Lowry himself. *Under the Volcano* might be one of those rare novels that approximate "absolute perfection," but most of Lowry's other works, although for the most part "marvelously promising," are either "incomplete" (not to mention "fragmentary" and "half-finished": Lowry's redundancy on this point is significant), or "juvenile," or "damned," while virtually all of them are "posthumous." Like the subjects of his analysis, Lowry was a perfectionist, at least with respect to his art, and he found it difficult to let go of his work and mail it off to a publisher, perhaps because he feared rejection (a lesson painfully learned from the numerous refusals of the 1940 *Volcano* draft), but also because he could always see ways to improve his manuscript.[1] Indeed, in his 1951 "Work in Progress" statement, written four years after publication of *Under the Volcano*, Lowry still referred to the *Volcano* as "a more or less finished novel, that has already been published, but which is a cub that can still stand a little further licking" (WP 77). The purpose of further revisions would have been to integrate the novel into the sequence of *The Voyage That Never Ends*, where, in the guise of *The Valley of the Shadow of Death* by Sigbjørn Wilderness, it would be a novel-within-a-novel, apparently twice removed from Lowry's own life and yet even more intricately entangled with it. Sigbjørn, meanwhile, although based on Lowry, would not be identified absolutely either with Lowry himself or with the persona that he adopts as the creator (or dreamer) of the entire *Voyage*.

By 1951 Lowry's concept of *The Voyage That Never Ends* had changed drastically from his original plans for a trilogy modeled after *The Divine Comedy*, with *Under the Volcano* as the *Inferno*, *Lunar Caustic* as the *Purgatorio*, and *In Ballast to the White Sea* as the *Paradiso* (SL 63, 113–14, 255). Several experiences were crucial in reshaping the *Voyage* sequence: the loss of the *In Ballast* manuscript in June 1944; Lowry's 1945–46 trip to Mexico, which provided him with the raw materials for *Dark as the Grave* and *La Mordida;* and his July 1949 fall from a pier, which resulted in his being hospitalized in Vancouver. The very success of *Under the Volcano* encouraged Lowry to attempt an even larger and more ambitious project, one that would incorporate both his life and the "whole bolus" of his fiction within one major cycle of works. Finally, there was Lowry's interest in "organic form," which, as a metaphor for literary art, values "the promise of the incomplete, and the glory of the imperfect," implying "a complex inter-relation of living, indeterminate, and endlessly changing components" rather than a fixed set of mechanical relations (Abrams 220). The concept of organic form also reinforced Lowry's tendency to see life and art as interchangeable (or, on another level, as substitutes for one another), and it made bringing the *Voyage* to a conclusion even more of a problem, for as Sigbjørn Wilderness realizes, "an organic work of art, having been conceived, must grow in the creator's mind, or proceed to perish" (DG 154).

In the revised *Voyage* sequence, outlined in the "Work in Progress" statement, the 1949 hospital experience—fictionalized in *The Ordeal of Sigbjørn Wilderness*—became the framing device for the entire series of works. While undergoing treatment for a back injury, Lowry's protagonist has a psychic experience that Lowry described as "a sort of battle between life and delirium, in which life . . . is fighting to give that delirium a form, a meaning" (WP 74). Once again, life seems to be dependent upon art, for as the dying man's life flashes before his eyes, he reshapes it, through a process of "artistic selection," into a series of works that constitute the "form" or "meaning" of the "delirium" that has been his life. The order of the works, at least as Lowry planned at that time to arrange them, is given on the cover sheet for the description:

—WORK IN PROGRESS—

THE VOYAGE THAT NEVER ENDS

THE ORDEAL OF SIGBJØRN WILDERNESS   I

UNTITLED SEA NOVEL   LUNAR CAUSTIC

UNDER THE VOLCANO   ←The Centre

DARK AS THE GRAVE WHEREIN MY FRIEND IS LAID

ERIDANUS   } Trilogy

LA MORDIDA

THE ORDEAL OF SIGBJØRN WILDERNESS   II

(WP 72; UBC 32:1)

The relationship between the untitled sea novel (a revision of *Ultramarine*) and *Lunar Caustic*, Lowry said, would parallel that between *Under the Volcano* and *Dark as the Grave* (WP 75). Although the "Work in Progress" statement provides few details on this score, other notes indicate that in the revised *Lunar Caustic*, Bill Plantagenet was to have been replaced by the Earl of Thurstaston, apparently the fictionalized author of *Ultramarine* (UBC 15:12). The parallel with *Dark as the Grave*, then, is that one reason for the Earl's stay at the psychiatric hospital would be so that he can learn to deal with the influence of a novel by a Scandinavian author (Nordahl Grieg) on his own sea novel—just as, in *Dark as the Grave*, Sigbjørn Wilderness is plagued by other people's suspicions that he stole his material for *The Valley of the Shadow of Death* (*Under the Volcano*) from *Drunkard's Rigadoon* (*The Lost Weekend*).

The protagonists of all of the novels in the *Voyage* would be versions of the protagonist of *The Ordeal of Sigbjørn Wilderness*, whose unending voyage, which Lowry equates with "life itself" (WP 75), is one of self-discovery and self-creation. All of these characters are artist figures, in accordance with Lowry's belief that "man himself is . . . a sort of novelist," and death is "the accepted manuscript of one's life" (WP 74). At the conclusion of the *Voyage*, Lowry planned for "the end of La Mordida [to] merge into Sigbjørn Wilderness' recovery in hospital after his near fatal accident" (WP 96). Since the author, or dreamer, of all these "manuscripts" does not die, the manuscript of his life is apparently rejected, which is another way of saying that the structure of the *Voyage*, like that of *Under the Volcano*, is cyclic.[2] The idea that Lowry's entire corpus was planned as something comparable to an unfinished or rejected manuscript makes the whole enterprise seem fundamentally ironic, but given Lowry's association of completion with death, the comparison seems inevitable. On another level, since Sigbjørn imagines the world as a rejected play or novel—his own novel, in fact (DG 12)—the implied parallel between the *Voyage* and a rejected manuscript further complicates the relationship between text and world, art and life. Finally, since Lowry tends to equate the author with the work, the *Voyage* can never be completed (it is, after all, *The Voyage That Never Ends*) but must undergo continual revision, at least figuratively—as a text that accumulates new meanings with every reading or with new events in the author's life that alter the significance of what he wrote before. For Lowry, the danger lies in taking this metaphor of rejection and revision too literally and coming to fear the completion and acceptance of his magnum opus on the grounds that the work, like its author, must always be in progress.

At the center of the series is *Under the Volcano*, a novel that "represents something in the nature of a psychological objective triumph" for the protagonist of the *Voyage* (WP 77). Nonetheless, even apart from the whole issue of *The Lost Weekend*, the success of *Under the Volcano* presents a problem for Sigbjørn Wilderness, who, on his return to Mexico, repeats Lowry's post-*Volcano* sensation of being trapped within his own novel. The proposed trilogy of *Dark as the Grave*, *Eridanus*, and *La Mordida* emerged out of Lowry's experiences during his 1945–46 trip to Mexico, during which he was constantly involved in events that seemed to come directly out of the pages of his own novel. In Cuernavaca, for example, the Lowrys stayed at the house where Jacques Laruelle had lived in the novel, and when the letter arrived to tell Lowry that *Under the Volcano* had been accepted by Reynal and Hitchcock, it was brought by the same postman who had delivered Yvonne's long-overdue card to the Consul. There were, of course, such familiar sights as the sign reading ¿*Le gusta este jardín que es suyo?* (which Lowry now realized he had miscopied, and mistranslated, during his earlier visit), but most startling of all was the discovery that his friend Juan Fernando Márquez had been shot to death in a drunken cantina argument six years earlier. Márquez, whom Lowry renamed Fernando Atonalzin in "Garden of Etla" and Juan Fernando Martinez in *Dark as the Grave*, was the proponent of *la vida impersonal*; in *Under the Volcano*, both Dr. Vigil and Hugh's friend Juan Cerillo are based on him. Given his growing inclination to believe that he was living in a world influenced by his own writings (a view directly opposed to *la vida impersonal*, for whatever that is worth), Lowry could not help feeling that the parallels between the Consul's death and that of Juan Fernando Márquez were more than coincidental. The fact that his trip involved him in serious difficulties with the Mexican police did nothing to improve Lowry's state of mind, even though his own legal problems (being arrested for alleged nonpayment of a fine during his previous stay in Mexico) resulted merely in his deportation rather than in his death.

At one point, Lowry planned to increase Sigbjørn's sense of being trapped within a fiction by introducing a new character, a French movie director named L'Hirondelle, supposedly the person upon whom Sigbjørn had patterned Jacques Laruelle. L'Hirondelle does not appear in the manuscripts of *Dark as the Grave* or *La Mordida*, both of which were well under way before the 1949 accident that gave Lowry the idea of using the *Ordeal* as the frame for the *Voyage*; his appearance in the "Work in Progress" description seems to indicate a new development that Lowry never really carried out. The plans for the *Voyage* involved introducing L'Hirondelle—who, like the Wildernesses, is traveling to Cuernavaca—at the San Francisco airport, where he spots Sigbjørn and wonders if he is someone L'Hirondelle knew years earlier. At the next stop, the Los Angeles airport, Sigbjørn leaves the manuscript for *The Valley of the Shadow of Death* at a bar, where L'Hirondelle finds it, begins reading, and recognizes himself—*sortes Shakespeareanae!*—as the original of Laruelle. Eventually Sigbjørn and L'Hirondelle meet in Cuernavaca, where Sigbjørn and Primrose are staying at a house owned by L'Hirondelle, and in *Eridanus*, Lowry planned to have the Wildernesses invite L'Hirondelle to dinner and tell him about their life in Canada.

Little was ever written of *Eridanus*, however, and most of that was absorbed into *October Ferry to Gabriola*, which takes place entirely in Canada.[3]

In the final volume of the trilogy, *La Mordida*, Sigbjørn sees bad omens everywhere and believes that his daemon is controlling him for some sinister purpose. During a sight-seeing trip to Acapulco, Sigbjørn is arrested by the Mexican police, who claim that during his previous trip to Mexico he stayed longer than his visa allowed, failed to pay a fine, and should not have been allowed to reenter Mexico. While detained at his hotel until his legal problems are cleared up (preferably through payment of *la mordida:* "the bite," Mexican slang for the expected small bribe), Sigbjørn learns that *The Valley of the Shadow of Death* has been accepted for publication, but he and Primrose have little opportunity to enjoy his "triumph" amidst the "endless tortures" inflicted on them by the Mexican officials (WP 92). Eventually, however, they are released and travel back to Canada. At the end of *La Mordida*, Lowry planned to return to the framework of *The Ordeal of Sigbjørn Wilderness*, where we now realize that the idyllic conclusion of *La Mordida* has in fact been succeeded by the accident that set in motion the entire *Voyage* sequence. The whole visionary experience has been beneficial, for now the protagonist has been given a religious vision that allows him to see his life and work in perspective. Lowry planned to conclude the *Ordeal* with a scene borrowed from "The Forest Path to the Spring," one that portrays the protagonist and his wife "watching the tide bearing the ships out upon its currents that become remote, and which, like the Ice, becoming remote, return" (WP 97). Significantly, the terrible isolation that follows the Lowryan protagonist throughout *The Voyage That Never Ends* was to have given way to an affirmation of the importance of love.

The Ordeal of Sigbjørn Wilderness exists in a 160-page typescript that is now stored at the University of British Columbia library (UBC 22:19). Although numbered consecutively, the pages do not all belong to a single draft but involve some over-lapping, fresh starts, and revision. Moreover, in a pattern typi-cal of Lowry's drafts for his later works, the typescript includes not only material that has been more or less worked into shape but a great deal of undigested matter: Lowry's meditations on the function of literature, newspaper articles copied directly into the typescript, notes on such diverse sources as Arthur Lovejoy's *The Great Chain of Being*, Annie Besant's *The Ancient Wisdom*, and Michael Williams's *The Catholic Church in Action*, drafts of Lowry's letters (including one to T. R. Henn, the Yeats scholar, who had been one of Lowry's professors at Cambridge), and the like.

In the narrative itself, which begins on page 29 (with a new draft beginning on page 78), the protagonist lies "on a stretcher in the old hospital of St. Nicolas de Barri's in Burrard Street Vancouver," suffering from a broken back (UBC 22:19, 78).[4] One confusing issue is what this protagonist is named: both the title of the work and Lowry's "Work in Progress" statement call him Sigbjørn Wilderness, but in the typescript his first name is consistently given as Martin. Moreover, although Martin and his wife, Primrose, are referred to as "the Trumbaughs" (UBC 22:19, 34, 43), Martin claims that he is in fact Martin Striven, author of *The Valley of the Shadow of Death*. (The claim is dis-counted by the hospital personnel, who believe Martin is under a delusion.) To further complicate matters, Martin at one point imagines himself as Martin Sigbjørn Wilderness (UBC 22:19, 131), suggesting that Sigbjørn Wilderness is his adopted iden-tity or alter ego. Perhaps all of this merely reflects Lowry's ex-perimentation with different names and his collation of drafts in various stages of composition, but it is also possible that the protagonist's "real" name is Martin Trumbaugh, that he has written a novel under the pen name Martin Striven, and that in the dream-vision of *The Voyage That Never Ends* he assumes the additional identity of a character named Sigbjørn Wilderness.[5]

In the hospital, Martin imagines that he sees and hears people from his (or, rather, Lowry's) days at Cambridge. One such person, called James, is based on Lowry's friend James Travers, who had died during World War II.[6] Although dead, James claims to be "certainly not as dead as you think," but his appearance here involves no great revelations from the after-life; instead, he and Martin mainly discuss books, especially Hemingway's *The Sun Also Rises*, to whose popularity, rather than the influence of T. S. Eliot, Martin attributes the revival of interest in John Donne (UBC 22:19, 132–38). It is hard to see what Lowry hoped to accomplish by introducing this ghost from Martin's past, although the discussion of reading might eventually have been related to a subsequent section entitled "Martin's reading," which presents the self as both the origin and the terminus of reading and emphasizes the significance of coincidence (UBC 22:19, 140–42). In general, however, James's presence in this draft is typical of the work's accumulation of elements that are never adequately developed or integrated into the work as a whole.

Of somewhat greater moment is a woman modeled after Charlotte Haldane, in whose 1932 novel *I Bring Not Peace*— cited by that title in the *Ordeal* (UBC 22:19, 87)—Lowry had been disguised as James Dowd. That Lowry had been a char-acter in someone else's novel a year before the publication of his own first novel might well have seemed significant, if rather threatening, to him at a time when he worried about the pos-sibility that he was "being *written through*" (UBC 22:19, 3). Indeed, recalling "that godawful book of hers," Martin won-ders "to what extent she had created him in real fact, as he was now, physically, sixteen years after he'd last seen her" (UBC 22:19, 58). Certainly the appearance of this person contrib-utes to our impression that Martin—hospitalized with a broken back and unable to persuade Miss Ford, his nurse, that he is also the Martin Striven whose book, *The Valley of the Shadow of Death*, is being discussed on a radio broadcast—is subject to forces well beyond his control.

In the *Ordeal*, Charlotte Haldane is initially called Roxy McEwin; the name is later changed to Ann Roxy-Evans, Anne Sully, and Roxy Anne Sully, although the typescript once refers to her as Charlotte. Martin hears Roxy and an unidentified man carrying on a conversation in which the man derides all of Martin's accomplishments, claiming even that *The Valley of the Shadow of Death* was "lifted practically word for word" from *Drunkard's Rigadoon* (UBC 22:19, 65). The whole treatment of this conversation is confusing, probably because Lowry had not decided how to handle it. First, Roxy and her friend appear to be talking elsewhere (perhaps, Martin speculates, at a club for biochemists); then they are in the room with him, looking down at him while he sleeps (but still knows they are there); then, Nurse Ford says that the two are in the next room—although Martin soon hears them talking as they walk away from the hospital. At last, an explanation of sorts is provided by the nurse, who finally can hear the voices and says that they are being transmitted by the hospital's "new acoustic system" (UBC 22:19, 123).

Despite all this confusion, what Lowry tried to achieve with the Roxy character and her male friend (who somewhat belatedly is given the name "Izzard") was both complex and serious. Charlotte Haldane was a writer as well as someone out of Lowry's own past, and therefore a figure who could bring together the autobiographical and aesthetic dimensions of his art. Martin's relationship to Roxy, who is in some sense his creator—but also now, within the *Ordeal*, his creation—is an example of how closely intertwined art and life were for Lowry, each emerging out of (and in turn exerting pressure on) the other. Hearing Roxy praise his arms, whose muscular nature he attributes to the way she described them in her novel, Martin thinks of her praise as something like "Pygmalion in reverse: the reverse too of what he had been trying to get in his novel about Under Under the Volcano [*Dark as the Grave*] where . . . he had returned to Mexico to look for his character Dr. Vigil and to see how he had developed in his absence in real life" (UBC 22:19, 67–68). The reversal of the Pygmalion myth apparently involves gender, with the creator being female (perhaps the only time that happens in Lowry's entire corpus), but the more significant reversal involves Lowry's return to Mexico to seek "Dr. Vigil"—Juan Fernando Márquez in real life, Juan Fernando Martinez in *Dark as the Grave*. There, Lowry-Martin-Sigbjørn returns to find someone he "created," gave fictional form, in one of his works; now he is himself a fictional character revisited by his creator.

In Haldane's *I Bring Not Peace*, Lowry is transformed into James Dowd, an amiable but irresponsible American sailor who has studied at Cambridge; his interests include jazz composition, Rimbaud, and drinking, the three merging in a composition entitled "Bateau Ivre—Variations on a Jazz Theme" (Haldane 201). In Paris, he meets Michal, the novel's heroine, who hears him fall down drunkenly outside her apartment and soon finds herself sexually attracted to him. She realizes that he is also in love with her, but she holds back from sexual involvement with him, partly because she also loves another man, Jean, and partly because she senses that "He has an inner voice. He lives an intense and strange life of his own that is not much affected by his relations with other people, at any rate by me" (Haldane 193). That description neatly summarizes one side of Malcolm Lowry's character, the side that he himself described in *Under the Volcano*, through the Consul.

Of all the unhappy relationships in *I Bring Not Peace*, the saddest involves a homosexual Englishman, Dennis Carling, who falls hopelessly in love with Dowd. Feeling sorry for him, and hoping to restore him to health through his friendship, Dowd returns with him to England, but his patience wears thin when Carling, who is blackmailed over some letters he has written, threatens suicide. Dowd refuses to take the threat seriously, telling him, "If you kill yourself, when I'm taking all this trouble to get those damn-fool letters, I shall never forgive you" (Haldane 286). Carling does commit suicide, by carbon monoxide poisoning, and Dowd feels responsible.

As Bradbrook has shown, Dennis Carling is based on Paul Leonard Charles Fitte, a Cambridge friend whom Lowry had met in Germany (*Malcolm Lowry* 113–14). Fitte was blackmailed, and Lowry either misunderstood or ridiculed his suicide threat; when Fitte killed himself, Lowry was called to the coroner's inquest as a witness. At this remove, it is almost certainly impossible to ascertain with any degree of accuracy how much responsibility Lowry really bore for Fitte's suicide; possibly, like Geoffrey Firmin's guilt in the *Samaritan* affair, this one was largely fabricated. If so, the fabrication probably owed a good deal to *I Bring Not Peace*, which might be part of what Martin means when he says that Roxy had created him. Not content with another person's portrayal of his guilt, Lowry made the theme his own, for one of the central themes in *October Ferry to Gabriola* is Ethan Llewelyn's obsession with his responsibility for the death of Peter Cordwainer, a Cambridge friend who committed suicide two decades earlier. Likewise, in his planned revisions of *Lunar Caustic*, Lowry intended to transfer the guilt to the Earl of Thurstaston, who should have prevented the suicide of a college friend (UBC 15:12, "Lunar Caustic" ts. 10–11).

The theme is only touched on briefly in *The Ordeal of Sigbjørn Wilderness*, but it is there in embryonic form, with Fitte-Carling-Cordwainer now called "Wensleydale." Although the responsibility for Wensleydale's death might actually lie with Roxy's companion, Izzard (UBC 22:19, 130), it seems likely that a fully developed *Ordeal of Sigbjørn Wilderness* would have had Martin working through his own guilt rather than blaming Izzard. There is also a second reference to Wensleydale in the *Ordeal* typescript, one that Douglas Day finds "totally enigmatic" (ML 141). This reference, in the "Martin's reading" section, follows a summary of Roald Dahl's story "The Sound Machine," in which a man named Klausner constructs a machine that allows him to hear the sounds made by plants.[7] At the story's end, Klausner makes a doctor come over to his house so that the doctor can hear the sound of a tree being struck by an ax, but a branch falls on the sound machine and smashes it. Klausner pleads with the doctor to paint the tree's wound with iodine, and the doctor, obviously convinced that Klausner is mad, does so. Following his summary, Lowry writes that Martin found the end of Dahl's story "rather feeble" and "was relieved that it had little to do with his subject," although he found the story plausible. Suddenly Martin "remembered that a man named Dahl had been at college with him." The recollection inspires this puzzling sequence:

> This related again to Wensleydale. It related to Guldbransen [Nordahl Grieg]. Dahl after all, a promising young writer, perhaps some genius even of the future, would not be the same person: but Dahl itself was a vibration. It is perhaps in a word such as "vibration" that is to be sought the reason for a natural repugnance towards such systems. This was because the day before he had been reading Annie Besant which Primrose had brought him from the library. (UBC 22:19, 141)

Clearly, it took little to set Lowry (or Martin) off on an uncontrolled series of associations. Lowry reads a story with a theme vaguely reminiscent of his own work (since it involves coming in touch with a reality beyond the normal range of human experience), realizes that he went to school with a person who had the same last name as the story's author, and probably associates Dahl with Nordahl (although Grieg is here disguised as Guldbransen, a name also found in drafts of *Dark as the Grave* written before Lowry changed Grieg's fictional name to Erikson). In *Under the Volcano*, Lowry showed that he recognized the danger posed by the tendency to read personal significance into every event; here, however, it is apparent that the need to find patterns everywhere was Lowry's as well as the Consul's. Nonetheless, the reference to "a natural repugnance towards such systems," and the description, on the following page, of Martin's struggle "with the inverted cones of Yeats," indicates that if Lowry was attracted by the possibility of incorporating all experience within a large scheme—including the one he was cobbling together out of a combination of personal experience and numerous philosophical and occult books—he also felt a personal resistance to the "systems" that threatened to overwhelm him.

In keeping with its role as the framing fiction for the entire *Voyage*, *The Ordeal of Sigbjørn Wilderness* emphasizes the importance of visionary or transcendental experience. Numerous citations of stories involving paranormal or supernatural experiences, sometimes under the influence of morphine or other drugs, indicate that Lowry was experimenting with ways in which to justify the hallucinatory theme of his work. The pattern of the *Ordeal*, and indeed of the entire *Voyage*, was to have been one of constantly expanding consciousness, beginning with Martin's own past and developing outward from the individual to the universal. As Sherrill Grace has demonstrated, Conrad Aiken's "use of serial form and his concept of the evolution of consciousness" undoubtedly influenced the overall pattern of the *Voyage*, while one of Aiken's most famous stories, "Mr. Arcularis," describes "a man's imaginary sea voyage through time until he relives and comes to terms with his past before dying peacefully on an operating table" (*Voyage* 124, 127).[8] The completed *Voyage That Never Ends* would have been an immeasurably more complex version of "Mr. Arcularis," one whose conclusion did not close the cycle of life but renewed it. Yet Lowry drafted only part of Part I of the *Ordeal*, never getting far enough to make the transition to the works that were to have been sandwiched between the two halves of the *Ordeal*; Part II apparently was not drafted at all.

Writing never came easily to Malcolm Lowry, whose successful works were typically the products of incessant and determined revision. Even *Under the Volcano* evolved from drafts that contain some painfully bad writing, especially in the dialogue, along with other material good enough to survive into the novel's final text. Moreover, as Sherrill Grace maintains, *The Ordeal of Sigbjørn Wilderness* "involves one of the most unusual and challenging concepts in modern fiction" (*Voyage* 11), a judgment that tempts us to believe that if Lowry had just had more time and fewer personal problems, and if he had stayed away from the bottle, the *Ordeal* might have developed into a fiction worthy of his ambitious plans for it. Completed, *The Voyage That Never Ends* would ideally have provided a means of integrating world, text, and self in an elaborate autobiographical-philosophical-visionary metafiction on the scale of Proust's *Remembrance of Things Past*, one of the many works to which Lowry refers in the *Ordeal* typescript (UBC 22:19, 15).

Nonetheless, even the most "finished" sections of the existing *Ordeal* typescript show that in that novel, on which the whole *Voyage* depended, Lowry probably was facing greater problems than he ever could have resolved. The very form of the *Ordeal*—the hallucinatory vision—offered a temptation to Lowry, since it held out the possibility of transcending natural experience and taking a short cut to ultimate truth. While Lowry might have recognized the danger in assuming that truth lay within an alcoholic vision (even if that realization failed to deter him from monumental bouts of drinking), he made the mistake of assuming that a re-creation and elaboration of his hospital experiences could substitute for the difficulties of real life, which would be subsumed (and thereby bypassed) by his vision. Brief references to the allegory of the cave in Plato's *Republic* (UBC 22:19, 44, 69, 86) seem to indicate that Lowry hoped to move beyond the experience of the natural world and into an apprehension of a higher reality, but his attempt to include all reality within a single hallucinatory sequence led only to a fragmented vision of the self and the world it inhabits.

In the next chapter I will consider *Dark as the Grave* and *La Mordida*—the two other unfinished novels that would have been incorporated within *The Voyage That Never Ends*—along with *October Ferry to Gabriola*, which evolved from the abandoned *Eridanus*. Here, it is necessary to consider why the *Voyage*, and for that matter the bulk of Lowry's other post-*Volcano* fiction, was never completed.

Several reasons immediately present themselves, not necessarily in order of importance. To begin with, we might consider the impact on Lowry of what Harold Bloom has termed "the anxiety of influence," a writer's quasi-Oedipal battle against a powerful literary precursor who must be misread, transformed, and overcome so that the younger writer may "clear imaginative space" for himself (Bloom 5). While the Bloomian model of poetic misprision might not prove altogether satisfactory in Lowry's case,[9] there is little doubt that Lowry felt anxious about the extent to which other writers exerted their influence on him.[10] This anxiety is apparent throughout Lowry's fiction, from *Ultramarine* on, but it became especially acute after the publication of *Under the Volcano*, perhaps because reviewers frequently called attention to ways in which Lowry's novel resembled those of other authors. The reviews contained innumerable references to *The Lost Weekend*, which Lowry read as implications that he had plagiarized from that book. There was also Jacques Barzun's harsh judgment that *Under the Volcano* included "long regurgitations of the material found in *Ulysses* and *The Sun Also Rises*" and was little more than "an anthology held together by earnestness" (Barzun, 69–70). The apparent influence of Joyce on Lowry's work, which was assumed by numerous reviewers of *Under the Volcano*, was one Lowry had explicitly denied in his long 1946 letter to Jonathan Cape, where he claimed that his work was a simplification of something he had experienced "in far more baffling, complex and esoteric terms," and therefore quite different from Joyce's technique (SL 66). That reference seems at least to confirm Lowry's familiarity with *Ulysses*,[11] yet in his response to Barzun, Lowry said that he had never read Joyce's novel all the way through, and a few years later he told Albert Erskine that only recently had he "read (your gift of) *Ulysses* through—essentially—for the first time" (SL 144, 319).

On the other hand, it would have been impossible for Lowry to deny his intimate knowledge of Conrad Aiken's work, even had he wanted to do so. In chapter 1, I argued that it is an exaggeration to say that Lowry was always guilt-ridden over his indebtedness to Aiken, and terrified that it would be discovered. Instead, I noted, Lowry seems to have sought out Aiken partly because he saw Aiken as someone he could learn from and then surpass; moreover, far from denying that he had learned from Aiken, Lowry often called attention to Aiken's influence on his fiction. Yet when the *Volcano* reviews raised other literary models (while generally overlooking Aiken, whom Lowry regarded as a more significant force), Lowry's sensitivity about all sorts of influence may well have extended to Aiken. Aiken's story "Mr. Arcularis" provided little more than a starting-point for *The Ordeal of Sigbjørn Wilderness*, but under the circumstances even that would have been enough to raise the level of Lowry's anxiety. That anxiety could have surfaced in a number of ways, including, if Clarissa Lorenz is accurate on this point, Lowry's attempt to prevent Margerie from reading Aiken's *Ushant*, where all of the Aiken-Lowry conflicts are re-created from Aiken's perspective (Lorenz 219).

It is also interesting that in the 1951 letter to David Markson that constitutes our single most important source of information about *In Ballast to the White Sea*—a novel about the way anxiety and influence may eventually be overcome—Lowry called attention to Aiken's powerful influence on him while insisting that the novelist about whom his protagonist develops an obsession was not based on Aiken (SL 248–49, 256). In his continuation of the letter, after repeating that "X was not Aiken," Lowry argued for the creative potential that lay within strongly felt literary influences such as the one he had described in his lost novel, citing Aiken as his authority:

Aiken once told me that he considered [the transcendence of influence] primarily an operation of genius. Genius knows what it wants and goes after it. He told me . . . that he was once drawn to Eliot's work in the same way. Eliot himself—who owes a great deal to Aiken himself that has not been acknowledged—has called this identification "one of the most important experiences (for a writer) of adolescence." . . . I surmise an identification on Eliot's part with Laforgue. On the tragic plane you have Keats' identification with Chatterton, leading, Aiken once suggested, to a kind of *conscious* death on Keats' part. (SL 264)

Here, the identifications and influences proliferate and turn back on one another until they appear to be the one inescapable fact of a writer's life. Meanwhile, the level of Lowry's own anxiety has been reduced—and his debt to Aiken obscured—by the citation of Aiken as an authority who quickly becomes lost in the same maze of influences that seems to entrap all writers.

Lowry's alcoholism undoubtedly contributed to his inability to bring his projects to a conclusion. Drinking was a prominent factor in Lowry's life, just as the representation of drinking plays a large role in his fiction, but there is reason to believe that it was at least as much a symptom as a cause of his writer's block. In an 1974 interview, Margerie Lowry responded to a question about her husband's alternation between productivity and blockage:

Yes, he'd get writer's blocks from time to time and then he'd get into a real despair and that's when he would drink, when he couldn't write. I think it was because as long as he could work, as long as his writing was going well—of course he never took a drink during all the years, the last three or four years that he was doing the final draft of the *Volcano*. . . . He said it would cloud his critical vision of [his work]. So he said that you might get certain inspirations under the influence of alcohol but you'd better sit down the next day stone cold sober, take a good hard look at them and throw them all away. (Deck 17)

In Margerie Lowry's view, then, far from inspiring his work, Lowry's drunken binges generally emerged "out of a sense of despair when something was going wrong and he couldn't work" (Deck 17). Thus he drank because he couldn't write— and then, of course, the drinking made writing that much more difficult.[12]

Robert B. Heilman has characterized Lowry as a "possessed" artist, a description that is obviously related to Lowry's drinking. Whereas the "self-possessed" artist "uses his materials as an instrument," Heilman notes that in the case of the "possessed" artist, "the materials appear to use him as an instrument, finding in him, as it were, a channel to the objective existence of art, sacrificing a minimum of their autonomy to his hand, which partly directs and shapes rather than wholly controls" (Heilman 18). Signs of "possession" may be found throughout Lowry's work, for example in the Consul's "familiars" and in Sigbjørn Wilderness's obsession, in *Dark as the Grave* and *La Mordida*, with his "daemon." Heilman's observation that the hand of the possessed artist is not altogether in control of the work (or, for that matter, under the control of the artist) is dramatically confirmed by Dr. C. G. McNeill's memoir of Lowry's 1949 visit to his office. Dr. McNeill found, among other things, that Lowry was unable to hold a pencil or pen and that he could only compose by dictating to Margerie while standing up, leaning "with the back of his hands on the top of the desk" (McNeill 158). Lowry proved unable to autograph a copy of *Under the Volcano* for Dr. McNeill and took two months to manage the four-word note that he eventually wrote to the doctor. Lowry apparently had trouble signing his name on other occasions, and, in the Haitian sequence in *La Mordida*, transferred the dilemma to Sigbjørn Wilderness, who seems actually to fear writing his own name, as if to do so were to mean accepting an identity that he finds troubling. In Port-au-Prince, when Sigbjørn finally signs his name, he rationalizes that "I have not signed my name hard enough to make

any impression on the carbon" (UBC 13:23, 170). Clearly, signing his name had become a traumatic experience for Lowry,
one that cannot be explained simply by the fact that he must
often have had the shakes, either from overdrinking or from
alcoholic withdrawal.

In the most thorough study to date of writer's block, Zachary
Leader considers the problem first from a psychological per-
spective and then as an aspect of literary or cultural history.
Although there are important differences among the theories
Leader surveys, the psychological accounts of writer's block
among British object-relations theorists such as Hanna Segal,
Marion Milner, and D. W. Winnicott are especially interesting
because they bear an obvious relevance to cultural-historical
explanations of writer's block; to the cases of Wordsworth and
Coleridge, which Leader considers at length; and to Malcolm
Lowry, whom Leader never mentions.

A recurrent theme in psychological accounts of blockage is
that it involves the writer's anxiety over the relationship between the self and the external world of objects. In *Art and
Artist* (1932), Otto Rank argued that literary or artistic creation involves a desire to set oneself apart from the world,
or in Leader's terms, "a wish for separation or emergence."
Ironically, Leader observes, "the individuating impulse is itself,
ultimately, a longing for community or merger, for 'the potential *restoration* of a union with the Cosmos, which once existed
and was then lost'" (Leader 67). Hanna Segal described a
writer, one of her patients, who regarded the use of words as
an attack on the essential unity of the world. For this person,
writing was "an aggressive act" that "meant acknowledging
the separateness of the world from herself, and gave her a feeling of loss." Moreover, underlying her dread of writing was her
fear of death, the ultimate separation of the self from all other
reality (Leader 89–90). Likewise, Marion Milner, who believed
that "development is marked by the ability to tolerate 'the difference between the feeling of oneness, of being united with

everything, and the feeling of twoness, of self and object,' "
found that artists need to be able to accept both merger ("oneness") and differentiation ("twoness") in order to work (Leader
93–94). Thus, writer's block may be caused by either of two
related fears: first, of isolating oneself by asserting an identity
apart from the world; second, of losing that sense of individu-
ality and finding the line between self and other hopelessly
blurred.

A complementary explanation of blockage may be found
within the attitude toward language, especially written language, throughout Western culture. Plato and others viewed
writing with distrust, associating it with deceit and regarding it as "inhuman or thinglike"—one reason why writing is
evocative of death (Leader 221–22). By the late eighteenth century, as the traditional description of literature as a species of
imitation gave way to an emphasis upon originality and subjectivity, the relationship between the writer and the written
work became highly complex; hence the frequent representation, in literary works, of the dangers or difficulties involved in
creative actions, and the emergence of the fragment as a characteristic literary form. With the romantic doctrine that poetry
must be both original and highly subjective also came a new
dread of plagiarism, a fear reinforced (and in part created) by
print technology, which had led to "a new sense of the private
ownership of words" that could not be maintained in an oral
culture (Ong 131; see also Mallon 4).

Leader's analysis of the way these forces affected Coleridge
is especially intriguing for the light it sheds on Lowry's situation. Here, only a few of the more obvious parallels need be
mentioned. Leader calls attention to the way "Coleridge's obsession with the ideal of originality" led both to solipsism and
to a fear of his own imaginative projections, with the result
that "he either completely stopped writing, was blocked, or
resorted to a borrowing so consistent and transparent as to
earn the name of plagiarism" (Leader 99–100). Coleridge also

found the external world of objects unstable and unreliable, a fragmented and self-contradictory realm in which the essential unity of nature is overwhelmed by its very "richness and amplitude" (Leader 193–97). Moreover, Leader argues that Coleridge distrusted writing, and especially dreaded the "self-contained or autonomous, and hence falsifying, character" of the completed work, a fact that led him to resist completion and closure by resorting instead to conversation and to "a variety of unofficial 'writings,' such as the letter, the marginal comment, the Notebook entry" (Leader 213–14). Finally, Coleridge's bias against writing may be regarded partly as an expression of his preference for an oral culture in which there is a direct involvement or dialogue between two people. This preference led him to attempt to transform writing "into conversation, either by labeling it as such or by surrounding the actual 'text' with glosses and prefatory qualifications that approximate the explanatory or dialectical features of spoken interchange" (Leader 222).

All of these factors are already present in *Under the Volcano*, where Lowry discovered a means of accommodating his anxieties and turning them to good use. The unstable and threatening nature of the external world, with its constantly proliferating correspondences to the Consul's situation, makes it impossible for the Consul to develop any secure sense of his identity; meanwhile, the world seems to be peopled with projections of his imagination, not only his familiars and the "spiders" who he believes watch him but also the various animals who represent aspects of his fragmented identity. The distrust of writing may be found everywhere in the novel: in letters that are never sent and postcards that arrive too late, in signs that are chillingly misread, and in an unfinished poem, written on a bar tab, whose text is surrounded and circumscribed by other writings and drawings. The incorporation of other "texts" within *Under the Volcano*, which develops a Bakhtinian dialogue among the various discourses of the novel, allowing the texts to interrogate one another and refusing to establish an unalterable hierarchy of meanings, may be partly due to the same fear of the fixed, written word that contributed to Coleridge's writer's block and led him to seek forms that approximated the condition of dialogue.

The characteristics of writer's block became even more evident after 1947, indicating that Lowry's ability to transform his problems into the materials of art did not lead to their elimination (any more than his description of an alcoholic's death enabled him to stop drinking). There are, of course, the numerous abortive projects themselves, not to mention such extreme signs of blockage as that described by Dr. McNeill.[13] In a 1948 letter to Albert Erskine, Lowry said that he wrote "5 novels in imagination" each night but could not write a single word in reality; "even this silly little note," he added, had cost him an "incredible effort" to write (SL 165). Explicit references to writer's block appear in Lowry's works as early as 1938–39, in the poems "A dried up river is like the soul" and "A poem about a poem that can't be written" (CP 74, 75), but they are far more numerous in such post-*Volcano* projects as *The Ordeal of Sigbjørn Wilderness, Dark as the Grave Wherein My Friend Is Laid, La Mordida,* "Through the Panama," "Elephant and Colosseum," "Strange Comfort Afforded by the Profession," and "Ghostkeeper."[14] In these works, we generally discover a paranoid writer who is afraid of his own success and, even more, fears being unmasked as a plagiarist; who undergoes hallucinations and believes himself possessed; who thinks, alternately, that he cannot write and that he is being "written" by his daemon; who finds the external world unstable and menacing, and wavers between seeing events as malign products of his imagination and as part of a "Law of Series" that shapes his fate; and who, despite his belief in the importance of originality, finds his own identity hopelessly entangled with those of other writers. Lowry's experimentation with marginal notes and glosses in *La Mordida* and "Through the Panama" certainly owes a great deal to Coleridge (especially since glosses from *The Rime of the Ancient Mariner* are incorporated within those of "Through the Panama") and appears to reflect the same desire to simulate the openness of dialogue and thereby keep the work, and its author, alive.

The dilemma Lowry faced is perhaps most succinctly described in *Dark as the Grave*, where Sigbjørn tells Dr. Hippolyte that "the artist's despair" derives partly from his knowledge that the universe is unfinished, constantly "in the process of creation." Likewise, the artist's creation stays alive only so long as it remains a work in progress:

> An organic work of art, having been conceived, must grow in the creator's mind, or proceed to perish. . . . The author, while working, is like a man continually pushing his way through blinding smoke in an effort to rescue some precious objects from a burning building. How hopeless, how inexplicable the effort! For is not the building the work of art in question, long since perfect in the mind, and only rendered a vehicle of destruction by the effort to realize it, to transmute it upon paper? (DG 154)

Sigbjørn's conception of the work as something perfectly conceived in the imagination but imperfectly translated into a written text (and even damaged by the process of being written down) recalls Plato's belief that language always diminishes or distorts whatever it attempts to represent. Even closer is Shelley's declaration, in "A Defence of Poetry," that "when composition begins, inspiration is always on the decline, and the most glorious poetry that has ever been communicated to the world is probably a feeble shadow of the original conception of the poet" (Shelley 504).[15] Sigbjørn extends this feeling of loss a step further, for when the writer awakens in the morning he discovers that the work has changed: "it is as if during the night invisible workmen had been monkeying with it, a stringer has been made away with in the night and mysteriously replaced by one of inferior quality" (DG 155). Short poems, he says, "in part manage to outwit the process" because they involve the briefest interval between conception and composition.

While Sigbjørn extols the virtues of lyric poetry, however, Lowry embarked upon precisely the opposite sort of project, an ambitious cycle of novels that would raise fundamental questions about self and world, art and life, language and identity, originality and influence. These are essentially the same questions that Lowry had dealt with—often painfully—throughout his fiction, and that he raised in his filmscript for *Tender Is the Night*,[16] but the scale of *The Voyage That Never Ends* dwarfed anything that Lowry had previously attempted. Sherrill Grace argues that "Lowry's concept of voyage as continuous withdrawal and return" is central to his work (*Voyage* xv), and this pattern seems to be fundamental to his plans for *The Voyage That Never Ends*; it is even given a reprise in his statement that the sequence would end "with the Wildernesses watching the tide bearing the ships out upon its currents that become remote, and which, like the Ice, becoming remote, return" (WP 97). Ironically, however, the path of withdrawal and return, or separation and reimmersion, is one that blocked writers find most difficult to negotiate (in many cases, it seems to *cause* blockage). Thus Lowry's attempt to write *The Voyage That Never Ends* involved him in a heroic, and perhaps impossible, battle against the very fears and obsessions that he had always faced as a writer, one that may well have doomed the *Voyage* sequence from its inception.

SIX

After the Volcano: *Dark as
the Grave, La Mordida,* and
October Ferry to Gabriola

Dark as the Grave Wherein My
Friend Is Laid is an unfinished novel about a writer whose life
and art have become so hopelessly entangled with one another
that he finds it impossible to write, and almost as difficult to
live. It is a novel with obvious flaws—the dialogue, for example,
is generally clumsy, and the narrative as a whole is loosely
stitched together—but there are passages worthy of *Under the
Volcano;* for the most part, the book's characterization is weak,
yet Sigbjørn Wilderness emerges as a complex and strangely
engaging figure. Above all, it is in this book, where Lowry
chronicled his own fears and obsessions, attempting to justify
or transcend them by turning them into art, that he found himself overwhelmed by the very problems that he was trying to
write through; but the record of Lowry's attempt to face those
problems carries its own conviction as evidence of his artistic
dedication and seriousness. If *Dark as the Grave* is in some
respects an artistic failure, it is a most instructive one.

In a 1949 letter to Frank Taylor, Lowry described the theme
of *Dark as the Grave* as "the identification of a creator with his

creation—Pirandello in reverse, or, Six authors in search of his [sic] characters; or otherwise stated, Every Man his own Laocoön." Lowry added ominously that "since the philosophical implications might prove fatal to myself, I have to preserve a certain detachment" (SL 180). The Laocoön metaphor, which Lowry had already used in an early draft of *Dark as the Grave* (UBC 8:3, 12), figures more prominently in later drafts, assuming a complex function in the edited version of the book:

> Coincidences, yes, the sort of coincidences in [Sigbjørn's] life of which there seemed no end. But were they, strictly speaking, coincidences? Were they something less, or more? A maze of complicated suffering and interrelated nonsense! Yes, but still, what a more-than-Pirandellian theme was here for someone, if not for him. Every man his own Laocoön! As Daniel [Conrad Aiken] might say. And here would be the trick, he thought, in one's life to be amused by them, in one's work, rather to study them, to be the detached haruspex of them. For were he to take them all seriously, and he was still thinking of only a fraction, he might well go the way of that protagonist, or of the late owner of his elegant corduroy trousers. (DG 43)[1]

Here, in the guise of Sigbjørn Wilderness, Lowry once again associates the Laocoön with Pirandello's complex entanglement of author and character, life and art. More significantly, Lowry observes his own need to remain detached, to stand apart from the work in which he planned to examine the nature of coincidence and entrapment. Yet in *Dark as the Grave*, while Sigbjørn constantly seeks to "preserve a certain detachment" from the analogies between art and life that seem to accumulate during his trip, he is unable to draw a clear line between the Mexico that he sees around him and the one he has described in his unpublished novel about an alcoholic British consul, *The Valley of the Shadow of Death*. Correspondences between his present experiences and the Consul's appear especially menacing to Sigbjørn, who nonetheless recognizes that part of himself, which he imagines as *another* Wilderness (or, on a different level, his daemon), desires and even helps to create these analogies.

In a letter to Albert Erskine, Lowry noted that Sigbjørn is terrified by the suspicion "that he is not a writer so much as being *written*" (SL 332). *Dark as the Grave* returns almost obsessively to Sigbjørn's growing conviction that he is "standing *within* his book" and is "haunted by his characters" (DG 158–59, 192). Even before reaching Mexico, he imagines the world as a rejected play or novel "like, for instance, *The Valley of the Shadow of Death*, by Sigbjørn Wilderness" (DG 12–13). Once in Mexico, he finds himself not only reliving events from his novel—meeting people on whom he had based characters, staying in Laruelle's tower, encountering a sign that asks *¿Le gusta este jardín que es suyo?*, ordering Alas cigarettes—but actually living within the world of a parallel novel composed by his daemon (DG 85–87). The daemon's novel, which in practical terms is identical with the one we are reading, is an unfinished book, one "*being* written as they went along" (DG 103). The difficulty Sigbjørn experiences in distinguishing between the novel he has written and the one in which he believes he is living gives us an extreme version of the struggle between life and art, a theme found in Lowry's work from *Ultramarine* on. The problem is exacerbated by Sigbjørn's inability to determine the precise nature and extent of his involvement with the "book" he is experiencing: whether he is its author, or one of its characters, or simply one of its readers. His multiple roles undermine his attempts to arrive at a secure sense of his relationship to the world about (and within) him and lead to much the same disintegration of identity that we observe in Geoffrey Firmin.

In his characteristically Lowryan role as a reader of the world as book, an interpreter of the forest of symbols that is at least partly his own creation, Sigbjørn finds both personal and cosmic meaning in the world of external objects and phenomena.

As in *Under the Volcano*, these phenomena include the various writings that Lowry's protagonist encounters: a copy of Julian Green's *The Dark Journey*, which Sigbjørn opens to a passage that seems to refer to his return to Mexico, a newspaper article, a tourist folder, advertisements for *Drunkard's Rigadoon*, the reader's report on *The Valley of the Shadow of Death*, the *Le gusta este jardín* sign, and so forth. Among these apparently symbolic writings are the men's room graffiti—"*Kilroy was here. El Grafe was looking*" (DG 21, 30–31, 101–2)—that begin to assume a vaguely sinister import, leading Sigbjørn to complain of "being pursued down the coast by this Kilroy moron" (DG 31). Kilroy, who has chosen "to establish his immortality in a public urinal," is perhaps on some level a comic version of the successful writer Sigbjørn aspires to be, but the introduction of El Grafe also associates Kilroy with Sigbjørn's guilt and self-consciousness. Since El Grafe is another writer of graffiti, one who mocks Kilroy's literary efforts, the two might be regarded as the halves of a divided imagination struggling against itself: Kilroy claims hegemony over the walls of the urinal, and El Grafe then establishes his primacy by enclosing Kilroy's writing within his own.[2] The Kilroy motif recurs several times in *La Mordida*, where at one point Sigbjørn identifies Kilroy as a symbol of "American Civilization" (UBC 13:20, 112);[3] likewise, in *Dark as the Grave*, Kilroy seems to represent an aspect of American culture from which Sigbjørn is at pains to disassociate himself. Since Sigbjørn is neither American nor Mexican, his apparent identification both with Kilroy and with El Grafe might reflect his expatriate status, but his exaggerated response to the writing on the wall still seems hard to explain as anything other than a symptom of paranoia.

Equally paranoid is his reading of a newspaper article about a wife-slayer, which he sees while flying from Los Angeles to El Paso. In a passage reminiscent of scenes from *Under the Volcano*, Sigbjørn reads himself into the story: "Wilderness Returned Here for Trial, *he read*. Canadian Police Ignore U.S.

Ban. Bring Murder Suspect Back via Airlines. . . . Sigbjørn Wilderness, *he read*, accused of the murder of his thirty-nine-year-old wife, in Eridanus last June 6, was returned to Vancouver today to stand trial for his life" (DG 54–55). The source of this sequence was a newspaper clipping, now deposited in the Malcolm Lowry Archive (UBC 10:13), which Lowry in turn transcribed almost verbatim in a longer draft of this passage (UBC 9:1, 110–13). A comparison of that draft with the published version indicates not only how much material has been deleted from the edited text, but also how the newspaper article, as read by Sigbjørn, has been altered to reinforce the idea that he is somehow the murderer. For example, the final sentence quoted above differs significantly from the corresponding sentence in the draft: "Percy Jean Baker, he read, accused of the murder of his 30 year old wife, in Port Moody last May 21, was returned to Vancouver today to stand trial for his life." Apart from changing the name of the murderer to Sigbjørn Wilderness, the edited version adds other details that tie it to Sigbjørn's situation: the place is changed from Port Moody to Eridanus, a fictional (and symbolic) name for Dollarton, where the Lowrys lived; the wife's age is increased to thirty-nine to correspond with Primrose's age (DG 9); and the date of the murder has been moved from May 21 to June 6, the anniversary of the fire that destroyed the Wildernesses' shack in Eridanus. It seems apparent that Sigbjørn's reading of the article involves a conscious or unconscious substitution of his own name for the one in the newspaper, but since we are never allowed to see a "correct" text of the article—one that exists independently of Sigbjørn's mind—we have no means of judging whether the other details that appear to link Sigbjørn to the murderer are coincidences or the product of his imagination.

In the longer, unpublished version of this scene, Sigbjørn reads that "pretty airline stewardess Ann Sherlock" called the returned murderer "a model passenger," and he remembers that in chapter 12 of *The Valley of the Shadow of Death* he had

posed the question, "Why did people have to be called Sherlock" (UBC 9:1, 111). This passage refers to the final chapter
of *Under the Volcano*, where the Consul reads Yvonne's letters at the Farolito while imagining himself "another kind of
drunkard"—one who, unable to grasp the fact that his wife is
leaving him, recalls his conversation of the previous night with
a barman, in which he talked about a house burning down.
The Consul wonders, "why is the barman's name Sherlock? an
unforgettable name!" (UV 344). In their commentary on this
passage from *Under the Volcano*, Ackerley and Clipper note the
association with Sherlock Holmes and observe that the Consul
might worry that the detective-barman is helping the police
investigate the fire. On another level, they say, Sherlock refers to the owner of the inn where Lowry made the last few
annotations on the manuscript of *Under the Volcano*—an event
transferred to the life of Sigbjørn Wilderness (DG 169–70)—
while the fact that there is a Sherlock Court at St. Catharine's
College, which Lowry associated with the suicide of Paul Fitte,
might add a further level of meaning (A&C 424). Whatever
the merits of the longer version of this passage, its dependence
upon a fairly obscure sentence in *Under the Volcano*, as well as
on events from Lowry's life, indicates how difficult Lowry and
Sigbjørn found it to separate life from art or to see any event
in simple and direct terms rather than as part of an elaborate
series of coincidences.

The question is to what extent Sigbjørn is responsible for
creating the intricate symbolic meanings that he finds wherever he looks. For the most part, Fernando's term for Sigbjørn,
"old maker of tragedies" (DG 24), seems an apt description
of a man who appears bent on finding portents of his destiny
everywhere. As Sigbjørn himself realizes, his tendency to read
the world symbolically is stimulated, or reinforced, by alcohol: "With the beer, he thought now, or rather the habanero,
the butterflies had become more than butterflies, the stream
more than a stream, just as with the rumpope, the hill had

become more than a hill, and earlier thanks to his matutinal inspirational habanero, the bus drive more than a bus drive. And for that matter, of course, Sigbjørn more than Sigbjørn, and Primrose more than Primrose" (DG 176). Elsewhere he quotes William James on the subject of alcoholic inspiration: "fundamentally the truth, or part of the truth, about his own drinking was to be found in William James. 'It heightened the metaphysical consciousness in man,' he said. . . . And had not James said somewhere too that it was the poor man's symphony?" (DG 29).[4] Even more revealing is Sigbjørn's belief that "in mescal lies the principle of that god-like or daemonic force in Mexico that, anyone who had lived there knows, remains to this day unappeased" (DG 60). Sigbjørn, and to some extent Lowry, has persuaded himself that by drinking he can establish direct contact with the universal and elemental. Inevitably, his immersion in this forest of symbols, often to the exclusion of the life around him, reinforces his identification with the Consul by burying his own identity under the proliferating meanings and analogies that he discovers—or creates.

Lowry's notes for *La Mordida* indicate that he hoped to strike a balance between Sigbjørn's responsibility for his circumstances and his role as victim: "—as a matter of fact the construction, though it ties up with "The Maker of Tragedies"—that [Sigbjørn] has done or is doing all this himself is too hard for him to take, and possibly not wholly true (The Daemon)—there is a sense of something *outside* him—but always remember that what is happening to Wilderness will lose its dramatic effect unless we continually harp on his sense of persecution—" (UBC 13:24, 239). Although presented here as an external force, the daemon is at times regarded as an aspect of Sigbjørn's own mind or will, and in *Dark as the Grave* we even learn that "Sigbjørn Wilderness . . . often thought of himself as less a man than some species of daemon" (DG 199). The conception of the daemon in *Dark as the Grave* and *La Mordida* is in fact rather ill-defined, but the frequent references to the daemon as the author of the book in which Sigbjørn is a character—alternating with Sigbjørn's suspicion that he is enclosed in his own book—indicate a fundamental split in his character.

As described in *Dark as the Grave* and *La Mordida* (where he appears even more prominently), the daemon may be in some respects like Yeats's Daimon, a kind of mask or anti-self through which the poet hopes to discover himself. In *A Vision*, where the union of self and anti-self leads to knowledge, it is necessary for the poet to seek out and embrace his opposite.[5] The Yeatsian Daimon is thus a sort of muse: a "tutelary gent," as Sigbjørn puts it (DG 86). Yeats even notes that the "philosophic voices" that spoke to him and his wife "insisted that the whole system [of *A Vision*] is the creation of my wife's Daimon and of mine, and that it is as startling to them as to us" (Yeats 22). Despite Sigbjørn's talk of a benevolent daemon "wanting us to do good, to be good" (DG 86), however, his daemon generally appears in a more sinister light than Yeats's: instead of revealing fundamental truths about the nature of the universe, the daemon often seems to be bent on destroying Sigbjørn, or at least on making him appear ridiculous. The daemon may be responsible for the numerous symbols and omens that Sigbjørn sees (perhaps even including the Kilroy inscriptions) as well as for the coincidental encounters with people and events from Sigbjørn's own past, or from his novel.

One of the primary reasons for Sigbjørn's visit to Mexico is his desire to see Juan Fernando Martinez, his Zapotecan friend and advocate of *la vida impersonal*. At the end of *Dark as the Grave*, however, Sigbjørn and Primrose learn that Fernando died in December 1939, shot—like the Consul—during a drunken quarrel. The similarity between Fernando's death and the Consul's once again suggests that Sigbjørn's life and art are intricately related, but Sigbjørn's recognition that Fernando is dead also appears to release him, at least temporarily, from his bondage to the world he created in *The Valley of the*

Shadow of Death. Thus Sigbjørn's final vision is of a vibrant, fertile world, a "garden" created by the financial policies of the Banco Ejidal, for which Fernando worked. To attain the awareness of life around him that he possesses at the novel's end, Sigbjørn must undergo a trial that involves a descent into the dark night of the soul, a half-hearted suicide attempt, and his own symbolic death (a tour through Monte Albán, where he enters "dark tomb number seven" and later glimpses life's "meaninglessness" through a syphilitic skull [DG 226–28]). At some point, Lowry must have intended to treat Fernando— whose death is revealed shortly after the encounter with "dark tomb number seven"—as a daemon or arranging presence within the novel, since in *La Mordida* Sigbjørn reads a newspaper article about the archaeological discoveries at the tomb and later has a conversation with the dead Fernando, who says that he sent Sigbjørn a "warning" in the form of "Tomb number 7" (UBC 13:18, 47; 13:26, 279).[6] Tomb number seven is also where Sigbjørn learns that the ancient Mexicans often killed a dog and buried it with its master, a practice that reminds him of the Consul's fate, so the warning here might have been about the danger to which Sigbjørn's novel has exposed him. Lowry never fully developed this portrait of Fernando as a benevolent daemon, however; instead, he concentrated on a more sinister portrayal of the daemon. Thus, according to the "Work in Progress" statement, Sigbjørn's apparent triumph over the daemon at the end of *Dark as the Grave* is an illusion since the daemon is just biding his time until *La Mordida* (WP 87).

In a thoughtful essay on *Dark as the Grave*, J. A. Wainwright asks whether we might best regard that novel as evidence of Lowry's inability "to detach himself from his artistic creations and hold a wholly objective view of them" or as "a remarkable explication of such a dilemma in fictional terms" (Wainwright 82). Opting for the latter view, Wainwright argues that Sigbjørn "resolves a very real dilemma about the relationship of [art and life], a dilemma that Lowry could not resolve for himself in his lifetime" (Wainwright 85). Although this reading of the novel makes sense when *Dark as the Grave* is considered in isolation, it does not adequately explain the complex role Lowry planned for the novel within *The Voyage That Never Ends*. It does not, for example, take into account Lowry's view that, despite the various signs of spiritual renewal and equilibrium at the end of the novel, this book is just a prologue to *La Mordida*, where the daemon will return in force. Moreover, according to Lowry, throughout *Dark as the Grave*, Sigbjørn "becomes ever more and more trapped in the machinery of his own work . . . and becomes more and more like the Consul" (WP 83), a description that contradicts Wainwright's more optimistic reading of the novel.

Since *The Voyage That Never Ends*, which centers on *Under the Volcano*, provides the context for *Dark as the Grave*, it seems curious that Wainwright believes that Sigbjørn and *The Valley of the Shadow of Death* needn't be "directly connected" with Lowry and *Under the Volcano*, and that Sigbjørn "is not haunted by his art per se but by the content of his life which includes within its borders the content of his art. Lowry emphasizes this by having Sigbjørn 'living' rather than writing *Dark as the Grave*" (Wainwright 83–84, 86). Wainwright fails to note that Sigbjørn's real problem lies precisely in his inability to write, or create, the present life he is experiencing: in short, his conviction that he is neither living nor writing, but is "being written." Thus the fact that on the bus ride to Cuernavaca Sigbjørn "does not have a notebook on hand to allow him to alter the novel he has already written" (Wainwright 93) should not be read as an indication that Sigbjørn realizes that the life around him represents a greater reality than that of his own novel, as Wainwright argues. A more important reason why Sigbjørn does not take along a notebook in which he could record possible changes in *The Valley of the Shadow of Death* is that Lowry is focusing on the way Sigbjørn's manuscript has already transformed the life he is now living, not on the way his present life might transform the book. If Sigbjørn knows that life is superior to art, he is generally incapable of acting on his awareness.

Nonetheless, there *is* progress in the novel, and if we read *Dark as the Grave* in its published form, without reference to *La Mordida*, we can certainly find reasons to be optimistic about Sigbjørn's psychic and emotional development. Cynthia Sugars, for example, makes a good case for interpreting the narrative in terms of the stages of separation, transition, and incorporation that constitute a rite of initiation. Sugars concludes that at the novel's end, when "Sigbjørn leaves Mexico with the ability to appreciate the pure joy of being alive once again," he can return to Canada with the realization that he has redeemed his misspent past by transforming it into art (Sugars 159). Unfortunately, even the edited version of *Dark as the Grave* says only that the Wildernesses are leaving the state of Oaxaca, not all of Mexico. If we read *Dark as the Grave* as part of the sequence that includes *La Mordida*, we are forced to recognize that yet another, more terrible, phase of Sigbjørn's life will rise up to torment him before he is allowed to escape from Mexico.

Even so, Sugars is astute in pointing to Sigbjørn's meditations on Jean Epstein's 1928 film *The Fall of the House of Usher* as crucial to our understanding of his progress, particularly his desire for reunion with Primrose (Sugars 156–58). Remembering having seen the film in London, Sigbjørn thinks of the way Epstein gave the story "a happy, or a hopeful ending," transforming Edgar Allan Poe's "despairing" tale into his own version in which "the entombed [Madelaine] was Usher's wife and not his sister, [who] came back in time, as it were with the doctor's help, to save him" (DG 248–49). This description implies a parallel with *Under the Volcano*, in which the wife also returns (although not "in time . . . to save him"), but Sigbjørn turns at once to his present experiences rather than to his novel, wondering if he could emulate Epstein by taking charge of his own life and turning "apparent disaster . . . into triumph" (DG 249). Sigbjørn certainly expresses his hope for a deeper reconciliation with Primrose when he wonders if he can be "the director of this film of his life," but it is significant that he immediately moves away from this claim of responsibility, speculating that his life might be directed by God or the devil, while he is only an actor who must appeal to God "to change the ending" (DG 248). And if we are tempted to regard Sigbjørn's vision of his life in cinematic terms as an unambiguous sign of his progress, we need to consider that the same metaphor occurs early in the novel, where the posters for *Drunkard's Rigadoon* lead Sigbjørn to imagine "yet another advertisement for a movie":

> Sigbjørn Wilderness in *Wilderness's Rigadoon*. Featuring Primrose Wilderness. With Don Fernando Martinez and Bjørnson Erikson. And an unprecedented cast of omens, joys, terrors, delights, demons, dentists, doctors and coincidences. Bottoms up, Gabbler Hooples. (DG 26)[7]

Although the comparison with Epstein's *Usher* implies a far more positive view of his life than this imagined poster, Sigbjørn remains an actor whose life is directed by someone else, and there is no clear indication that he is willing or able to assume control of his life.[8]

That life is, or ought to be, a creative act comparable to directing a film or writing a novel is an idea that underlies much of Lowry's fiction: an idea, moreover, that he used to justify his fixation on artist figures. Responding in 1953 to Albert Erskine's qualms regarding "fiction about writings and writers," Lowry described Sigbjørn Wilderness as "Ortega's fellow, making up his life as he goes along," adding that "according to Ortega, the best image for man himself *is* a novelist" (SL 329, 331). Earlier, in his "Work in Progress" statement, Lowry had told Harold Matson that "man himself is a cutter, and a shaper; indeed as Ortega observes, a sort of novelist,

God help him" (WP 74). The relationship of Lowry's work to
the ideas of José Ortega y Gasset has been discussed by several critics, most notably Sherrill Grace, who observes that
Lowry's belief that we are continually in the process of invent-
ing ourselves—a concept that is fundamental to the overall
plan for *The Voyage That Never Ends*—was suggested or at
least confirmed by his reading of Ortega's *Toward a Philosophy
of History* (Grace, " 'Consciousness of Shipwreck' ").[9] In view
of Grace's thorough and judicious consideration of Lowry's response to Ortega, I will only comment briefly on some negative
implications of Ortega's theory of self-creation for *Dark as the
Grave* and *La Mordida*.

For Ortega, the power to invent their lives was what set
human beings apart from the other animals: "In the vacuum
arising after he has left behind his animal life [man] devotes
himself to a series of nonbiological occupations which are not
imposed by nature but invented by himself. This invented life—
invented as a novel or a play is invented—man calls 'human
life,' well-being." Thus man is "a sort of novelist of himself
who conceives the fanciful figure of a personage with its unreal
occupations" (Ortega, *Toward a Philosophy* 107–8). For Lowry,
however, if the invented life was potentially a source of power
it was also a source of terror, not only because it meant that
he had to accept responsibility for his life but also because on
another level he could never fully believe that he was writing
his life rather than being written—or that in his fiction he was
not, to some extent, a plagiarist. William New succinctly traces
the way an idea like Ortega's could take on a sinister connota-
tion for Lowry: "Lowry was enchanted with the notion that the
novelist was the ideal metaphor for man. That a writer could
create a character (who could be a writer-creator who could
ostensibly in his turn do the same thing) suggested to him that
the writer himself might be a character in the purview of an
unknown artist/perceiver" (New, *Malcolm Lowry* 12).

Thus in *Dark as the Grave*, Sigbjørn's belief that he is "enclosed in his own book" produces an ambiguous response: "In one sense it gave him a feeling of power, and in another he felt like a puppet. Or would God close the book upon him, as if he were an insect?" (DG 195). The question, of course, is who wrote *The Valley of the Shadow of Death,* and whether it can be distinguished from the world around him, God's "strange dark manuscript" from which he might at any time be deleted (DG 142). In *La Mordida* the ambiguities multiply, as Sigbjørn is forced to admit his "indecent admiration for the daemon," whom he compares to "some unearthly novelist in some other dimension"; when he finally is released from the custody of the immigration officials he even imagines that the daemon initially meant to kill him off but then realized that without Sigbjørn he would have no one left to write his book (UBC 14:3, 324; 14:9, 343). If Lowry believed that human beings ideally are novelists who create their own lives, he feared that he was not the true author of his own life but a secretary or amanuensis (or, unconsciously, a plagiarist) who wrote down a life that was being directed by some force outside himself. This fear, which Sigbjørn seems almost to overcome in *Dark as the Grave,* becomes even more intense in *La Mordida,* where it is one of the book's central themes.

Shorn of the projected meeting with L'Hirondelle, which would have greatly complicated the plot, *Dark as the Grave* seems to be the story of a failed quest that nonetheless concludes in a vision of hope. At the end of the novel, Sigbjørn has encountered all the worst aspects of his past (he meets John Stanford, whom he associates with his self-destruction, rather than Fernando), and he seems no closer to having *The Valley of the Shadow of Death* accepted or to writing its sequel, but the conclusion of the novel, with its vision of an Edenic world created by the Banco Ejidal and the memory of a candle that Sigbjørn lit in a church, seems to promise renewal. *La*

Mordida, however, only plunges Sigbjørn into an even darker night of the soul, one in which he is forced to face the terrifying possibility that his entire excursion to Mexico has been an elaborate trap arranged by his daemon.

For several months after his return to British Columbia in May 1946, Lowry was primarily occupied with final revisions and corrections for *Under the Volcano.* Soon, however, the Lowrys found time for two trips: a short one in October to Gabriola Island, which furnished some of the raw material for *October Ferry to Gabriola,* and a much longer one, lasting from late November until early March. The second trip took them across the United States to New Orleans, then to Haiti, up to New York to celebrate the publication of *Under the Volcano,* and to Niagara-on-the-Lake, Ontario, to see Gerald and Betty Noxon. The Lowrys returned to Vancouver separately, Malcolm flying in on 10 March and Margerie arriving a week later by train, only to discover that her husband had not been to Dollarton to ready their shack for her, as he had promised, but had spent the week "drinking and raving" at Maurice Carey's house in Vancouver (ML 384). Before Margerie arrived, however, Lowry was interviewed for the somewhat ludicrous story entitled "Hollywood Seeks Hit Novel Written Here" that appeared in the Vancouver *News Herald* on 15 March 1947. According to this article, Lowry had earned $250,000 from *Under the Volcano,* a novel whose film rights were sought by Orson Welles and other film industry luminaries. Moreover, "Lowry has written a new book, 'La Mordida.' 'It's horrible,' he said Friday, 'the history of a man's imagination. It's about Mexico.' " [10]

Lowry's description of *La Mordida* as the history of an imagination is somewhat more accurate than the rest of the article, including the statement that he had actually written the book; in fact, he was only just beginning it and might not have accomplished much beyond arranging and transcribing some notes. By June he had gotten much further, and he reported to Albert Erskine that he was "working hard" on the novel, which he compared to a difficult and complicated golf course that he had to design while playing it (SL 150). The analogy suggests that Lowry's difficulties with *La Mordida* were conceptual as well as practical, and that he was still working out the fundamental design of the novel. Two months later, when he wrote to Erskine that he was writing what he called *Dark Is the Grave* (SL 151), he had set *La Mordida* aside, and over the next five years his attention shifted to other projects: to *Dark as the Grave, The Ordeal of Sigbjørn Wilderness, October Ferry to Gabriola,* and *Hear Us O Lord from Heaven Thy Dwelling Place,* as well as to the filmscript for *Tender Is the Night* on which he and Margerie collaborated. Despite the elaborate plans for *La Mordida* announced in Lowry's "Work in Progress" statement of November 1951, he had clearly done little work on the manuscript since 1947. The process of describing the book in the statement might have revived his interest in it, since four articles from the Vancouver *Sun* of 27 November 1951 were included in the 1952 typescript that Lowry deposited in a bank vault to guard against the loss of yet another novel.[11] After that draft disappeared into the bank, however, it was largely forgotten—although Lowry used a number of its themes in other works—and *La Mordida* was not among the manuscripts that Lowry took with him in August 1954 when he left Dollarton, never to return.

The intervention of other projects, the numerous trips, and the bouts of drinking all help to explain Lowry's abandonment of *La Mordida,* but a more fundamental reason might lie in the nature of the project itself, which Sigbjørn Wilderness prophetically calls "something never dreamed of before, a work of art so beyond conception it could not be written" (UBC 14:7, 295). The complications do not lie in the narrative line, which is fairly straightforward and basically episodic: the Wildernesses leave their hotel in Cuernavaca for a trip by way of Taxco and Iguala to Acapulco, where they are detained by

Mexican immigration officials who say that they have an out-
standing fine of fifty pesos against Sigbjørn from 1938 and that
he has returned illegally to Mexico. The remainder of the book
recounts the endless delays and frustrations involved in this
Kafkaesque encounter with bureaucracy, which ends finally
when they are taken under guard to Nuevo Laredo, where a
sympathetic sub-chief of the immigration office allows them to
make their escape across the border into Texas. The later chapters are of greater interest to the biographer than to the literary
critic, since they are mainly transcriptions or adaptations of
the notebooks in which Malcolm and (more often) Margerie
recorded their experiences. Earlier chapters, however, involve
a complex array of materials: not only the narrative itself but
marginalia copied from a tourist brochure about Acapulco,[12]
Lowry's notes to himself about revisions, and other miscellaneous items. Much of chapter 6, for example, consists of a
long "dream" sequence based on the notes that the Lowrys
took during their trip to New Orleans and Haiti at the end of
1946—a dream followed in the typescript by a Gospel Mission-
ary Union tract on the reality of Hell and by newspaper stories
about death or disaster.

The incomplete and somewhat haphazard state of the *La
Mordida* typescript means that we cannot judge this work as
we might judge Lowry's more "finished" works. Even *Lunar
Caustic, Dark as the Grave*, and *October Ferry to Gabriola* were
at least sufficiently well developed so that posthumous editions could be published, although it is doubtful that those editions come very close to representing what Lowry would have
wanted to produce. *La Mordida*, by contrast, is not so much a
novel, or even a novel-in-progress, as the record of a stage in
Lowry's life and career. As such, it is important for what it can
tell us about what Lowry hoped to achieve with a work like this
(and of course for what it reveals about the relationship between his aesthetic theories and psychological problems in the
late 1940s and early 1950s). It also provides evidence as to why

Lowry's *Voyage* project, so grand in conception, was probably doomed from the outset.

La Mordida amply demonstrates Lowry's intense belief that all experience is interconnected, and in particular that his fiction and his (or Sigbjørn's) present experience are inextricably linked. Nothing just happens: it happens in relation to, or even because of, something else, and it is in those relationships that we can best understand individual events and begin to see the substantial reality that underlies our sensory experience. The idea is never explicitly developed in the typescript, but it is implicit in a passage from P. D. Ouspensky's *Tertium Organum* that Lowry found significant enough to include in the *La Mordida* draft (UBC 14:1, 299–300). For Ouspensky, as for so many others from Plato on, the world of natural phenomena is just a reflection of a "world of causes" that we experience only indirectly, through "the forms of the three-dimensional phenomenal world." It is symptomatic of Lowry's plight that his extensive quotation from Ouspensky concludes on a note of bewilderment: "In this dwells the tragedy of our spiritual questings: *we do not know what we are searching for.* And the only method by which we can escape this tragedy consists in a preliminary *intellectual* definition of the properties *of that of which we are in search.* Without such definitions, going merely by indefinite feelings, we shall not approach the world of causes or else *we shall get lost on its borderland*" (Ouspensky 196).

For Sigbjørn and, at this stage, for Lowry as well, this belief in an unseen world of causes is a source of confusion and terror: since he has only his "indefinite feelings" to guide him, Sigbjørn cannot help feeling lost on the "borderland" between the world of causes—the daemon's realm—and the phenomenal world in which he lives. Moreover, there is his unshakable belief that the Mexico that he now sees around him is somehow shaped by his writing of *The Valley of the Shadow of Death.* In the first chapter, for instance, a glimpse at a newspaper tells Sigbjørn that there is a meningitis scare in Chilpancingo.

Rather than worry about this possible danger to his health, he is immediately concerned about the way this outbreak of disease seems strangely connected to his novel:

> But it was not this that worried him so much and made him look forward to leaving Chilpancingo as soon as possible, as that he had suddenly remembered that he had invested, in the Valley of the Shadow of Death, his character Yvonne's child by a first marriage with "la Terrible Meningitis Cerebrospinal," and that he had caused that child, in a paragraph that made play with the number 7, seven years before the book began, while at the same time remembered that it was 7 years almost to the day since he had last left Acapulco himself with Bousfield. What a passion for order in all things there seemed to be, down to the minutest detail. No wonder one pined in wars against ignorance and superstition. Nevertheless, if he were to be honest, this was the way he thought. And the way he thought was the way of madness. (UBC 13:18, 48)

Sigbjørn's "passion for order" seems a strange concept in a work so apparently chaotic as *La Mordida*, but the belief that everything somehow relates to everything else provided Lowry with a rationale for his inclusion of such disparate materials in the typescript. Obviously, too, the interplay of different discourses, whose true relationship could be seen only through their effect on the protagonist, was to have been a major feature of the work, perhaps even more so than in *Under the Volcano*. The question was how to fashion these heterogeneous materials into something meaningful: how, in other words, to reconcile the passion for order with the desire for an encyclopedic inclusiveness that threatens to overwhelm the entire structure and render futile all attempts to make sense of this forest of symbols.

On the biographical level, *La Mordida* could be regarded as part of Lowry's ongoing effort to free himself from his own creation, *Under the Volcano*, and specifically from the Consul. David Falk argues that the "almost naked autobiographical

impulse" underlying much of the post-*Volcano* fiction reveals
Lowry's desire for "self-mastery" rather than "self-discovery":
in other words, that he wrote the later works in order to keep
from being taken over by the Consul. Unfortunately, as Falk
notes, Lowry's "attempt to achieve psychic distance" from his
protagonists involved him more fully than ever in his own
creation, so that in "Through the Panama" the line between
creator and creation becomes hopelessly blurred ("Beyond the
Volcano" 26–28). More recently, Falk has observed that "one
of the central ways that the struggle to attain self-mastery is
enacted in the late fiction is as a battle between form and
formlessness" ("Aesthetics of Salvation" 54). To put the matter
another way: Sigbjørn reflects Lowry's deepest fear that any
form he might impose upon his experience is either borrowed
from another writer (which could make him a plagiarist) or
conceived by his daemon (so that Sigbjørn is a puppet con-
trolled by an unseen force). Alternately, there is Sigbjørn's
"fear of any *action* I may take" (UBC 14:3, 328). On its most
immediate level, that fear is what paralyzes him, making it impossible to pay the mordida and somehow extricate himself and
Primrose from the Mexican bureaucracy; on the broadest level,
it is the fear, more terrifying than any ever felt by J. Alfred
Prufrock, that whatever action he takes could upset the balance of the universe and make him responsible for the result.
Moreover, insofar as it applies to Sigbjørn's role as a figure for
Lowry the writer, his fear of taking any kind of action is related to the two forms of Lowry's writer's block: his inability to
write at all or, more often, his inability to stop writing, to bring
a given work to a conclusion and regard it as completed.[13]

One of the fundamental ironies of *La Mordida* and other
later works is that basing his life on his art, and his art on
his life, leaves Lowry in much the same bind as Sigbjørn
Wilderness: he cannot overcome, transcend, even forget the
past because he continually reenacts it in the process of writing
about it. If "La Mordida is also involved etymologically with

remorse" (UBC 13:23, 154–55), as Lowry believed, then one question posed by the book might be what degree of remorse is sufficient: can the debt ever be erased, the fine paid? When Sigbjørn wonders what other parts of his past—like the fine—are still there, waiting to resurface and confront him (UBC 13:20, 111), he voices the basic fear that Lowry felt not only throughout his return visit to Mexico but also, I suspect, in his attempts to write about that visit. Like paying a fine, writing was for Lowry a means of expiation and transcendence, but every move was perilous because in writing about his experience he also half-created it, by giving it a form that it would then carry into his future life. Sugars observes that in *Dark as the Grave* Sigbjørn discovers that he has not transformed his past by writing about it in *The Valley of the Shadow of Death;* instead, he "must physically relive the past and actively steer it into a more positive direction" (Sugars 153). But it is also true that in *Dark as the Grave* and *La Mordida,* one problem that Sigbjørn faces is that the past, the world he is reliving, has been changed, and that *he* changed it by writing *The Valley.*

In his letter to Jonathan Cape in defense of *Under the Volcano,* Lowry argued that his book might be read in various ways—as "a prophecy, a political warning, a cryptogram, a preposterous movie, and a writing on the wall"—adding that "it can even be regarded as a sort of machine: it works too, believe me, as I have found out" (SL 66). For Lowry, the idea of the book as a machine seems inevitably sinister, and in fact *Under the Volcano* presents both book and world as infernal machines: only a few pages before taking a ride on La Máchina Infernal, an infernal version of the Wheel of Fortune, the Consul glances at Jean Cocteau's *La Machine infernale,* whose title applies not only to Cocteau's play but to the cosmic mechanism that lies behind its action. The description of Lowry's work generally, and especially *Under the Volcano,* as a sort of diabolical mechanism recurs significantly in the later writings. In *Dark as the Grave,* as Rankin notes, the airplane carrying the Wildernesses to Mexico is associated with the Infernal Machine that Sigbjørn's book has become ("Writer as Metaphor" 321). Later, in "Through the Panama," Sigbjørn comments on the process through which *"The Valley of the Shadow* worked like an infernal machine" (HL 36).

In *La Mordida,* the idea that his own work is a kind of "machine" threatening Sigbjorn alternates with his belief that he is the victim of a malign universe. Chapter 7 presents both of these images of Sigbjørn, first by associating him with someone who is to be hanged the next morning in a disused elevator shaft (UBC 13:24, 226–27). When Sigbjørn reminds himself that he "was not indeed going to be hanged or shot in the morning . . . he was merely going to be tortured, and at that more by himself than any other outside agency," his thoughts immediately turn to someone else, a man he recalls having seen in a newsreel. The man had invented a flying machine ("one of the first helicopters," as Sigbjørn recalls), and the newsreel showed the man shaking hands with his friends, mugging for the camera, climbing into the machine, and taking off. Then the film, which had begun rather comically, suddenly turned disastrous:

> The invention met with some kind of disaster, came apart in mid-air, fell to pieces. You saw this, and this was bad enough, but not yet terrible. You did not quite believe it: and anyway it was only a machine, so that it was almost abstract. What was dreadful was not that but what followed almost immediately after. You saw the inventor falling feet first from his contraption, frantically kicking his legs, as if trying to run on the air, falling falling all the way to the ground, kicking his helpless legs, over which the individuals who had been playing such a good humored part only a moment before were now frantically running. It was not only that these moments, before the man hit the ground, while he was still alive—what was he thinking?—was he thinking?—were so horrible: it was that the whole thing was in such dreadful, as it

were, taste, as if in a two reel Laurel and Hardy comedy Laurel, say, would actually be killed. (UBC 13:24, 228)

It is perhaps unnecessary to belabor the symbolism here: to show in detail that the inventor represents the artist who becomes literally entangled in, and ultimately killed by, his own creation, the entire sequence being captured on a motion picture reel, one more image of mechanical circularity and inevitability.[14] The reference to a Laurel and Hardy film in which Laurel is really killed introduces an equally important dimension into the passage, as it demonstrates the terrible consequences of failing to distinguish clearly between life and art. Ironically, although Sigbjørn recognizes this danger, he is unable to avoid it, and he immediately identifies himself with the inventor in the newsreel: "Sigbjørn yesterday was the man in the plane smiling: Sigbjørn now was the man falling, and nothing—he felt—could save him" (UBC 13:24, 229). We might gather from this passage how far Sigbjørn (and perhaps Lowry) is from being able to act upon Ortega's insistence that we are "shipwrecked," cast adrift, forced to move our arms to keep ourselves afloat and thereby compelled to accept responsibility for what we are and what we represent ("In Search of Goethe" 136–37). Consciousness of shipwreck, for Ortega, "constitutes salvation"; it is a source of freedom, since it throws the responsibility for creating our lives back upon us. But Sigbjørn's belief that his life is a kind of tragedy works in the opposite way, since it enables him to deny that he now has any control over his life.

Barry Wood's observation that "if Lowry was not lost in his own landscapes, he was lost in those of other artists" ("Metafiction" 18) applies as well to Sigbjørn, whose life and art both seem to be defined and circumscribed by those of other authors. This is hardly a new theme in Lowry's works, which from *Ultramarine* on feature autobiographical protagonists who struggle to establish their own identities in a world in which their stories seem already written. The tendency for Lowry's protagonists to read their experiences in literary terms becomes even more of a threat to their own identities in works written after *Under the Volcano*, including *La Mordida*, where Sigbjørn recalls having been used as a character in a story by Sherwood Anderson (UBC 13:21, 124–25). Likewise, in *Dark as the Grave*, he wonders, "Had he not identified himself with a character of Daniel's—if not with Daniel himself? And a similar thing had happened with Erikson" (DG 41). Daniel and Erikson are recognizable as Conrad Aiken and Nordahl Grieg, with whose works Lowry felt a profound sense of identification, while Sigbjørn's repeated encounters with advertisements for *Drunkard's Rigadoon* call attention to the less welcome, if unavoidable, connection between *Under the Volcano* and *The Lost Weekend*. Nor are these the only such identifications in *Dark as the Grave*, or even necessarily the most important ones: when Sigbjørn imagines that he hears church bells ringing as they do in Hart Crane's "Purgatorio" (which he misquotes— DG 63),[15] envisions himself as "Herman Melville, masquerading as Redburn" (DG 20), or compares his situation to those in Julian Green's *The Dark Journey* and Arthur Schnitzler's *Flight into Darkness* (DG 45–46), the imposition of literary paradigms on his experience demonstrates his inability to cope with the reality around him in any other terms.

La Mordida is even more obsessively "literary" than *Dark as the Grave*, and although we might assume that Lowry would eventually have reduced the mass of literary allusions and parallels, or at least introduced them in a less obtrusive manner, the sheer number of these references in a working draft may be used to gauge the extent to which Lowry's response to his own experience was shaped by his reading. Some of the references are casual and even wry, as when a hotel's advertisement that it has two penguins prompts Sigbjørn to speculate that they are "on loan doubtless from Melville's Encantadas" (UBC

13:18, 63), but a memo such as "intellectually speaking there can be resemblances between this and Measure for Measure" (UBC 14:9, 332), inserted into a scene whose connection with *Measure for Measure* is not especially apparent, suggests that Lowry was straining to build literary parallels into his narrative. Numerous literary references—to "Mario and the Magician," *Crime and Punishment*, Flaubert's *Salammbô*, Hudson's *The Purple Land*, and O'Hara's *Appointment in Samarra*, for example—are worked into the typescript, and notes such as "This is a wonderful opportunity for a sort of good soldier Schweik scene" (UBC 13:24, 243) indicate that Lowry might well have increased their number if he had revised his novel.[16]

As it stands, *La Mordida* is little more than a set of sketches and notes for a novel—if "novel" is the right word for the work that might eventually have emerged from a revised text. Such a work would have involved a central narrative: the Wildernesses' journey to Acapulco, arrest, and escape across the border, a kind of emergence from the underworld. This narrative would have been played off against the marginalia; moreover, the highly self-conscious nature of the protagonist would have made the entire work a kind of extended meditation on a host of aesthetic, psychological, and philosophical questions, and its inquiry into these issues would have been broadened and deepened by the allusions with which the text is studded, as well as by the larger context of *The Voyage That Never Ends*. Although biographical in its origins, *La Mordida* was meant to pose essential questions about the nature of human existence, but the progressive entanglement of life and art was fatal to this project, and to most of the other works written after *Under the Volcano*. Even in its unfinished state, however, *La Mordida* is essential reading for anyone undertaking serious study of Lowry's life and works, if in fact there is a significant difference between the two. It also demonstrates the anxiety—in fact, the sheer terror—that underlay his attempt to return, imaginatively, to *Under the Volcano*. A reading of *La Mordida* (and for that matter *Dark as the Grave*) shows why Lowry positively needed to escape his own creation. His most extended attempt to make that escape involved the composition of another novel, *October Ferry to Gabriola.*

Begun as a short story that developed out of notes taken during the 1946 trip to Gabriola Island, *October Ferry to Gabriola* soon burgeoned into a novella and ultimately into the increasingly long and complex novel-in-progress that occupied much of Lowry's attention during the 1950s. In October 1951 Lowry told Harold Matson that the work "deals with the theme of eviction, which is related to man's dispossession, but this theme is universalized"; it was, he added proudly, "a hell of a fine thing" (SL 267). He was still working on "a rewritten (and I hope terrific) *October Ferry to Gabriola*" in January 1953, worrying that the novel was "not quite subdued and cut to size" and that it threatened to absorb material he planned for *Eridanus,* the "intermezzo" scheduled for insertion between *Dark as the Grave* and *La Mordida* in *The Voyage That Never Ends* (SL 328). Torn between his commitment to the multivolume *Voyage* and a new novel that would not quite fit into the sequence, Lowry felt guilty about the time he was spending on *October Ferry* but unable to abandon a book that "has cost me more pains than all the *Volcano* put together," as he told Albert Erskine in April 1953 (SL 334).[17] Later in the same letter, he detailed some of those pains, caused in part by the fact that his "daemon" had turned *October Ferry* from "an innocent and beautiful story of human longing" into a "guilt-laden" and "quite Satanically horrendous" work. If it was not an "artistic triumph," Lowry claimed, the unfinished novel was at least "a psychological triumph of the first order," one whose power and impact are attributable to "the bloody agony of the writer writing it." Admitting that it had numerous faults—inadequate characterization, obvious symbolism, repetition—and might be considered "a total failure," Lowry argued that "the important thing though is that I should have written it—touch wood!—at all" (SL 338–40).

Lowry *hadn't* written it, of course; or at least he hadn't finished writing it, and he never would. In one of his last letters, written to Ralph Gustafson in April 1957, Lowry said he was "now writing a huge and sad novel about Burrard Inlet called *October Ferry to Gabriola* that I sometimes feel could have been better stated in about ten short poems—or even lines—instead" (SL 409). The published text includes an editor's note in which Margerie Lowry points to two elements that Lowry had hoped to develop further: Jacqueline's father, The McCandless, was to have played a more prominent role, and the reason for Ethan Llewelyn's abandonment of his law practice—his discovery that a man whom he had defended against, and believed innocent of, a charge of murder was in fact guilty (OF 7)— was to have been spelled out (OF 336). Other possible changes might be deduced from Lowry's notes: Kilgallin, for example, points to marginalia that indicate Lowry's concern with the accumulation of literary allusions in the manuscript and with passages that are "far too done, too final and too pseudo-intellectual" ("The Long Voyage Home" 221). Nonetheless, the texture of *October Ferry* became increasingly complex as Lowry enlarged it to accommodate numerous cinematic, literary, and philosophical allusions that carry much of the novel's weight of meaning.

Lowry's belief that his daemon had gotten hold of the novel's composition is revealing. For better or for worse, *October Ferry* is a different sort of novel from the one Lowry appears to have intended: "a more classically objective form of novel," as Binns puts it ("Anti-Novel" 109). *October Ferry* seems "objective" only by comparison with *Dark as the Grave, La Mordida,* and other similar works that Lowry was attempting around the same time: all of the work's narration is filtered through the consciousness of Ethan Llewelyn, whose sensation that he is "merging into [the world around him], while equally there was a fading of it into himself," indicates that he suffers from the characteristic inability of Lowry's protagonists to distinguish between inner and outer reality, between self and world. Day calls Ethan Llewelyn "Lowry's earnest attempt not, for once, to write about an artist" but admits that Ethan "is finally yet another projection of the author's personality" (ML 438).[18] Despite Wood's claim that *October Ferry*'s "remarkable promise . . . rests in its escape from the involution of metafiction" ("Metafiction" 24), Lowry's last novel is a highly reflexive work that uses some of the same themes, techniques, and situations, and poses many of the same questions, as his other post-*Volcano* fiction.

Still, Ethan Llewelyn is not Sigbjørn Wilderness (although we learn that Sigbjørn—along with Roderick Fairhaven, the protagonist of "Present State of Pompeii"—lives nearby, in Eridanus). Ethan is a retired attorney who has been living with his wife, Jacqueline—and, when he is not at boarding school, their son, Tommy—in a squatter's shack in Eridanus, across the Burrard Inlet from Vancouver. Threatened with eviction by a local government that wants to turn their land into a public park, Ethan and Jacqueline decide to look into the possibility of relocating to the even more remote Gabriola Island, a ferry's ride from Nanaimo, on Vancouver Island. The frame for the narrative is their journey by bus and ferry toward Gabriola, during which "Ethan's mind is divided between the immediate sensations of the journey toward the future and the memories and guilt that continue to hold him back from hope of that future" (MacDonald 49). Whether or not Ethan will overcome his past is in fact a major issue in this novel, one that relates it to virtually all of Lowry's other major undertakings.

Throughout the journey, Ethan's mind returns obsessively to two traumatic aspects of his past: the suicide of a college friend, Peter Cordwainer, and a series of mysterious fires that drove the Llewelyns from Niagara-on-the-Lake, Ontario, to the seclusion of Eridanus. Like the trip to Gabriola itself, both of these events have their origins in Lowry's experiences, although a number of details have been altered. Cordwainer, of course, is yet another version of Paul Fitte (the "Wensleydale" of *The Ordeal of Sigbjørn Wilderness*), but the university where he committed suicide has been changed from Cambridge to South Wales, the cause of death from gas poisoning to hanging, and the date of the suicide from 15 November to 7 October 1929. Since we are told that 7 October is also the date of Edgar Allan Poe's death (OF 212, 215), the change in date reinforces the book's theme of coincidence and gives Lowry an excuse to introduce references to Poe that suggest the weight of guilt and terror that Ethan carries with him. Moreover, "Ethan had often been told that he looked rather like Edgar Allan Poe,"[19] so a process of association would appear to connect Ethan with Cordwainer by way of Poe; but when Ethan looks into the rearview mirror of the bus, the face that looks back seems to accuse him of murder, thereby reinforcing his role as the self-destructive criminal/victim (OF 215–16). Likewise, the change in the cause of Fitte's death is thematically relevant, for it permits Lowry to connect Ethan's guilty past with his desire to redeem himself by defending a teenage boy who has been sentenced to hang for murder.[20]

The fires that seem to follow Ethan around also come from Lowry's experience, although they are not directly traceable to the fire that burned down the Lowrys' Dollarton shack in June 1944, taking with it the manuscript of *In Ballast to the White Sea*. That fire plays a significant role in the background of *Dark as the Grave*, where the image of the burning house haunts Sigbjørn with its implications of personal and artistic failure, but the fires in *October Ferry* are mainly based on a series of mysterious conflagrations in Ontario, where Lowry went after the Dollarton fire. Lowry's belief that he had somehow aroused "demonic forces" by dabbling with occult matters, and that he was being "pursued by the element of fire" (ML 303), is reflected in Ethan's meditations on the fires which he first believes are caused by a demon that seeks to destroy him; later, after reading the works of Charles Fort, Ethan comes to regard the fires as the products of his own mind. Once again, as in *Under the Volcano, Dark as the Grave,* and *La Mordida,* Lowry opens the question whether his characters create the worlds in which they suffer—whether, in short, they are "makers of tragedies"—or whether they are the victims of a malignant and absurd universe.

In its themes and techniques, *October Ferry* constantly uses material that may be found elsewhere in Lowry's fiction. The use of "Frère Jacques" to represent the sound of a boat's engine recurs in five of the stories in *Hear Us O Lord,* while a curious reference to juke boxes playing "White Christmas" repeats a line already used in *Dark as the Grave* and *La Mordida.* The phrase "some correspondence between the subnormal world and the abnormally suspicious" is repeated from *Under the Volcano* (UV 34, 355; OF 320),[21] along with the chilling word "farolitos" (OF 249); references to Popocatepetl, Oaxaca, and Ixtaccihuatl relate this journey to the infernal geography of *Under the Volcano* and even seem to imply that Ethan has spent time in Mexico, although nothing else in the novel supports that idea (OF 4, 171, 299). We have reworkings of the theme of eviction, the idea of a divided consciousness, the obsession with informers, and the use of simultaneous conversations; signs and other printed materials appear throughout the book, and the numerous references to movies carry a good deal of thematic weight, far more even than in *Under the Volcano.* There is even a variation on *sortes Shakespeareanae* when a randomly chosen passage from *The Books of Charles Fort* tells Ethan that J. Temple Thurston—known to him as the author of a play about the Wandering Jew, which had been made into a movie that could almost have been about Ethan—died in a mysterious fire. Like almost all of Lowry's protagonists, from Dana Hilliot to Sigbjørn Wilderness, Ethan tends to see representations of his own situation wherever he looks.

Even so, Lowry planned to strike out in a new direction with *October Ferry*. The trips by bus and boat are reminiscent of those in other works, but there is a difference: if *October Ferry* does not quite conclude with the grand affirmation that Lowry planned for *In Ballast to the White Sea*, the journey at least culminates in a willingness to accept, and even embrace, ambiguity and change. Keith Harrison argues that because the book ends without the Llewelyns' having reached Gabriola, the "success of their quest [is] uncertain," but uncertainty is probably an essential aspect of the book's structure and vision since, as Bradbrook argues, the novel demands that we recognize "that Paradise is no permanent place, that what is loved must be recognized to be transient" (Harrison, "Balancing Time" 121; Bradbrook, "Intention and Design" 150). Sherrill Grace has cited an unpublished letter in which Lowry compared *October Ferry* to Kafka's *The Castle* but noted a crucial difference between the two novels: according to Lowry, Ethan and Jacqueline "have more trouble getting to Gabriola than K to the castle though Gabriola is not a castellan symbol; it *is*, finally, the future" (Grace, *Voyage* 76). Precisely what sort of future Gabriola represents is not altogether clear, but it seems to involve the acceptance of ambiguity and change.

One crucial difference between *October Ferry* and the other novels may be illustrated through the opening chapter's description of the bus ride, which invites comparison with chapter 8 of *Under the Volcano*. Lowry had begun his narration of the Consul's fated journey with a paragraph consisting of the single word "Downhill . . .," a word repeated at a strategic point late in the chapter to emphasize that nothing has happened to arrest the Consul's downward flight (UV 231, 252; the ellipsis appears in both passages). In his letter to Jonathan Cape, Lowry had stressed the thematic importance of the direction taken by the bus: "Here the book, so to speak, goes into reverse—or, more strictly speaking, it begins to go downhill. . . . Downhill (the first word) toward the abyss" (SL 78). At first, Ethan's bus is headed in the same direction: "Downhill: and to the right hand beyond the blue sea, beneath the blue sky, the mountains on the British Columbian mainland traversed the horizon" (OF 3–4). Even the topography of this journey seems to mirror that of the earlier novel, as Mount Baker appears "like a remote, unanchored Popocatepetl." Quickly, however, the book reverses directions: "The bus changed gear, going up a hill: beginning: beginning: beginning again: beginning yet again: here we go, into the blue morning" (OF 5). In most of Lowry's works, this movement up and down hills would probably invite a parallel with the myth of Sisyphus, as it does in *Under the Volcano* (see Barnes 12–18), but in *October Ferry* Lowry puts a less sinister interpretation on the pattern. The conclusion of the penultimate chapter (OF 322) echoes this passage, and it seems apparent that "beginning yet again" refers to Lowry's writing career as well as to Ethan's search for a new life.

In fact, on one level the opening sequence of *October Ferry* is a rewriting of the bus trip with which *La Mordida* begins. There, the journey quickly turns ominous as Sigbjørn, traveling along the new road to Acapulco, feels the presence of the "inconceivably more terrible . . . old road [that] still existed running parallel with the new paved one" (UBC 13:18, 35). The parallel routes of the old and new roads appear to lead Sigbjørn directly into his own past, just as *La Mordida* proclaims Lowry's entanglement with his personal and artistic past. *October Ferry* at least holds out the possibility that the journey may lead to new territory, even if the landmarks along the route often seem all too familiar.

Another significant difference between *October Ferry* and most of Lowry's works involves Ethan's awareness of, and concern for, other people. It is true that in many respects he is a typical Lowryan protagonist, self-pitying and obsessed with a past that continually arises to haunt him in the form of advertisements for Mother Gettle's soup, with their pictures of a young Peter Cordwainer that remind him of his callous treatment of Cordwainer. There is, however, another side to Ethan's character as well, one that increasingly emerges as the journey progresses. For one thing, as Doyen remarks, Ethan's chance meeting with Henry Knight, an innocent man whom he had successfully defended against a charge of murder, marks a significant stage in his experience, since "the rediscovery of the past leads to an acceptance of the self" ("From Innocent Story" 179). In virtually all of Lowry's other works from *Under the Volcano* on, encounters with the past take on a sinister form, and people who arise unexpectedly out of the past are often somehow threatening, like Stanford in *Dark as the Grave* or the stool pigeon in *La Mordida;* alternatively, when Yvonne returns to the Consul, he proves unable to respond appropriately because he believes too firmly that the past is fixed and that he is unable to will his own salvation. Ethan's concern for other people is present in his meditations about the case of the teenage boy who has been condemned to hang, but if we want to see this as a sign of Ethan's commitment to social action we have to recognize that he really does nothing about the case except to think about it, even though, as a prominent attorney, he is one of the few people capable of actually helping; moreover, his vision of himself as a heroic lawyer pleading for the boy's life at the bar of public opinion is severely undercut by his tendency to see himself as the accused criminal victimized by an uncaring society.

A better sign of Ethan's willingness to see other people as more than mere projections of himself, and his concern for their welfare, may be seen on the boat to Gabriola when Mrs. Neiman, an elderly woman who has just had all her teeth extracted, begins bleeding so badly and is in such pain that the boat has to be turned around so that she can be returned to Nanaimo. Ethan does not have to risk his life to help her, as Dana Hilliot would have if he had jumped into the bay to save a shipmate's pigeon, nor does he risk being arrested for coming to the aid of someone else, as Hugh Firmin does when he

wants to help the dying Indian. The extent of Ethan's involvement with Mrs. Neiman's situation is that he gives her a drink
of gin to help relieve the pain, expresses sympathy for her, and
accepts with equanimity the fact that he and Jacqueline will
be delayed in getting to Gabriola. Still, all of this is at least
a move in the right direction, and the fact that he is able to
open the gin bottle for Mrs. Neiman, whereas a few minutes
earlier he had been unable to open it for himself, is certainly a
positive sign.

One final difference between Ethan and most of Lowry's
other characters is that he becomes aware of the danger of seeing his life largely in terms of aesthetic models (in his case,
films) and of trying to fit his life into a preconceived pattern
rather than being open to the more ambiguous and fluctu-
ating nature of individual experience. Lowry has Ethan and
Jacqueline join a film society, a rather contrived device that
allows him to introduce films that parallel their lives in one
way or another. In an early passage, Ethan thinks about "the
eerie significance of cinemas in our life . . . as if they related
to the afterlife, as if we knew, after we are dead, we would
be conducted to a movie house where, only half to our surprise, is playing a film named: *The Ordeal of Ethan Llewelyn*,
with Jacqueline Llewelyn"; the conceit is worthy of Sigbjørn
Wilderness, who imagines his life as a movie entitled *Wilderness's Rigadoon* (OF 26–27; DG 26). "Films had more reality
to him than life until he had found his little house," Ethan
realizes (OF 61), but by the end of the novel he seems able to
put some distance between himself and the films he sees. In
chapter 28, where "the billboards and advertisements took on
a new significance . . . as if man's spiritual pilgrimage on earth
too were eternally between these hoardings," Ethan is amused
by an advertisement for a cinematic double bill whose titles,
Mr. Blanding's Dream House and *The Long Voyage Home*,
might well have seemed more ominous, and in chapter 36,
when Jacqueline suggests that they see the two films, Ethan's
thoughts move in another direction (OF 225, 317).

The conclusion of *October Ferry to Gabriola* is one of the most positive in Lowry's corpus, comparable to the endings of *Dark as the Grave* (when it is read on its own, and not as part of a sequence that includes the darker *La Mordida*) and "The Forest Path to the Spring." This is not to say that it is a highly successful novel, or that it could ever have been a masterwork on the level of *Under the Volcano*. But it is a significant attempt on Lowry's part to begin again, using some of the same materials—themes, narrative techniques, images—as *Under the Volcano* and his other work to achieve a somewhat different end, creating not a *Paradiso* (despite its background in the Northern Paradise of which Yvonne and the Consul dreamed) but a *Purgatorio* from which both Ethan and his creator emerge with renewed faith in themselves. Completed, *October Ferry* would have been in some ways like *The Voyage That Never Ends*, since Ethan spends his voyage delving into his own past and coming to terms with himself and with the world; and it seems likely that the ultimate form of the novel would have justified Lowry's description of it as "a psychological triumph of the first order" (SL 339). Of all the novels Lowry attempted after *Under the Volcano*, *October Ferry* almost certainly held out the greatest hope for just such a triumph, and even in its published form, with all its weaknesses, we can discern Lowry's almost heroic effort to re-create himself.

SEVEN

Apparently Incongruous Parts:
*Hear Us O Lord from Heaven
Thy Dwelling Place*

Despite his frequently expressed desire for simplicity, Lowry's work suggests that he was in fact a writer "to whom no simple truth was true," as he put it in his poem "God help those and others who" (CP 79). The tendency for Lowry's projects to become longer and more complex may be seen in the way *Under the Volcano* and *October Ferry to Gabriola* evolved from short stories into substantial novels, as well as in the great overarching structures, like *The Voyage That Never Ends*, that he hoped would lend significance to his individual works. The same tendency is apparent even in Lowry's only attempt at a short story collection, *Hear Us O Lord from Heaven Thy Dwelling Place*, ostensibly the narrative of a composite protagonist whose descent into obsessive self-involvement and eventual affirmation of the value of the simple life in close contact with nature describe what Lowry hoped would be the pattern of his own life.

The exact makeup of the book changed over time. An October 1951 letter to Harold Matson lists six stories—"Through the Panama," "October Ferry to Gabriola," "In the Black Hills,"

"Strange Comfort Afforded by the Profession," "Elephant and Colosseum," and "The Forest Path to the Spring" (SL 267–68)—but in the yet-unpublished *Hear Us O Lord* section of the "Work in Progress" statement that Lowry wrote the next month, the order of the stories is slightly different and "October Ferry" is dropped in favor of "The Bravest Boat," which he had just written (UBC 12:13). The statement also describes several more stories that could be included in the collection, among them "Battement de Tambours" (a version of the Vancouver-to-Haiti trip in chapter 6 of *La Mordida*), "We're All Good Ducks Here" (the story of a Canadian game warden), and a winter's tale that moves from despair to affirmation, "Nocturnal Genius." By 1953 the number of anticipated stories had grown to twelve, possibly as part of an attempt to establish a parallel with the twelve chapters of *Under the Volcano*. Moreover, the nature of the project, with the significance and even the genre of each story changing according to the context in which it is read, is more complex than ever:

> As things stand, *Gabriola* . . . is—or will be—a novel. But so is "The Forest Path to the Spring" another short novel. *Gabriola* and "Forest Path" taken together make, as you will see, *another* kind of novel. "Ghostkeeper," "Pompeii," *Gabriola* and "Forest Path" make yet *another* kind of novel. *Hear Us O Lord*—with its 12 chapters—would be, if done aright . . . yet *another* kind of novel: a kind of—often far less serious, often much more so—*Volcano* in reverse, with a triumphant ending. (SL 338)

The version of the collection that Margerie Lowry published in 1961 contains only seven stories, but it does culminate in the much-desired "triumphant ending." Moreover, the general shape of the collection, which involves a geographical and psychological movement from British Columbia to Europe and back to the Canadian Eden—or, on another level, a fall from unity into division and then a return to oneness, psychic harmony, or grace—is certainly consistent with Lowry's plans. Yet as Brian Moore noted in his review of the collection, despite the "note of lyrical affirmation" with which the book ends, "we have glimpsed once again the dread, doomed figure of the Consul" (Moore 157). Doom always had more reality for Lowry than salvation, and if *Hear Us O Lord* is framed by two relatively idyllic stories, with the tone of the other stories lightened by comic moments, the overriding impression given by the volume is that we are dealing with typical Lowryan characters whose preoccupation with their own problems is both the principal source of the stories' interest and the reason why Lowry found it so hard to give this book a shape and identity of its own, apart from his other works.

Lowry's difficulty with relatively simple themes and with stories that do not focus on the problems of obsessive and self-involved writers is evident in the opening story, "The Bravest Boat." Read on its own terms, the story is a rather slender fable that depicts the idealized relationship between Sigurd and Astrid Storlesen, whom we encounter as they stroll through a version of Vancouver's Stanley Park. It is now March 1951, and in three months they will celebrate the twenty-ninth anniversary of the event that ultimately brought them together. For on 27 June 1922 Sigurd, who was then ten years old, launched a toy boat, sealed with a message inside, from a wharf in the state of Washington.[1] The boat "wandered" for twelve years before it was found by seven-year-old Astrid, who was born five years after the boat set out on its brave journey. The story does not explain how Astrid's discovery of the boat and the message led her, some years later, to marry Sigurd (who would have been twenty-two when Astrid found the boat), but they have now been married for seven years. The story, in fact, takes place on their seventh wedding anniversary.

The boat, with its message of hope tightly sealed inside to protect it against the turbulence of the sea, is the story's central symbol. The best passages in the story describe the boat's imagined journey—"imagined" because it was unwitnessed and can only be created by the imagination: as in his other works, what Lowry's characters *think* in this story is generally more interesting than what they *say* or *do*. The boat's survival, against all odds, is mirrored when a squirrel ventures too near a lynx's cage and narrowly escapes being killed by the "demonic" lynx (a scene that in turn reminds us of the insect's miraculous flight from the mouth of Mr. Quincey's cat in *Under the Volcano*). On another level, the return of the boat is like the cycle of the seasons. While the "desolate beach" is strewn with "wreckage, the toll of winter's wrath," the narrator reminds us that spring is not far behind: "Nor was it possible to grasp for more than a moment that all this with its feeling of death and destruction and barrenness was only an appearance, that beneath the flotsam, under the very shells they crunched, within the trickling overflows of winterbournes they jumped over, down at the tide margin, existed, just as in the forest, a stirring and stretching of life, a seething of spring" (HL 26). Nature, ultimately, is both destructive and creative: the ocean attempts to destroy the boat but eventually delivers it to Astrid, and even the ferocious lynx is last glimpsed in a domestic scene, "solemnly washing his mate's face" (HL 23).

A far more sinister force is the city, Enochvilleport, that surrounds and menaces the park. Intruding onto the park through a loudspeaker that blares out messages, typified by "dilapidated," "broken," and "soulless" structures, peopled by a bourgeois citizenry intent (as in *October Ferry*) on hanging a sixteen-year-old boy for murder, Enochvilleport is just as infernal as the New York of *Lunar Caustic*. Indeed, the narrator says that the city, with its "numerous sawmills relentlessly smoking and champing away like demons, Molochs fed by whole mountainsides of forests that never grew again," would be recognizable to "anyone who had ever really been in hell" (HL 17).

The city threatens the park, and the natural world generally, almost from the beginning, where Lowry describes "the tragic

Seven Sisters, a constellation of seven noble red cedars that had grown there for hundreds of years, but were now dying, blasted . . . dying rather than live longer near civilization" (HL 13). The Seven Sisters were named for the Pleiades, but the cosmic implications of the name have long been lost on the people of Enochvilleport, who imagine that the trees "were named with civic pride after the seven daughters of a butcher, who seventy years before . . . had all danced together in a shop window." In view of Geoffrey Durrant's Neoplatonic reading of "Through the Panama" as the soul's voyage through the world of gross matter in order to return to "the heavenly region of the stars—the true home from which it has been exiled" ("Death in Life" 158), it is probably significant that the citizens are oblivious to the astral origin of the name given to the trees by their forebears, people who were in closer contact with the natural (and therefore the ideal) world. As in *Under the Volcano*'s recurrent myth of lost harmony between the physical and spiritual realms, "The Bravest Boat" implies that the modern world is fallen from a state of grace into one of division.

The story's themes and motifs—the journey, the pattern of separation and return, the necessity of love, and the opposition between civilization (or at least material progress) and nature —are characteristic not only of this volume but of Lowry's work generally: thus it is hardly surprising to find an ominous phrase like *"Your weight and your destiny"* repeated from *October Ferry* (HL 14, 15; OF 233, 234). If at first it appears that Sigurd, unlike almost all of Lowry's other protagonists, is not an artist figure, we might observe that he is at least the author of a note that ultimately reached Astrid, and that in this sense he may be regarded as a successful writer: perhaps even the converse of Geoffrey Firmin, whose letter never reaches Yvonne because he lacks the courage to mail it. Given the way stories like "Through the Panama" and "Strange Comfort Afforded by the Profession" play with the nature of writing and its relationship to fact and memory, it is also intriguing to see that Sigurd's original letter survives as an artifact, or relic, that Sigurd and Astrid have made so much a part of themselves that they "read" it from memory even though the actual document is now "hardly legible" (HL 25). The events of the past, particularly Sigurd's launching of the boat and Astrid's discovery of it, form the basis for the identity that they have forged together, one that they re-create by reciting the story of the boat, each of them chiming in and repeating the other's story so that it is hard to tell them apart.

"The Bravest Boat" also sets up other themes and images of *Hear Us O Lord*. The laughter at its conclusion is echoed in different ways at the ends of "Strange Comfort Afforded by the Profession," "Elephant and Colosseum," and "The Forest Path to the Spring," for example, while the symbolic significance of the toy boat is made explicit in "Through the Panama": "How can the soul take this kind of battering and survive? It's a bit like the toy boat" (HL 40). Richard Cross argues that "man's estrangement from the earth is in fact the major theme not just of this story but of the entire collection," and Keith Harrison finds in the first story of *Hear Us O Lord* a positive treatment of one of the book's dominant concerns, the significance of the past (Cross 89; Harrison, "Malcolm Lowry's *Hear Us O Lord*" 246). And of course it is in "The Bravest Boat" that we first hear the refrain of "Frère Jacques" that will recur in four of the remaining six stories, as well as in *October Ferry* and the *Tender Is the Night* screenplay.

Taking the story on those terms, we may well analyze "The Bravest Boat" in relation to the narrative and thematic patterns of *Hear Us O Lord* as a whole, arguing, for example, that the story should be read as an "overture" to the volume (Grace, *Voyage* 103–5).[2] Critics who have evaluated the story by itself, however, have almost invariably found it deficient. Ronald Binns, for example, regards "The Bravest Boat" as "a rather schmalzy sentimental piece" whose 1954 publication in *Partisan Review*, at a time when Lowry's more significant work could not find an outlet, stands as an indictment of literary taste during the 1950s ("Lowry and the Profession" 168). It is hard to see much merit in the story apart from its relationship to the other stories in the volume: by itself, it is little more than a poorly developed and inadequately motivated narrative, with flat characters and a stereotypical description of the relationship between the City of Man and the Edenic world of nature. Since Lowry conceived and wrote the story as part of *Hear Us O Lord*, a volume that in turn was to have encapsulated the pattern of *The Voyage That Never Ends*, however, the story itself cannot really be regarded as finished until all of the other works associated with it are completed and their reverberations of one another have been fully assimilated into the structures of *Hear Us O Lord* and the *Voyage*. Despite its separate publication and Lowry's expression of fondness for it in a 1956 letter to David Markson (SL 385), "The Bravest Boat" is less interesting for its own sake than as a fragment of a larger vision that Lowry never completed.

Of all the stories in *Hear Us O Lord*, the most ambitious (and, from the viewpoint of the present study, the most important) is "Through the Panama," a complex metafictional work that plays with numerous levels of artifice and reality. Subtitled "From the Journal of Sigbjørn Wilderness," the story originated in a notebook that Lowry kept during a trip from Vancouver to France in late 1947, aboard the *Diderot*, the French ship on which Sigbjørn and Primrose Wilderness travel through the Panama Canal. The subtitle implies that the story is a direct (although selective) transcription from a writer's journal rather than an enlarged or polished version of the journal, but it also calls attention to the way much of Lowry's later work began with notes taken during a trip and then grew into a projected phase of *The Voyage That Never Ends*. For like his creator, Sigbjørn is trying to write an increasingly complex series of novels called *The Voyage That Never Ends*, centering on yet another author, Martin Trumbaugh, who—in a volume called *Dark as the Grave Wherein My Friend Is Laid*—"becomes enmeshed in the plot of the novel he has written, as I did in Mexico" (HL 30). The "I" of that sentence, the author-protagonist who became "enmeshed" in his own novel, is supposed to be Sigbjørn, but it is ultimately, inevitably, Malcolm Lowry as well.

The relationship of these various "authors" to one another, and to their protagonists, is intricate and fascinating. Sigbjørn occasionally tries to distinguish between himself and Martin, as when he portrays Martin with delirium tremens and adds, not altogether persuasively, "This gentleman with the d.t.'s is not myself" (HL 44). At other times, however, the distinction is not so clear. As the ship sails past Acapulco, Sigbjørn writes, "Acapulco is also the first place where Martin ever set foot in Mexico. November 1936. Yes, and on the Day of the Dead. I remember, going ashore, in a boat, the madman foaming at the mouth, correcting his watch. . . . That is also when the Consul began. Scene of first mescal is now abaft the beam" (HL 42). What begins as a passage about Martin quickly turns into one about Sigbjørn and then into one about the Consul, who is simultaneously a character in Sigbjørn's *The Valley of the Shadow of Death* and in Martin's book of the same name, not to mention *Under the Volcano*. Likewise, the "first mescal" referred to in this passage is presumably Lowry's, Sigbjørn's, Martin's, and the Consul's as well. Given the complex entanglement of Lowry's (or Sigbjørn's) life and art in this story, it is easy to see why Douglas Day reads this passage as one that gives us a probable date for Lowry's own 1936 arrival in Mexico, even though the story never directly makes that claim (ML 214–15).

As in *Dark as the Grave* and *La Mordida*, Sigbjørn Wilderness is fundamentally a version of Malcolm Lowry, and his problems, including those that he inflicts on Martin Trumbaugh, are also Lowry's. The journal itself is Sigbjørn's substitute for the novel(s) he is unable to write, much as Lowry, at the same time, was busily writing letters and elaborate statements about works that he had hardly begun, or that he could not complete. Ironically, the journal *becomes* a literary work in its own right: not the novel that Sigbjørn believes he should be writing, of course, but an interesting metafictional narrative nonetheless. Sigbjørn's hope that he can turn all of Martin's agonies "into triumph: the furies into mercies" (HL 31) is of course what Lowry was attempting in his own *Voyage That Never Ends*, as it was earlier in *In Ballast to the White Sea*, and it is the aim of "Through the Panama" as well. And we can readily see Lowry's own obsessions with originality, authorship, "being written," and the daemon in Sigbjørn's comparison of the Panama Canal to "a novel—in fact just such a novel as I, Sigbjørn Wilderness . . . might have written myself" (HL 62). As Sigbjørn imagines him, the author of such a novel would be analogous to the operator of the canal's locks:

> that man sitting up in the control tower high above the topmost lock who, by the way, is myself, and who would feel perfectly comfortable if only he did not know that there was yet another man sitting yet higher above him in *his* invisible control tower, who also has a model of the canal locks before him, carefully built, which registers electrically the exact depth of everything *I* do, and who thus is able to see everything that is happening to me at every moment—and worse, everything that is *going* to happen—(HL 63)

There is a playful and ironic tone in this description of the writer's dilemma—his recognition that although he is apparently in control of his fictional world he is really part of a larger fiction—but it is hard to miss the undercurrent of genuine terror in the passage. Likewise, when Sigbjørn writes, "Man not enmeshed by, but *killed* by his own book and the malign forces it arouses. Wonderful theme" (HL 38), he calls attention to Lowry's obsession with the idea that *Under the Volcano* had left him at a dead end, "killing" him by making it impossible for him to write outside the design of his masterwork.

If Martin is a little paranoid, as Sigbjørn suggests (HL 76), then what of Sigbjørn himself? Reading other events and sights of his journey, Sigbjørn, like almost all of Lowry's protagonists, associates them with his own life and works, so that the world becomes a forest of symbols representing his private obsessions. The whole sequence of *The Voyage That Never Ends*, we learn, involves a "dream of death," a "dissociation" or loss of individual identity, and is indeed "like going through the Panama Canal" (HL 39–40). Various critics have observed that Sigbjørn's description of his trip through the canal, especially the way he imagines himself imprisoned within locks that resemble teeth, suggests any number of fears and anxieties, including "birth trauma and separation anxiety" (Nordgren 503). Sigbjørn's fears of separation (from the home that could be destroyed while they are away, from Primrose, from the natural world, from his mother) are evident throughout the trip. At the same time, however, Sigbjørn is afflicted with the converse of separation anxiety: he regards himself as fatally entangled not only with his works but with everything around him, and his identity always seems on the verge of fragmentation or dissolution. Recalling Marion Milner's belief that artists may experience blockage because they fear the "merging of identities, or melting of boundaries, between self and other," or, on the other hand, because of "a fear of separation" (Leader 94), we can easily understand why the canal trip is associated so closely with Sigbjørn's writer's block. It is also apparent why, exiting from the canal, he looks back to see "De Lesseps' old canal [leading] into a swamp, a sad monument to unfinished projects, though actually *it is worse than that*" (HL 63). The only thing worse than an abandoned project, we might suspect, is a completed one like the Suez Canal or *Under the Volcano:* one that haunts its creator by setting a standard he will not again meet.

Among the more prominent features of "Through the

Panama" are the marginalia that appear throughout much of the story, and to some degree any assessment of the story's success as a work of experimental fiction is apt to be based on an analysis of the nature and purpose of these marginal writings.[3] The marginalia of this story have a more complex function than those of *La Mordida*, citations from an Acapulco guidebook that are used principally for the purpose of ironic contrast with the experience of the protagonists. In "Through the Panama," the marginal notes are generally inserted by Sigbjørn, so that the entire text both reflects and analyzes his state of mind, revealing a divided consciousness engaged in fashioning a version of itself in yet another text: the unwritten *Voyage* of which this trip through the Panama Canal is a small-scale model. Thus Martin Bock contends that the marginalia "demonstrate the diary author's schizophrenic perceptions and social disorientation," presenting "divergent perspectives that reflect the physical disorientation of ship travel and the psychological disorientation of the diarist" (Bock 122). More generally, as William New observes, "the splitting of the story into independent but concurrent columns . . . reflects the fragmentation of identity that we have already seen Lowry/ Wilderness/ Trumbaugh undergo" (*Malcolm Lowry* 16).

If most of the marginalia are directly traceable to Sigbjørn's mind, the immediate source of the glosses lifted from *The Rime of the Ancient Mariner* is not so obvious, and their inclusion in the text might be attributed either to Sigbjørn or to Lowry. Since the main text also presents Sigbjørn as simultaneously the author of the journal and a character in a story written by someone else (perhaps even by Malcolm Lowry), the alternation between the journal and the *Ancient Mariner* citations presents us with "a collision of texts, the authorship of both being in doubt" (Hassam 44). Moreover, the function of the glosses in Lowry's story differs from the way they are used by Coleridge, although it is generally possible to see a thematic link between the marginal text and the main text that it is presumably interpreting: the first gloss, for example, plays Martin's thoughts about "the fixity and closed order" of the stars against the Ancient Mariner's condition of "loneliness and fixedness" in which he "yearneth towards the journeying Moon, and the stars that still sojourn, yet still move onward" (HL 38). A few pages later, Sigbjørn's description of a death dream that leads him to "St Catherine's College, Cambridge, *and the very room*"—presumably the room where Paul Fitte committed suicide, an event that also is recollected in Sigbjørn's superstition about sailing on 15 November—is juxtaposed against glosses that describe the curse in the eye of the Mariner's dead crew members and the spirits' demand that the Mariner do penance for his crime.

Lowry's appropriation of material from Coleridge and other sources raises questions about literary proprietorship, inevitably invoking the specter of plagiarism, but in fact this is one of the most imaginative—even original—elements in the story. By placing the glosses in a new context, Lowry transforms them into part of the interplay of voices in Sigbjørn's journal as well as in his mind. But since we are never allowed to forget that the glosses previously operated in another context—that of Coleridge's poem—their appearance here necessarily reminds us that texts do not exist in isolation but are created from a combination of personal experience (the journal, deriving from Lowry's notebook) and antecedent texts. The differences between the functions of the glosses here and in *The Rime of the Ancient Mariner* imply that, on some level, Lowry's story is a modernist burlesque of Coleridge's romantic poem.

"Through the Panama" also shows how a writer's sense of identity is created out of various texts, and how his mind in turn reshapes the texts that it encounters and subsumes. Even more than in *Under the Volcano*, the typographic form of "Through the Panama" calls attention to a number of competing discourses, undermining our faith in the validity or authority of any single perspective. The journal records impressions and experiences, including signs (*"Watch the Hook It Can't Watch You"*) and documents (an immigration questionnaire) that Sigbjørn sees around him. The technique is akin to the stream-of-consciousness style that Lowry used as early as *Ultramarine,* but it differs in that, instead of recording these other texts directly as they impinge on his protagonist's mind, Lowry absorbs them into his text, filtering them through Sigbjørn's reconstruction of the day's events.

What Sigbjørn sees around him is a world that almost invariably reflects his own experience and the inner world of his art: even an immigration inspector, he imagines, has an "unfinished novel" (HL 49). The descriptions of the trip are typically related in some way to the recurrent concerns of Sigbjørn's life and art, as for example when the Mexican mountains resemble the cones of Yeats's *A Vision,* suggestive of the great cosmic patterns that influence individual life (HL 37). Passing down the coast of Mexico, Sigbjørn sees Acapulco: "There is Larqueta, with the lighthouse going past so slowly, and it even seems we can make out the Quinta Eulalia" (HL 41). Significantly, he does *not* see La Roqueta and the Quinta Eugenia, but substitutes the names Lowry had used in *La Mordida* for the island and the hotel.[4] Another transformation (this time on Lowry's part) occurs when Sigbjørn reads a newspaper story about John Firmin, an American researcher who killed an albatross (HL 33). Victor Doyen, who has traced this article to one that appeared in the Vancouver *Sun* on 15 September 1951, notes that the alteration of the researcher's name from John Slipp to John Firmin is the only change Lowry has made in the article. Even had Sigbjørn not mentioned a few pages later that the Consul was "likewise named Firmin" (HL 37), the point would be clear enough: the mind of Lowry's protagonist constantly fastens on, or creates, points of contact between the texts of the external world and those of his own imagination.

The same observation might be applied to Lowry's citations of other writers, which generally imply a reading of their lives

or works in the context of his own. The marginal glosses from
The Rime of the Ancient Mariner are an obvious case in point,
as is the attribution to Coleridge of a notice about the need to
conserve water aboard ship (HL 51). Moving from romanticism
to modernism, Sigbjørn rewrites the next sign—a safety notice
about the use of a lifebelt—in the prosaic verse style used in
much of *Paterson,* signing it "Wilderness Carlos Wilderness"
to make the identification clear. The question of authorship
also surfaces when Lowry quotes the last four lines of his poem
"I tried to think of something good," adding, "I know you
think Tennyson wrote that, but I did" (HL 50; see CP 184).
Elsewhere, he cites a comment allegedly made by D. H. Lawrence about Joyce's *Ulysses:* "The whole is a strange assembly
of apparently incongruous parts, slipping past one another"
(HL 34, 98). What Lawrence was describing, Sherrill Grace
notes, was not *Ulysses* or any other aspect of Joyce's work, but
the nature of existence itself; far from being a disparaging
remark about Joyce, Lawrence's comment—from "Why the
Novel Matters"—emphasizes the necessity for rejecting fixed
or absolute visions of reality (see Grace, " 'A strange assembly' " 187, 221–22). Since Lawrence does not mention Joyce
anywhere in this essay, Lowry's pretense that the description
refers to Joyce is clearly a deliberate distortion of Lawrence's
text, an appropriation of an antecedent text for Lowry's own
purposes. In applying the description to *Ulysses,* Lowry once
again implies that art and reality are closely and complexly
intertwined, not only in *Ulysses* but in a story like "Through
the Panama" as well. At the same time, he preempts one of
the most obvious criticisms of his own story by associating its
heterogeneous form with that of Joyce's modern epic.

Some of Lowry's most revealing comments on his role as
a writer are incorporated into "Through the Panama," where
they refer to Martin Trumbaugh, so that they are apparently
twice removed from Lowry himself. At one point, Martin com-
plains about modern critics and teachers of literature, "the

non-creative bully-boys and homosapient schoolmasters of English literature" whose "dictatorship of opinion" threatens him. He proclaims, moreover, that "I have to forget that there is such a thing as so-called 'modern literature' and the 'new criticism' in order to get any of my old feeling and passion back" (HL 75). The anxiety evident in this declaration is analyzed a moment later, when Martin adopts the persona of one of his own reviewers and declares, "Neurosis, of one kind and another, is stamped on almost every word he writes, both neurosis and a kind of fierce health. Perhaps his tragedy is that he is the one normal writer left on earth and it is this that adds to his isolation and so his sense of guilt" (HL 77). Martin's "isolation," his estrangement from modern literature, is again apparent when he describes a writer "who *simply cannot understand,* and never has been able to understand, what his fellow writers are driving at" even though he subscribes to literary magazines and "heroically reads a few pages of William Empson's *Seven Types of Ambiguity* each night before going to sleep," all in a desperate attempt to comprehend modern literature and criticism (HL 84–85). The reference to Empson, whom Lowry had known at Cambridge, is particularly interesting, since the critical method associated with Empson's work focuses on the verbal structure of a literary work rather than on the personal, cultural, or economic circumstances that led to its creation, whereas Lowry's work always resists being read strictly as a verbal icon, ambiguous or not. As Binns remarks, " 'Through the Panama' is a New Critic's nightmare. Outside the context of Lowry's life and *oeuvre* it is incomprehensible" (*Malcolm Lowry* 82).

Even within the context of Lowry's life and work, "Through the Panama" is a remarkably complex story, and it is not altogether clear whether the narrative presents a version of a writer who successfully navigates his way through his problems or whether Sigbjørn simply imagines that he has weathered the storm. Lowry himself told Harold Matson that the story "reads something like [Fitzgerald's] *The Crack-Up*, like Alfred [sic] Gordon Pym, but instead of cracking the protagonist's fission begins to be healed" (SL 267). In this view, "Through the Panama" is a miniature version of the longer journey of *Hear Us O Lord*, itself an abbreviated *Voyage That Never Ends*. Keith Harrison's reading of the story is also positive. Observing that the *Diderot* (like Sigbjørn) was in danger of cracking up but eventually arrived safely in England, accompanied by a marginal note from *The Rime of the Ancient Mariner* that "prefigures Sigbjørn's recovery of his communicative powers," Harrison argues that "the freighter transmits a message of human contact through the chaos of the storm, this time through literary history" ("Malcolm Lowry's *Hear Us O Lord*" 248–49). Yet near the story's end we are again told that "*the whole is an assembly of apparently incongruous parts, slipping past one another—*" (HL 97), the slightly retouched quotation from Lawrence reminding us not to settle for the part as an adequate description of the whole. If "Through the Panama" concludes on a note of hope, the ending also seems rather contrived, as if Lowry were desperately trying to rewrite his own past—the trip to Europe that he had taken a few years earlier—in order to escape "the insatiable albatross of self" (HL 31). Robert Kroetsch notes that "the large boat moves, in 'Through the Panama,' as did the small boat in the preceding story: we deliver our small, absurd messages from ourselves to ourselves" (Kroetsch 254). Whereas the Ancient Mariner, in the passage inserted at the end of Lowry's story, vows "to teach by his own example, love and reverence to all things that God made and loveth," there is no evidence that Sigbjørn ever communicates his message of hope and love to anyone but us, the unobserved and unsuspected readers of his journal.

❧

Although it was not included in the text of *Hear Us O Lord* that Margerie Lowry edited for publication, "Ghostkeeper" merits consideration here because its themes and images are closely related to those of the other stories in the collection.[5] Built around a writer's effort to give his experience a shape and meaning by writing about it, and his recognition that the process of writing inevitably falsifies the experience, "Ghost-keeper" encapsulates all of the anxieties and entanglements that attended Lowry's complex vision of the relationships among world, text, and self.

The story focuses on yet another pair of surrogates for Malcolm and Margerie Lowry: Tom Goodheart, a Vancouver newspaper columnist and would-be fiction writer, and his wife Mary. Walking together in Stanley Park, where Tom gathers material for his column, they find a wrecked boat with the name H. Ghostkeeper written on it in chalk, and Tom may or may not have a conversation with a blind Englishman about the boat; later they meet a young Frenchman, who offers to sell them his gold watch, and they reprimand some teenagers for throwing stones at ducks. The pivotal event of the story, however, is their discovery of a watch that bears the name Henrik Ghostkeeper. The remainder of the story concerns Tom's efforts to return the watch to its owner, who turns out to be one of the boys who were molesting the ducks; Tom's meditations on the significance of all this in relation to his own life and to the newspaper stories that he reads concerning such matters as flying saucers, poltergeists, and the death of King George VI (which apparently occurred at exactly the time when Tom's own watch stopped); and his attempt to write a story about his experience.

Even without the textual note that tells us "This is not a 'finished' story, it is a first draft, with notes" (PS 202), it would be difficult for any reader to mistake "Ghostkeeper" for a completed work of fiction. Beginning with a series of six alternate titles, the story is peppered with notes that have been inserted in the text—memoranda about the work's themes, or about material that needs to be inserted somewhere, or about other ways in which the story could be handled. That at least one scene is based on an actual experience is evident from the passage that reads "Mem: Important: Use Margie's note here about the young Frenchman and his watch. (This note follows)" (PS 208). At this point the Goodhearts' names are dropped temporarily in favor of "Margie" (who becomes a first person narrator) and "Malc," indicating that little has been done to reshape Margerie's notebook entry into part of Malcolm's fictional narrative.[6]

The unfinished state of "Ghostkeeper" may be attributed to any number of possible causes, but what interests me the most about this story is the way it deals with a writer's difficulty in constructing a story out of his own experience, and at the same time constructing *himself* through the process of writing. Ironically, Tom Goodheart manages something that Lowry did not in this story: at the beginning he is a blocked writer, unable to compose a book of short stories in which an American publisher has expressed interest and virtually incapable of writing his column (PS 205), but at the end he has finished "Lex Talionis," the fictionalized version of his experience, and the fear that has overwhelmed him is "transformed into love, love for his wife" (PS 227). This movement from anxiety, isolation, division, and obsessive self-involvement into love and affirmation is one that Lowry attempts in a number of post-*Volcano* works, but in every case, apart from "The Forest Path to the Spring" and perhaps *October Ferry to Gabriola*, either the conclusion is highly ambiguous or its positive nature seems artificially engrafted onto a darker vision of things. In "Ghostkeeper," too, the doubts and anxieties that beset Tom Goodheart somehow ring truer than his sudden, belated, recognition of the power of love.

A constant theme in "Ghostkeeper" is the relationship between art and life, two realms that overlap and reflect one another but differ in significant ways. When Goodheart begins writing "Lex Talionis," whose title echoes the theme of justice that he plans to impose upon it, the story initially seems simple: "Boy stones ducks. Man warns boy, tells him he'll be punished. Man finds watch. Man discovers, roundabout, that watch is property of boy . . . [and] man returns watch. Boy has lesson. God moves in a mysterious way, would be the moral and the result a concise heartwarming little story" (PS 218). But immediately there are problems. For one thing, Goodheart wants to tie the story to everything else he has just experienced or felt—"the kaleidoscope of life, the complexity, flying saucers, the impossibility of writing good stories." Then there is the problem of Ghostkeeper's name, which he needs (to make the story's point clear) but might not be able to use (since it is a real person's name, an uncommon one at that). As to his own name, it is too blatantly allegorical, "too much like Pilgrim's Progress," for Goodheart to use—although obviously not too much for Malcolm Lowry to use it. One is reminded here of Sigbjørn's regret, in "Through the Panama," that he cannot use his own rather exotic name in his novel (HL 44); on another level, Goodheart's inability to use his Bunyanesque name in his fiction parodies Clarence Malcolm Lowry's obsession with shedding his prosaic given name in favor of such extravagancies as Eugene Dana Hilliot, Bill Plantagenet, the Earl of Thurstaston, Ethan Llewelyn, Sigurd Storleson, Kennish Drumgold Cosnahan, Roderick McGregor Fairhaven, and (above all) Sigbjørn Wilderness.

"Ghostkeeper," after all, deals quite directly with the way art and life may be regarded as versions of one another, and in particular with the way writers like Tom Goodheart and Malcolm Lowry attempt to create or discover a valid identity through a fictional reshaping of material based on personal experience. Shortly after regretting that he cannot use his own name in the story, Goodheart wonders about the significance of all he has seen and thought during the day. Unfortunately, any attempt to turn these events into a narrative involves a somewhat arbitrary selection of material, whereas the truth, he believes, must encompass everything. As a voice seems to tell him, any satisfactory story line will get at only one of many possible meanings, whereas "if you're going to get anywhere near the truth you'll have twenty different plots and a story no one will take" (PS 219).

The meanings of his experience—and of his life generally— are multiple, ambiguous, constantly proliferating; Goodheart's problem lies in the need to simplify all this, to impose a pattern on it, in order to make it an acceptable story. As he wonders, "How could you write a story in which its main symbol was not even reasonably consistent, did not even have consistent ambiguity?" (PS 219). The "main symbol" here is the watch, but Gordon Bowker astutely reads this question as a sign of Lowry's "apparently urgent need to discover a consistency in his past which could supply some anchored sense of identity" ("The Biographical Lowry" 154). It is easy to see that the watch is on one level an aspect of Goodheart's identity: his lack of a watch at the beginning of the story, his encounters with the blind Englishman (a sort of doppelgänger) and the Frenchman—one of them watchless, the other offering a watch for sale—and his discovery and return of Ghostkeeper's watch might all be fitted neatly into a scheme in which the various watches are associated with stages in his spiritual development or his awareness of himself.

At the same time, however, the watch is another infernal machine, a symbol of a mechanical universe that is utterly alien to Lowry's protagonist and yet perhaps in control of him. So, too, is his story, which Lowry compares to "Sigbjorn in relation to the Volcano" (PS 223). That story seems at times to be written by an external agent—something like the daemon of *Dark as the Grave* and *La Mordida*—and Goodheart speculates that "the *name* Henrik Ghostkeeper is the symbol" of that daemonic intelligence (PS 223). Returning once again to the basic problem of artistic creation, Lowry gives what may be his most concise description of the process by which his own work seemed to spin out of his control:

Perhaps what happens is something like this. The minute an artist begins to try and shape his material—the more especially if
that material is his own life—some sort of magic lever is thrown
into gear, setting some celestial machinery in motion producing events or coincidences that show him that this shaping of
his is absurd, that nothing is static or can be pinned down, that
everything is evolving or developing into other meanings, or can-
cellations of meanings quite beyond his comprehension. (PS 223)

This passage is soon followed by the almost inevitable reference to Ortega's conception of "a man's life [as] a work of
fiction, that he makes up as he goes along." The allusion to
Ortega seems ironic, since Goodheart believes that he has no
real control over his life, and that whatever shape he gives to
his story detracts from its truth, which lies in the numerous
coincidences and analogies that connected it to his life.

"Ghostkeeper" is in some respects a sophisticated critique of
the nature of narrative art. More important, however, it reveals Lowry's highly ambiguous relationship to his own fiction,
including his twin desires for artistic openness and closure. A
work of art, Lowry implies, has its own criteria, among them a
desire for coherence that is quite at odds with the messiness of
life. Thus art is false to the extent that it attempts to close off
meanings, to impose one set of relationships on matters that
ideally should have an infinite number of interlocking patterns
or meanings, all of which cry out for consideration. At the same
time, the story shows how Goodheart's attempt to understand
even the simplest events of his own life becomes impossibly
complex unless he reduces it somehow, as he does by reading it
as a relatively coherent narrative—one that even has a moral,
God help us. Whether we regard "Ghostkeeper" as a failed
attempt at a traditional story, a set of notes or a preliminary
draft for a story that Lowry never completed, a species of metafiction, or merely an intriguing fragment, there is little doubt
that the story revolves around precisely the same desire for perfection, the same difficulty in reducing the complexities of life

to a coherent pattern, that plagued Lowry throughout much of
his life and left so much of his work tantalizingly incomplete.[7]

Each of the three central stories of *Hear Us O Lord*—"Strange
Comfort Afforded by the Profession," "Elephant and Colosseum," and "Present Estate of Pompeii"—is set in Italy, the
composite protagonist of the volume having completed the first
half of his journey from the New World to the Old and back. The
individual protagonists of these stories are all North Americans
(although Kennish Drumgold Cosnahan was raised on the Isle
of Man before emigrating to America), and their journeys involve voyages into the personal or historic past. Two of the protagonists are writers, temporarily in Rome, who are separated
from their wives; the third, Roderick McGregor Fairhaven of
"Present Estate," is a "Scotch-Canadian schoolmaster" (HL
178) who is visiting Pompeii with his wife, Tansy. Although
Douglas Day observes that Fairhaven is "obviously based on
Lowry's friend Downie Kirk" (ML 454), he is also modeled
after his creator, whom he resembles in various ways. Like
Lowry, he tends to describe experience analogically (Pompeii is "this old Cuernavaca-cum-Acapulco of the Romans"
while life resembles "the desolation that comes to one eternally
wading through the poem of *The Waste Land* without understanding it" [HL 185, 188]) and he is always alert to "symbols
and presciences of disaster" (HL 197). The story culminates
in Roderick's sudden recognition that Pompeii symbolizes his
own fleeting existence, and he wonders if all humanity is "not
beginning to stand, in some profound inexplicable sense, fundamentally in some such imperfect or dislocated relation to his
environment as he" (HL 199). Our "imperfect or dislocated relation" to the natural world is a recurrent theme in *Hear Us
O Lord*,[8] but it is expressed here in terms as pessimistic as
an earlier work's "¿Le gusta este jardín que es suyo? ¡Evite
que sus hijos lo destruyan!" Unfortunately, "Present Estate"

is otherwise a poorly developed and motivated story in which memories of Eridanus (where the Fairhavens' neighbors include the Wildernesses and the Llewelyns) are loosely connected to Roderick's present experience and the meaning of the story's epiphany—if it can be called that—is unclear.

"Elephant and Colosseum," the longest of the Italian stories, involves a Manx-American writer, Kennish Drumgold Cosnahan, who has come to Rome without his wife, Margaret ("Lovey") L'Hirondelle, an actress who is currently playing the lead in summer theater on Nantucket, where they live. The story falls into three parts of roughly equal length. In the first part, Cosnahan sits at a sidewalk cafe drinking milk (his Italian apparently was not up to the task of ordering wine) and thinking about his life and work. In the second part, Cosnahan walks around Rome, again meditating on a range of memories and concerns, including his mother's death, the medal he once received from the Japanese government for helping to save the lives of a ship's crew during a typhoon, and the disparity between the American success and the European neglect of his novel, *Ark from Singapore.* Eventually he happens on the offices of his Italian publisher and stops in to see why the book has not yet been translated. The clerk appears not to have any knowledge of him or his novel, but the confusion is cleared up when we learn that this is just a sub-office, the real office— where presumably someone has heard of Cosnahan and *Ark from Singapore*—being in Turin.

So far, there is little to recommend "Elephant and Colosseum": even a device like the internal monologues in which the protagonist splits into two voices, "Drumgold" and "Cosnahan" (recalling the Consul's "familiars" in *Under the Volcano*), is never really explained or connected to anything else in the narrative. The last section, however, contains elements of the comic vision that Lowry wanted to achieve in the novella.[9] Finding himself at the zoo, Cosnahan wanders around, agreeing with the Swedenborgian doctrine that animals can be wicked and imagining that inside each of the "poor endlessly pacing schizophrenic lions" is "the soul of a Manx-American author" (HL 159–60). Eventually he arrives at the elephants, and after a long and comically exaggerated series of encomia to the elephant—"a profoundly meditative animal," even a "compassionate creature of titanic orisons" (HL 163)—he suddenly and unexpectedly discovers his long-lost love: Rosemary, the elephant that had been placed in his care years ago during the voyage that he had fictionalized in *Ark from Singapore*. For as Cosnahan should have recalled (and as the protagonist of a story by virtually anyone else *would* have remembered), Rosemary had been transferred to an Italian boat for delivery to the Rome zoo, where she has lingered for years, waiting for him. Cosnahan imagines that she recognizes him, and in his mind Rosemary becomes symbolic of unselfish love.

In *Dark as the Grave*, responding to Sigbjørn's complaints about the difficulty of sustaining an imaginative vision throughout the process of writing a work, Dr. Hippolyte says, "Perhaps you try to get too much in. . . . A little selectivity might be in order." Sigbjørn replies with an impassioned plea for understanding: "suppose," he says, "that you were in my position, haunted at every moment that a fire or some other disaster would step in and destroy what you have already so laboriously created before you have the chance to get it into some reasonably permanent form . . . would you not tend also to 'get too much in'" (DG 156). The scene shows Lowry's recognition of one of the major problems of his fiction (even *Under the Volcano*, although the years of revisions eventually allowed him to put that book's encyclopedism to good use); it also shows him defending his methods on grounds having to do with the author's fears rather than the final shape of the work. The incoherence that results from trying "to get too much in" a story is all too evident in "Elephant and Colosseum," a novella that Lowry was unable to bring under control and whose numerous concerns are never related to one another in a meaningful fashion. The central problem, as Richard Cross suggests, might be that Cosnahan is so isolated that the city around him never has much reality for Lowry's readers (Cross 96). Another way of putting the problem is that Lowry never manages to create either a vivid inner reality for his protagonist or a clear sense of the world around him. Presumably the meeting with Rosemary was meant to awaken Cosnahan to the importance of love and the reality of the external world, but the story as a whole is so overwritten and incoherent that it is hard to see a clear pattern in Cosnahan's development.

In contrast to the other pieces set in Italy, "Strange Comfort Afforded by the Profession" is a compelling story about a writer, Sigbjørn Wilderness,[10] whose meditations on the relationship between life and art lead him to a strangely comforting identification of himself with Keats, Poe, and other writers. For the most part, the external world of this story is reduced to a series of texts: letters, plaques, inscriptions, and documents—even advertisements and graffiti—that Sigbjørn has seen during his present visit to Rome or a previous one to Richmond, Virginia, and the notebooks in which he has copied these texts and written his observations. When he enters the Keats museum, for example, he hardly notices the house's contents, including the aromatic gums used in the cremation of Shelley, but he writes down the legend in the case next to the gums as well as the texts of Shelley's marriage license and two letters by Joseph Severn about Keats's death. (Somewhat more comically, Sigbjørn notes the titles of several books on the shelves and feels "a remote twinge" that none of his own books are present [HL 100–101].) Far from being damaged by Sigbjørn's isolation from the physical world, for which he substitutes a series of texts that symbolize aspects of his own situation, "Strange Comfort" is an intriguing exploration of the romantic writer's dilemma, as it is represented by "the special reality of Sigbjørn's notebook" (HL 110). "Strange Comfort" might well be Lowry's most seriously underrated story.

The story begins with Sigbjørn's entrance into the house where Keats died and continues at a nearby bar, where Sigbjørn reviews his notebooks. A process akin to *sortes Shakespeareanae* leads him to relate several experiences to one another: first the visit to the Keats museum, then an earlier tour of the Mamertine prison, and then a trip, two years before, to the Valentine Museum in Richmond, where he had copied a number of items related to Poe. Once again, Lowry associates himself with misunderstood, suffering writers whose lives are inseparable from their art. Thus Sigbjørn imagines that when Poe wrote to his foster father, John Allan, to describe his torments, "Poe must have felt that he was transcribing the story that was E. A. Poe" (HL 107). Moreover, in the "special reality" of his notebook, "Poe's cry from Baltimore . . . had already been answered, seven years before, by Keats's cry from Rome," both of their deaths becoming "part of the same poem, the same story" (HL 110). That the poem also includes Sigbjørn's life is made clear moments later, when he opens another notebook and finds a draft of a letter that he had written years earlier, in Seattle. Addressed to a Los Angeles attorney named Van Bosch, who was then charged by Sigbjørn's family with running his affairs,[11] the letter describes his despair at having to live with the religious-minded Mackorkindale family, who believe that "as a serious writer I am lousy" and that he should turn to writing advertisements. The letter concludes with a line that seems prophetic of his identification with Poe and Keats: "Surely I am not the only writer, there have been others in history whose ways have been misconstrued and who have failed . . . who have won through . . . success . . . publicans and sinners . . . I have no intention—" (HL 112). The ellipses and the dash are Lowry's, presumably deleting material over which Sigbjørn's eye skips as he finds the record of his own torment unbearable.

Earlier in the story, Sigbjørn made clear his romantic conception of the artist as someone who creates directly out of his own experience, and whose life is his greatest work of art. By contrast, he has little in common with modern poets who resemble bank clerks or advertising writers, and who destroy evidence of their despair rather than allow it to be preserved—like Keats's or Poe's—in a glass case.[12] When he reads the letter in which he had recorded his own despair, however, his first response is to begin destroying the evidence by crossing it out, "line by line." Then he regrets his action: "For now, damn it, he wouldn't be able to use it." But at the Keats museum Sigbjørn had copied down one of Severn's letters, including a passage that Severn had crossed out, so Sigbjørn's own attempt to destroy the letter by crossing it out may not succeed. The letter, in any case, remains intact for Lowry's readers, just as we are not prevented from reading the letter that Jacques Laruelle burns in *Under the Volcano*.

Sigbjørn's attempt to destroy the letter, followed by his regret that after it is destroyed he cannot use it in his art, reflects Lowry's antithetical desires to forget the more painful events of his past and to re-create them in his fiction. Keith Harrison observes a similar ambivalence in Sigbjørn's identification with Keats and Poe, which implies both an "early death" for the writer and the power of his art to transcend mortality ("Malcolm Lowry's *Hear Us O Lord*" 250). The point is reinforced at the story's end, when Sigbjørn "suddenly gave a loud laugh, a laugh which, as if it had realized itself it should become something more respectable, turned immediately into a prolonged—though on the whole relatively pleasurable—fit of coughing" (HL 113). As several critics have pointed out, the ending implies Sigbjørn's "relatively pleasurable" identification with a writer like Keats, whose fits of coughing are described in Severn's letters, or Kafka, another tubercular writer whose name is shortened to "Kaf" (HL 109). Moreover, this is one of four stories in *Hear Us O Lord* that end with laughter, and these conclusions are part of the book's recurrent attempt to turn adversity "into triumph: the furies into mercies" (HL 31). The laughter in "Strange Comfort," however, is only "*relatively* pleasurable," and it is succeeded by coughing, so that any attempt to draw a neat parallel between the transformation of personal suffering into art and the laugh's metamorphosis into a cough is bound to run aground.

"Strange Comfort" shows Lowry at his most self-aware, and

it depicts several important aspects of his personality and art, among them his writer's block, his reluctance to sign his name, his belief that every event is significant and that the world is filled with signs and portents referring to him, and his aversion to the New Critical emphasis on reading works outside the context of their authors' lives. The use of the notebook is especially intriguing, in part because it reflects Lowry's own means of gathering material for his work and shows his tragic sense of identification with other writers, an identification that toys with plagiarism as Sigbjørn copies Poe's letters and imagines them in the context of his own life. At the same time, the almost magical power of Lowry's writing to transform reality— a phenomenon he experienced on his return trip to Mexico, when he felt that he was living in a world created by his own book—is manifested in the "special reality" of the notebook, which appears to create a set of literary relationships that have a very real meaning for Sigbjørn. But it should also be emphasized that Lowry emphasizes the absurdity of Sigbjørn's (and his own) exaggerated response to his experiences, as for example when he compounds American advertisements with the opening of Keats's "Ode on Melancholy": "LIC-OFF-PREM, he thought. No, no, go not to Virginia Dare . . . Neither twist Pepso—tight-rooted!—for its poisonous bane" (HL 111). If "Elephant and Colosseum" shows the problems that Lowry can cause himself when he tries to "get too much in," "Strange Comfort" shows what he can accomplish when he transfers his obsessive desire for all-inclusiveness to his protagonist and pares his own materials down to a manageable set of related experiences.

The last two stories of *Hear Us O Lord* are set in British Columbia, where the protagonists' return to nature begins the process of renewal. "Gin and Goldenrod" describes the miniature pilgrimage of Sigbjørn and Primrose Wilderness to and from the home of a bootlegger to whom Sigbjørn owes money for a night of drinking with some local Indians. The story involves the same circular pattern as the collection as a whole, for once again we see a confrontation with the past and a successful return to the natural environment in which the journey begins. There is presumably a sort of spiritual growth at the story's end: one made possible not only by Primrose's support of her husband, and her insistence that he pay his debt, but by his successful negotiation past the "bourgeois horrors" of Dark Rosslyn, a housing development. As they walk home in the soft rain, becoming perhaps the only characters in all of Lowry's fiction to pass up a bus ride, Sigbjørn and Primrose experience several small signs of hope that accumulate until "in the cool silver rainy twilight of the forest a kind of hope began to bloom again" (HL 214). First, an ambulance pulls up at the house of a man whom they have seen working at a typewriter, but it turns out that the driver only stopped to get directions; the man with the typewriter—perhaps a representation of Lowry himself as a writer—is not ill or dead. Then, Sigbjørn and Primrose re-enter the forest, carrying sprigs of dogwood and goldenrod that could be regarded as their equivalent of the Homeric moly. Finally, as they return home they are greeted by their cat, a kindred spirit who followed them at the outset of the story but balked at entering the debased realm of civilization. The most important reason for Sigbjørn's optimism, however, is Primrose's confession that she had saved a bottle of gin that he had believed lost. Sigbjørn's realization that a drink is at hand might seem insufficient reason for us to share his hope, especially because throughout the story he suffers remorse over his self-destructive alcoholic binges, but Lowry probably meant for the unexpected survival of the bottle of gin to be taken more than half-seriously as a sign of renewal.[13]

The final story of *Hear Us O Lord* is a first-person narration (a rarity in Lowry's fiction), and despite some biographical differences between the unnamed narrator and his creator,[14] there is little doubt that the two are basically identical. Indeed,

"The Forest Path to the Spring" is dedicated "To Margerie, my wife," and the narrative describes a life in "Eridanus" that is closely modeled after the Lowrys' years in Dollarton. The narrator's fear of eviction, his tendency to see projections of his own mind in the external world, his attempt to escape the tyranny of his ego and to transcend his past, and his image of a work of art (in this case a jazz opera called *The Forest Path to the Spring*) that is "built, like our new house, on the charred foundations and fragments of the old work and our old life" (HL 271), all suggest that the narrator is yet another of Lowry's self-portraits.

In a larger sense, "The Forest Path" encapsulates a spiritual struggle that runs through *Hear Us O Lord* and that Lowry intended to dramatize in the entirety of *The Voyage That Never Ends*. In the description of the *Voyage* that Lowry wrote in November 1951, just about the time when he was completing a draft of "The Forest Path," he says that the last volume in the series would end "as it began (and as it is portrayed in the Forest Path to the Spring) on a note of happiness, with the Wildernesses watching the tide bearing the ships out upon its currents that become remote, and which, like the Ice, becoming remote, return" (WP 97). This description occurs twice in the story, both times in connection with the Tao—the Way— which represents the ultimate unity of reality that lies beyond the apparent dualities of the phenomenal world (HL 234–35, 282). Ending on a moment of harmony with nature and acceptance of the present, symbolized by the spring from which the narrator and his wife drink, "The Forest Path" gives us a vision of what Lowry wanted the rest of his life to be like.

Throughout the story, the narrator struggles to recover the primal innocence or oneness that he has lost in a life of egotism. In a shack facing the inlet and backed up by the wilderness, he hopes to find "something that man had lost, of which these shacks and cabins . . . were the helpless yet stalwart symbol, of man's hunger and need for beauty, for the stars and the sunrise" (HL 232). As the narrator and his wife row out in a boat, the reflections of the mountain peaks seem to follow them; but as his wife points out, this is not quite the same as "Wordsworth's famous peak, that strode after him" in the first book of *The Prelude*. Instead, it seems "a reminder of duality, of opposing motions born of the motion of the earth, a symbol even while an illusion, of nature's intolerance of inertia" (HL 229). What threatens him is not outside, in nature, but in his heart and mind. (Even when a mountain lion suddenly appears before him, the cougar seems more a projection of his own mind—something like the leopard, lion, and wolf that block Dante's path through the dark wood in the opening canto of the *Inferno*—than a real beast.) Thus it is significant that while the mountains' reflections seem benign, his own shadow is sinister: "One night, coming across the porch from the woodshed with a lantern in one hand and a load of wood under the other arm, I saw my shadow, gigantic, the logs of wood as big as a coffin, and this shadow seemed for a moment the glowering embodiment of all that threatened us; yes, even a projection of that dark chaotic side of myself, my ferocious destructive ignorance" (HL 233).

R. D. MacDonald contends that this image of the narrator's shadow as "a projection of [his] dark chaotic side" "makes little sense in relation to the whole," since the dark side does not manifest itself in a specific event. More generally, he argues, the story's images are confused because the setting is "little more than a convenient and sometimes ill-tuned sounding board for [Lowry's] larger concern of showing an isolated man coming to terms with his humanity and with nature" (MacDonald 42, 46). MacDonald's analysis is basically true, although it should be added that "The Forest Path" should not be read as a conventional narrative but as a prose poem in which the logic is subjective and emotional rather than empirical. On the other hand, the story depends to a large extent on Lowry's entire corpus, which means that if we do not see a specific form taken by the narrator's dark side, we are nonetheless certain that it exists because we have seen it elsewhere: in all of those artist-protagonists whose preoccupation with self is the condition of the hell they inhabit.

As Barry Wood observes, the story's central symbols are the spring, symbolic of the present moment, and the path to the spring, representative of past and future ("The Edge of Eternity" 185–86). Much of the story is involved with the narrator's attempt to come to terms with his past and to live in the present. Eventually he realizes that he cannot simply evade the past (the forest path to the spring) but must use it in his music so that the experience becomes available to others (HL 279). The story culminates in the narrator's recognition that it is "necessary to go beyond remorse, beyond even contrition" in his relationship to his past. In a passage suggestive of *la vida impersonal*, he characterizes the nature of his revelation as one that gives him a glimpse of realities beyond, yet subtly related to, his own disastrous past:

> Nothing is more humbling than the wreckage of a burned house, the fragments of consumed work. But it is necessary not to take pride in such masterly pieces of damnation either, especially when they have become so nearly universal. If we had progressed, I thought, it was as if to a region where such words as spring, water, houses, trees, vines, laurels, mountains, wolves, bay, roses, beach, islands, forest, tides and deer and snow and fire, had realized their true being, or had their source: and as these words on a page once stood merely to what they symbolized, so did the reality we knew now stand to something else beyond that that symbolized or reflected. . . . (HL 280–81)

Douglas Day regards this passage as the epiphany toward which "The Forest Path to the Spring," and indeed all of Lowry's life and work, has progressed: "Here it all at last was, the experience of that which Lowry all his life had known was there, but had been unable quite to perceive: that what one needs to know about reality is only that it is real" (ML 458). Indeed, the description of a realm where words attain "their true being" seems at first to imply a movement beyond appearances to true reality. But when Lowry tells us that *that* reality "symbolized or reflected" a still greater reality, we are once again caught up in the proliferation of symbols and levels of reality that characterizes Lowry's darkest visions. Moreover, as Falk points out, "every story in *Hear Us O Lord* ends with a vision of salvation that is undercut immediately as the next story opens" ("Beyond the Volcano" 37), which means that the tranquillity at the end of "The Forest Path" may indicate a genuine transformation in the narrator's life or may serve merely as prelude to another descent into the abyss of self.

That the writing of the story, the achievement of the final vision, did not transform Lowry's endlessly complex and obsessive life into the simple and harmonious one that he so obviously desired may be seen through Day's account of the "anticlimactic last months in Canada," from January to August 1954 (ML 460–64). Or it might be seen in the other projects in which Lowry involved himself in the five and a half years from November 1951, when he sent a completed (although not final) draft of "The Forest Path" to Harold Matson, until his "death by misadventure" in June 1957: "Ghostkeeper," the two versions of *Lunar Caustic,* transcriptions of notes for *Dark as the Grave, La Mordida,* and *The Ordeal of Sigbjørn Wilderness* (a sign that Lowry had certainly not transcended his own infernal past), and above all *October Ferry to Gabriola,* a book that became longer and more involved even as Lowry was praising the simple and direct apprehension of reality in "The Forest Path." It might also be seen in what Lowry did not try to do: he did not seriously attempt to publish "The Forest Path to the Spring," perhaps because the story was not, in his mind, really finished. Whether or not it could ever have been finished is unclear, for like the conclusion of *The Voyage That Never Ends,* "The Forest Path" ends with a vision of the simplicity that Lowry always wanted but was seldom able to find or accept.

Conclusion

From *Ultramarine* to *Hear Us O Lord*, Lowry's work illustrates several key concepts of romantic and post-romantic thought. Attributes of his fiction derived from romantic aesthetics and from symbolist and modernist reformulations of romanticism include the obsessive concern with the "self," which is somehow created by, or identified with, the work of art; the understanding of the artist or writer as both a model of the human condition and a visionary whose creations offer glimpses of truths inaccessible through ordinary experience; the belief that art has a complex and ambivalent relationship to life; and the conviction that artistic creation is potentially redemptive, since it enables us to grasp, imaginatively, the lost harmony between mind and world. Moreover, as George Woodcock has noted, Lowry was influenced "by solipsistic attitudes prevalent in modern European literature, which in their turn stem from the nineteenth century romantic cult of the artist" ("Art as the Writer's Mirror" 70). In some respects, it is true that "solipsism is at the heart of modern literature" (Josipovici, *World* 302), but few writers demonstrate the rich possibilities—and the potentially disastrous consequences—of the inward turn of modern literature more clearly than Lowry.

Malcolm Bradbury has called attention to the romantic strain in Lowry's writing, but he has also noted that the works are both romantic and modern (Bradbury 157–58). At times, in fact, Lowry seems precariously poised between romantic and modern concepts of art and reality, a situation that undoubtedly contributed to his anxiety over the nature of his work and made it even more difficult for him to complete his projects. Binns calls attention to "Lowry's incompatibility with the prevailing literary culture" ("Lowry and the Profession" 173), but at the same time Lowry's use of myth and allusions, his experimentation with narrative perspective and chronology, his presentation of consciousness, and other aspects of his work demonstrate clearly the influence of such writers as Aiken, Joyce, and Eliot.[1] Similarly, Lowry's frequent presentations of the self as fragmented or multiple, a linguistic construct rather than a unitary subject, seem typically modernist, but at other times he appears to agree with the romantics' view that the self is (or should be) fundamentally unitary and unique, one function of art being to recover that uniqueness.[2] When the Consul catalogues the liquor bottles in which he has "hidden himself" and asks, "How indeed could he hope to find himself, to begin again when, somewhere, perhaps, in one of those lost or broken bottles, in one of those glasses, lay, forever, the solitary clue to his identity?" (UV 292–93), he not only shows why he will fail in this attempt to "find himself" but reveals his (and Lowry's) affinity with the romantics' concept of individual identity.

A related division occurs between Lowry's romantic belief in the importance of originality and his more contemporary recognition that writing is basically a rewriting—in Lowry's terms, a plagiarism—of previous texts. The romantic emphasis on the freedom and uniqueness of the individual self, combined with the belief that the highest expression of individual identity lies within aesthetic creation, places a great burden on the writer who also believes that his ideas are often derivative. The strain is increased for a writer like Lowry, working in the aftermath of the modernists, for whom, as Eliot argued in "Tradition and the Individual Talent," tradition (connections with previous writers) was just as important as originality— "those aspects of [a poet's] work in which he least resembles anyone else" (Eliot 37). The modernist age tended to find innovation within continuity, as when Joyce's use of Homer is cited as one of the most original aspects of *Ulysses*, but Lowry always found the balance particularly difficult to maintain.

The split between romantic and modern concepts of the self and of the creative process is only one of many fundamental contradictions in Lowry's attitudes toward the world and toward his art. His religious views, for example, tend to waver between faith and doubt; or, to be more precise, they may be summarized as the desire of a skeptic for a faith that he cannot quite accept. Citing a note for "The Forest Path to the Spring," in which Lowry laments the dilemma of a writer whose impulse toward religion is countered by his skeptical "higher self," Bock observes that Lowry's work is based on "a Manichean, at times even schizophrenic, epistemology in which the mind of the novelist or a character simultaneously embraces or artistically balances visions of heaven and hell" (Bock 115). Bock's observation that "Lowry's characters vacillate between a longing for the stasis of death and an intense sense of the joyful if chaotic flux of an animistic world" (Bock 123) is also pertinent, since these contrary impulses parallel Lowry's desires to complete his artistic voyage and to continue it. The complex entanglement of life and art in Lowry's fiction provides evidence of yet another split, since at times Lowry seems to believe that art is directly dependent on life while at other times the reverse is true, and there is no clear indication that he was ever able to believe that either life or art was ultimately higher, or truer, than the other.

His belief that life and art continually respond to, and in turn influence, each other, combined with his inability to achieve an objective perspective on either one, made it difficult for

Lowry to complete any of his projects without simultaneously ending his life. Writing was Lowry's means of giving his life a shape and a significance that it would otherwise lack, but—in what might be regarded as a Lowryan version of Heisenberg's principle of indeterminacy—the act of writing about the life changed it, producing an endless sequence of new complications. Moreover, if Lowry could never know for certain that he was the ultimate author of his own life and that he was not somehow "being written" on another level, how could he claim credit for his works? Doubts and conflicts assailed him at every turn.

Perhaps the most fundamental of Lowry's doubts involve the relationship of the self and external reality. Coincidences and correspondences are important in Lowry's work, and for that matter in his life, partly because he could never decide whether we create, or merely apprehend, the reality that we find about us: analogy might be a sign of our connection to the universe, as Lowry hoped, or of paranoia, as he feared. While the ambiguous relationship of self and world is handled brilliantly in *Under the Volcano,* and in fact contributes to the richness of Lowry's novel, it also reveals Lowry's anxiety about his status in relation to the world about him and to the texts (his own and others') that played so great a part in his concept of his identity.[3] These conflicting visions of reality worked against Lowry's effort to bring his later works to a satisfactory conclusion, since as Leader has noted, the inability to come to terms with such an opposition is itself a recurrent factor in cases of writer's block:

> Blocked writers fail to negotiate rival or opposing claims, variously associated with pairings such as inner and outer, primary and secondary processes, emergence and embeddedness, independence and incorporation, inspiration and elaboration, defusion and merger, subject and object, written and oral, "male" and "female." These oppositions reflect a deep and basic conflict, one that the psychoanalysts argue is rooted in our earliest rela-

tions with the world, whether that world is conceived of in terms of Kleinian "objects" or of people. Writing asks of writers, even those who feel most alienated, that they be at home in the world, by which is meant using and shaping it, as well as recognizing its otherness and integrity. (Leader 251)

It is hard to imagine anyone describing Malcolm Lowry as "at home in the world," if that means having a stable sense of his relationship to the world of objects and events. Furthermore, he was out of touch with the world of modern industrial civilization that glowered at him from the opposite bank of the Burrard Inlet, where a burned-out S converted a SHELL sign to a threat of damnation; with the world of the New Criticism, which divorced the reading of a literary work from any consideration of the author or the circumstances in which it was written; and with the commercial world of publishing. Both desiring and fearing success, Lowry moved from *Under the Volcano* to a startling number of new projects, almost all of them potentially fascinating but unfinished (perhaps even unfinishable) because of their inherent contradictions.

Those contradictions were exacerbated by the perfectionism that led Lowry to try to incorporate everything within a grand totalizing vision. The encyclopedism of Lowry's work is one of its strengths and, at the same time, one of its inherent flaws, for as Day observes, "Lowry could not bring himself to finish a book, because there was always so much more to say" ("Of Tragic Joy" 362).[4] In such manuscripts as *The Ordeal of Sigbjørn Wilderness* and *La Mordida* we find evidence of Lowry's obsessive desire to include a heterogeneous collection of materials—newspaper articles, notebook entries, random observations, notes on connections with other texts (including his own), and so forth—in the hope that somehow, with enough effort, he could make it all cohere. In striving toward all-inclusiveness, he had a model in the epic works of modernist literature—*A Vision, The Waste Land, Ulysses, Finnegans*

Wake, Remembrance of Things Past, The Magic Mountain, and *The Cantos*—that aim at a totalizing vision in which the inherent contradictions of life are either held in suspension or subsumed into a higher, unitary vision. Whereas the authors of these intensely subjective works strove toward objectivity and impersonality, however, Lowry's fictions were entangled in his awareness of his own subjectivity and his romantic belief, as Höfele puts it, that "art must be the authentic expression of the artist's inner life, his true nature" (Höfele 205). Under these circumstances, how could the works ever stand apart from his own life?

The involvement of self and text provided a further, related, complication. Lowry was familiar with J. W. Dunne's argument that any vision that attempts to include everything must include the observer, an idea that led Dunne to imagine a series of observers, each incorporating the previous ones, culminating in a fourth-dimensional observer who sees events from a perspective outside sequential time.[5] Aspects of Dunne's theory appear throughout Lowry's work, but it is most prominent in the plans for *The Voyage That Never Ends,* where the ultimate protagonist is akin to Dunne's fourth-dimensional observer, who is enabled to see the pattern of his life clearly through the sequence of figures created in the dream-within-a-dream. The problem, of course, is that it is difficult to bring this process to a conclusion because Lowry could never imagine that he had attained an objective perspective on a life that was essentially his own: each observer (or author) could in turn be observed (or "written") by a yet more remote figure, like the ultimate operator of the canal locks in "Through the Panama."

There are numerous contradictions in Lowry's view of himself and of his work, but it would be unfair to conclude a study of Malcolm Lowry's fiction on such a negative note. I have said that one of the problems Lowry faced was his perfectionism, but another way of putting that would be to say that he took the conditions of his art very seriously and attempted to work through them. The effort was at times heroic, and Lowry paid dearly for it: in a sense, Lowry sacrificed his life in favor of his art. If that sounds melodramatic, it is a conclusion that seems justified by the magnitude and complexity of Lowry's projects, the honesty of his effort, the brilliance of his finest work, and the sacrifices that he and Margerie made to bring that work into being. Not only *Under the Volcano* but the "whole bolus" of Lowry's writing places him among the modern writers who have posed serious and fundamental questions about life and art, and who have sacrificed the most in the quest for answers.

Notes

Introduction

1. See also Susan Sontag's observation, in a 1962 essay on Cesare Pavese, that "the writer is the man who discovers the use of suffering in the economy of art—as the saints discovered the utility and necessity of suffering in the economy of salvation" (Sontag 42).

2. Lowry derived the phrase "the bitch-goddess, success" from "The Insufficient Man," an unsigned *TLS* article on Dostoevsky that appeared on the verso of the page on which *Under the Volcano* was reviewed. Since the source of the phrase is not cited in the *TLS* article, Lowry might have been unaware that it originated in a 1906 letter from William James to H. G. Wells. (My thanks to Ronald Newman for locating this phrase for me.)

3. In the *Selected Poems*, this poem is given the title "After Publication of *Under the Volcano*," and "disastar" is emended to "disaster." Chris Ackerley, in his notes to the *Collected Poetry*, argues that "disastar" is Lowry's attempt "to suggest that the fault lies not within ourselves but in our stars" (SP 78, CP 310).

4. Lowry was particularly stung by Jacques Barzun's charge that *Under the Volcano* was largely an adaptation of techniques from other writers: see Barzun's review of *Under the Volcano*, Lowry's letter to Barzun (SL 143–48), and Barzun's reply (SL 440). Phrases from Bar-

zun's review are quoted in *Dark as the Grave*, where they are part of a publisher's negative review of Sigbjørn Wilderness's *The Valley of the Shadow of Death* (DG 142; further down the page, the quote beginning "But in spite of this" reshapes phrases from William Plomer's yet-unpublished report on *Under the Volcano* for Jonathan Cape [UBC 1:11]). Lowry's resentment against Barzun (as well as his insecurity) may be gauged by his reference, in "Ghostkeeper," to "that fake Barzun" (PS 206) and by his notes on possible revisions of *Lunar Caustic*, where he half-seriously contemplated portraying Barzun as a patient at the mental hospital, "for writing a dirty review of the Volcano" (UBC 15:12, "Lunar Caustic" ts. 1).

5. Although Lowry's second wife, Margerie Bonner Lowry, was herself an author, Lowry seems always to have thought of the artist or writer in masculine terms. A study of gender issues in Lowry is beyond the scope of the present book; my pronouns merely reflect Lowry's conception of the artist.

6. See also Suzanne Kim's comments on the "inner compulsion for order" underlying Lowry's revisions of the poem known either as "Grim vinegarroon" (SP 27) or "My hate is as a wind that buffets me" (CP 194–96), which Kim relates interestingly to Lowry's inability to complete his later works and to his belief that the process of writing involves a search for a unified self (Kim 228, 230).

Chapter 1: The Search for Authenticity: Ultramarine, In Ballast
to the White Sea, *and* Lunar Caustic

1. The scene in which Dana twice offers to jump in to save the pigeon, and has to be restrained from doing so (U 160–62), differs considerably from the early version of this scene in "On Board the *West Hardaway*" (PS 31–32): there, Dana thinks he should try to save the pigeon, but he says and does nothing. The scene immediately following, in which Dana berates the quartermaster for saying that there was not time enough to save the bird, is also substantially different from the version in "On Board the *West Hardaway*."

2. Lowry planned extensive revisions for *Ultramarine* but died without completing them; Sherrill Grace notes that most of the changes in

the 1962 edition involve deletions of "gauche undergraduate remarks, cumbersome references to Eliot's *The Waste Land*, and ornate punctuation" (*Voyage* 25). One reference to *The Waste Land* remains in the 1962 edition: "For the sea is picking Andy's bones in whispers. . . . Oh you who throw the peel and look to starboard, 'acuérdate de Flebas, que una vez fué bello y robusto como tú' " (U 150). There are also references to "The Hollow Men" ("Between the Tarot and the cabbage . . ." and "Eyes I dare not meet in dreams . . ." [U 69, 198]), to "The Love Song of J. Alfred Prufrock" ("I wish. I were—what? A pair of ragged clauses scuttling between two dark parentheses?" [U 143]), to "Ash-Wednesday" ("Three white leopards—" [U 153]), and to "Sweeney Among the Nightingales" ("a fungus that sang, very sweetly, in a wood" [U 198]).

3. See especially Day, ML, passim; Durrant, "Aiken and Lowry"; Grace, *Voyage* 123–27, 142–43; and Sugars's edition of *The Letters of Conrad Aiken and Malcolm Lowry, 1929–1954*. For a Freudian reading of the Lowry-Aiken relationship, see Nordgren.

4. Aiken addressed a presentation copy of *Ushant*, now on file in the Malcolm Lowry Archive at the University of British Columbia Library, to "our beloved Malc-Hambo-Blackstone with all devotion from Conrad."

5. Lowry might also have read parts of *Ushant* long before beginning *Dark as the Grave*, since Aiken began working on *Ushant* around 1933 (Joseph Killorin, in Aiken, *Selected Letters* 290) or 1934 (Lorenz 10).

6. Michel Schneider combines Eliot's and Bloom's perspectives in his description of "the great innovators" who read "with errors, misinterpretations . . . beside, in reverse, while progressively carving out a literary space proper for their style and imagination. On the other hand, weak authors idealize their model and are held in an unproductive deference. The strong steal, loot, destroy, plagiarize. The appropriation of the object is its destruction. To become an author is thus to overcome the anguish of influence" (Schneider 319–20, translation mine). In connection with Lowry's avowed intention to absorb Aiken, see also Schneider's association of plagiarism with cannibalism (Schneider 300).

7. By prefacing Dana's comments about the artist as father of the

father with a reference to *Hamlet*, Lowry reveals another debt, this time to Joyce's *Ulysses*, where Stephen Dedalus makes a similar argument. The connection with the Joyce passage is noted by Cross (9).

8. On the date of the trip, see Dahlie, " 'A Norwegian at Heart,' " and Lowry's September 1931 letter to Grieg, published in Grace, *Swinging the Maelstrom*, as " 'Nordahl Grieg, I greet you!' " Dahlie doubts that Grieg ever gave Lowry his permission to dramatize *The Ship Sails On* (" 'A Norwegian at Heart' " 37).

9. Grieg died on 2 December 1943 (Malcolm and Margerie Lowry's third wedding anniversary), and Lowry's shack burned down on 7 June 1944. In the manuscripts for *Dark as the Grave*, Lowry originally used these dates, but later changed the anniversary of Sigbjørn and Primrose Wilderness's wedding and the date of Erikson's (Grieg's) death to 7 December and the burning of the Wildernesses' shack to 6 June, reinforcing his theme of coincidence by locating these events on the anniversary of Pearl Harbor Day and on D-Day.

10. Peter Shaw confirms the association between the romantic emphasis on originality and the romantic writer's "concern about plagiarism" (Shaw 327). Zachary Leader notes "a connection between plagiarism and blockage . . . in Coleridge's career" and connects both to "Coleridge's obsession with the ideal of originality, or the claims of subjectivity" (Leader 99). I explore the association of writer's block with plagiarism in chapter 5. For case studies of plagiarism, see Mallon. The most thorough discussion of Lowry and plagiarism is Grace's "Respecting Plagiarism." See also Grace's "Caravan of Silence"; Schneider, 93, 296–99, 301–302, 352; Vice, "Self-Consciousness" 162–70; and Vice, "The *Volcano* of a Postmodern Lowry" 128–31.

11. In 1954, annoyed at being excluded from an anthology of modern writers (while Lowry was selected for inclusion), Rascoe typed an extended note on the letter that Lowry had written to him in May 1940 and sent it, along with another letter accusing Lowry of plagiarism, to a friend named Edward. Lowry's 1940 letter to Rascoe, along with Rascoe's notes on the alleged plagiarism, is in the Burton Rascoe Collection, Special Collections, Van Pelt Library, University of Pennsylvania; the Malcolm Lowry Archive has photocopies (UBC 3:13). On the Lowry-Rascoe relationship, see Doyen, "Fighting the

Albatross" 46–47, 213–17, and Grace, "Respecting Plagiarism" 465; for information about Rascoe's career, see Hensley.

12. Doyen cites a pair of quotations or adaptations from Emerson and Carroll, and another from Aristotle and Catullus (Rascoe, "What Is Love?" 718, 722), locating parallel passages in the first edition of *Ultramarine* (pp. 93, 99). The passages remain untouched in the 1962 edition (U 118, 125), and "post coitum omne animal triste est," a Latin adage often attributed to Aristotle, resurfaces in *October Ferry* (OF 196).

13. For a more specific interpretation of the "certain pamphlets" of "The Plagiarist," see Thomas 236.

14. Day (ML xi, 196) gives the date as June 1935, a date that agrees with Clarissa Lorenz's recollection (Lorenz 190–91); Bowker (*Remembered* 58 and "The Biographical Lowry" 152–53) and Bareham (*Malcolm Lowry* 8) place it a year later. Sherrill Grace, who is editing Lowry's letters, confirms the 1936 date (personal correspondence to author, 28 December 1990).

15. From Rimbaud's *Une Saison en enfer:* "Veut-on des chants nègres, des danses de houris? Veut-on que je disparaisse, que je plonge à la recherche de l'*anneau?* Veut-on? Je ferai de l'or, des remèdes." ("Do you want Negro songs, houris' dances? Do you want me to vanish, to dive in search of the *ring?* Do you? I will make gold, remedies.") Later, Plantagenet quotes Rimbaud's "Mêlant aux fleurs des yeux de pantheres" ("Mingling flowers with the eyes of panthers"—from "Le Bateau ivre") as part of his analysis of Garry's stories (PS 293). Another Rimbaud-obsessed sailor-artist, also based on Lowry, is James Dowd in Charlotte Haldane's 1932 roman à clef, *I Bring Not Peace*. Dowd quotes the sixth and seventh stanzas of "Le Bateau ivre" in a note to Michal, tells Dennis Carling that he came to Paris because of Rimbaud, and writes a jazz composition called "*Bateau Ivre*—Variations on a Jazz Theme" (Haldane 52, 90–91, 201).

16. See, however, Dale Edmonds's argument that " 'Lunar Caustic' is less a study of the horror of the alcoholic's withdrawal from, and subsequent return to, drink, than an occasionally effective protest against stultifying bureaucracy and disgraceful inefficiency on the part of the staff of a public hospital. In this respect the story contains the most explicit social criticism of Lowry's published writings"

("The Short Fiction" 65–66). Likewise, Keith Harrison contends that in *Lunar Caustic*, "the very clinical framework from which any putative cure might emerge is inadequate, fraudulent, and perhaps even destructive" ("Lowry's Allusions to Melville" 180).

17. In *October Ferry*, Ethan Llewelyn thinks of "his house forlorn as Cézanne's painting 'Maison de Pendu' seen the day before yesterday in the art gallery at Ixion . . . a house where a man has housed himself: a house where a man has hanged himself" (OF 112). Cézanne's "La Maison de Pendu" (1873) is in the Louvre.

18. Plantagenet's obsession with *Billy Budd* does not end with his release, for as he wanders the streets of New York he keeps "an eye out for Melville's house" (PS 305). Presumably this is Melville's "last address," where he wrote *Billy Budd*. David Benham's suggestion that the early title for *Lunar Caustic*, "The Last Address," refers to " 'the last address' at which Melville finished *Moby Dick*" (Benham 60) has been echoed by several other critics; but whereas Melville wrote *Billy Budd* in New York, shortly before his death, he had finished *Moby-Dick* in Pittsfield, Massachusetts, four decades earlier. The confusion might have originated with Lowry, since in "Swinging the Maelstrom" Bill Plantagenet recalls sailing down the Hudson with Ruth and "pointing vaguely . . . to where—behind them now—Melville was supposed to have finished Moby Dick" (UBC 15:7, 15).

19. On the death of Paul Fitte, see Bradbrook, *Malcolm Lowry* 113–16, 161–62; Doyen, "Fighting the Albatross" 15–16; and Day, ML 138–44. Day, who apparently did not know Fitte's real name, took his information largely from fictional transformations of the event in which Fitte appeared as Wensleydale, in the typescripts for *Dark as the Grave Wherein My Friend Is Laid* and *The Ordeal of Sigbjørn Wilderness*, and as Peter Cordwainer, in *October Ferry to Gabriola*. The Lowry Archive contains negative photocopies of articles from the *Cambridge Daily News* of Friday and Saturday, 15 and 16 November 1929, dealing with Fitte's death and the coroner's inquest (UBC 36:16). The inquest included testimony from "Clement Milton Lowry" and resulted in a verdict of "suicide during temporary insanity."

Chapter 2: The Law of Series: Correspondence and Identity
in Under the Volcano

1. Lowry also referred to Baudelaire's phrase in "Hotel Room in Chartres" (PS 22) and, more significantly, in his long letter to Jonathan Cape in defense of *Under the Volcano* (SL 78).

2. Henri Peyre translates: "Nature is a temple where living columns / Sometimes murmur indistinct words [allow confused words to escape]; / There man passes through forests of symbols / That watch him with familiar glances" (Burnshaw 8–9).

3. The text says that the letter was "apparently written at least a year ago" (UV 193), but in fact Yvonne has been gone only eleven months, since December 1937 (UV 38). The error might reflect Geoffrey's confused perceptions and judgments or Lowry's inconsistent revision of the text. For a reliable chronology of the novel's events, see Walker, " 'The Weight of the Past.' "

4. Lowry was fascinated (and often troubled) by the operation of coincidence in his life, even speculating, in a 1945 letter to Aiken, that he might be "the chap chosen of God or the devil to elucidate the Law of Series" (SL 49; CA/ML 187). References to the Law of Series also appear in other letters as well as in Lowry's prospectus for *The Voyage That Never Ends*, where he noted that "the terrifying Law of Series" figures prominently in *Dark as the Grave* (WP 82). Chris Ackerley and G. P. Jones have both shown that the Law of Series is a theory developed by Paul Kammerer in *Das Gesetz der Serie* (1919), a book that influenced Jung's better-known theory of synchronicity (Ackerley, "After Lowry's Lights" 115–16; Jones 203). For discussion of Kammerer's seriality and its relationship to Jung's synchronicity, see Arthur Koestler, *The Roots of Coincidence* 82–104.

5. It is worth noting that during the 1936–38 stay in Mexico that provided much of the material for *Under the Volcano*, Lowry believed that he was being spied on, either by police detectives in dark glasses, as he suggested in an unpublished letter to his father (ML 237–38), or by a man named Mensch who was supposedly reporting to Lowry's father (CA/ML 97).

6. Lowry's difficulties with *A Vision* are also reflected in *The Ordeal of Sigbjørn Wilderness*, whose autobiographical protagonist "struggled with the inverted cones of Yeats" (UBC 22:19, 142).

7. A comic version of the Hermetic doctrine surfaces in *La Mordida*, when Sigbjørn thinks about a novelist, Walt Ferries—nicknamed "Pisspot"—who had made Sigbjørn a character in "a murder mystery of the cheapest sort": "Sigbjorn wondered about the generosity of authors. Truly, what is above is like what is below. And what was below was certainly Pisspot" (UBC 13:21, 122–23). Other references to "as above, so below" may be found in *The Ordeal of Sigbjørn Wilderness* (UBC 22:19, 142) and in Lowry's notes on *Tender Is the Night* (NS 34).

8. In the 1940 version of chapter 12, the Consul was joined at the Farolito by a German silver miner named Wilhelm Schmidthaus (the name was changed to Wilhelm Bunge in later drafts) whose unhappy personal life connects him with the Consul. At one point the miner tells the Consul, "Going to have some changes in this country, eh. Too many Jew bastards, eh" (UV/1940 343). Lowry might have deleted this character to emphasize the Consul's isolation, but his removal also diminishes Geoffrey's association with anti-Semitism. In the published text, the *Samaritan* affair introduces the Nazi theme in a more complex and subtle fashion.

9. Likewise, Asals observes that when Geoffrey wonders whether "he is in the bathroom now or half an hour ago," we have no way of knowing for certain which is the "real" time. Lowry's disruption of linear time suggests that "what seems the present reality may be hallucinatory, visionary, a warp of linear time that, even as we read the words, has already occurred half an hour ago and is thus over" (Asals, "Revision and Illusion" 100).

10. Cf. Don Birnam's belief, in *The Lost Weekend*, that he is "unobserved by others . . . the only one alive in the place, the only one who *saw*. Their preoccupation with each other, his own solidarity, completeness, self-sufficiency, aloofness, gave him a sense of elevation and excellence that was almost god-like. He smiled with tolerance at the room, and felt so remote and apart that he might have been unseen" (Jackson 30–31). Birnam's faith in his invisibility proves misplaced when he is caught trying to steal a woman's purse.

11. Cf. Roger Bromley's suggestive remarks on the relationship between "liminality" and *Under the Volcano*'s "cyclic regression to chaos as a prelude to a new creation, the deliberate, if agonized, pursuit of the abyss" (Bromley, "Removing the Landmarks" 150).

Chapter 3: Sortes Shakespeareanae: Reading in Under the Volcano

1. The association of the Alas cigarettes with fate is even more explicit in an earlier draft: "The Consul produced his blue packet of cigarettes with the wings on them. Alas! He looked up once more. Was it really too late to break out of this precipitous curve of his destiny, too late to make the wheels start moving in another direction?" (UV/1940 337).

2. The book's circular structure may also be implied by Laruelle's name: Kilgallin (*Lowry* 156) points to the overtone of "the Wheel (la roue) of Fortune," and Morton P. Levitt has suggested to me a further possible echo of Spanish *la rueda*, "the wheel."

3. The words Lowry used as his epigraph are spoken by angels who are carrying Faust's soul upward. Charles E. Passage translates the speech:

> Delivered is he now from ill,
> Whom we a spirit deemed:
> "Who strives forever with a will,
> By us can be redeemed."
> And if in him the higher Love
> Has had a share, to meet him
> Will come the blessed host above
> And warmly greet him.

Passage notes that "the quotation marks do not indicate a quotation, but are Goethe's own punctuation to signify the particular importance he attached to the words so enclosed," and he says that Goethe told Eckermann that the lines contain "the key to Faust's redemption" (Goethe 406).

4. It is also noteworthy that in the 1940 version of *Under the Volcano*, "Her lips suck forth my soul, see where it flies" was the second of three passages from *Doctor Faustus* that Laruelle read in chapter 1 (UV/1940 24). At that stage, the misquotation "Then will I fly . . ." was Lowry's error; later, when he realized that he had misquoted Marlowe, Lowry turned his own careless mistake into a thematically significant one by Laruelle.

5. On the dialogic nature of *Under the Volcano*, see also Schaeffer, *passim*, and Vice, "The *Volcano* of a Postmodern Lowry" 133.

6. Ackerley and Clipper note that Lowry's source for the Bunyan quotation was William James's *The Varieties of Religious Experience*, a fact that accounts for the "minor inaccuracies" in the quotation (A&C 1; cf. James 155). Further evidence of Lowry's unfamiliarity with *Grace Abounding*, apart from the citation in James, may be found in the 1945 typescript of *Under the Volcano* (version E in the University of British Columbia collection), in which the epigraph is first attributed to *Pilgrim's Progress;* that title is crossed out and "Grace Abounding for the Prince of Sinners" is substituted; finally, "Prince" is marked out and "Chief" inserted (UBC 27:6, epigraph page).

7. The phrase reappears in *October Ferry to Gabriola*, as Ethan Llewelyn thinks, "All very well too for him to counsel Jacqueline to seek some meaning in the disaster, a belief in some 'force beyond' (as if the words *'Les dieux existent, c'est le diable'* had been written in vain)" (OF 95).

8. On informal/infernal dancing, see Lowry's poem "Delirium in Los Angeles" (CP 71–72). Another significant misreading of a sign appears in the following notebook entry (UBC 14:18, blue notebook), which Lowry incorporated into *La Mordida* (UBC 14:9, 344, 350):

Hallucinations such as the following produced from trying to study hotel regulations at distance: Lovers must nattily look at clerk at 12 o'clock on the guilty line. (actually—

Guests must notify clerk at Hotel Office

By 12 NOON

    Etc.—

Likewise, in *October Ferry to Gabriola*, Ethan Llewelyn misreads "ACUTE HOUSING SHORTAGE" as "ACUTE HANGING SHORTAGE" (OF 53) and overhears a reference to Calgary as Calvary (OF 59), while the "SAFESIDE-SUICIDE" inscriptions on license tags not only warn drivers that passing on the right is suicidal but appear to observe the disastrous consequences of taking the wrong step. (On the license tags see New, "Gabriola" 231.)

9. There are also explicit references to the writing on Belshazzar's wall in chapter 5: "The Consul wouldn't have needed a practised eye to detect on this wall, or any other, a Mene-Tekel-Peres for the world" and, shortly thereafter, a reference to "kingdoms divided" (UV 145–46).

10. See ML 351 and *Dark as the Grave* 140–41, where Lowry's discovery of his error is portrayed as one of Sigbjørn Wilderness's experiences. Ackerley and Clipper cite a note which they say refutes "the apocryphal legend that [Lowry] was not aware of the correct version himself until the book was virtually finished" (A&C 311–12). In fact, however, this note (which is actually in Margerie's hand, although clearly a transcription of Malcolm's own note) was written in 1946 and incorporated into page 5 of the notes that Lowry attached to his letter of 22 June 1946 to Albert Erskine (UBC 2:5; the handwritten note cited by Ackerley and Clipper is now in 28:21). In all of the earlier drafts, the sign contains errors of spelling and grammar in addition to the punctuation error that Lowry retained in chapter 5 of the published text. In accordance with Lowry's instructions to Erskine in June and July 1946, extensive changes were made by hand in the copy of the final typescript used for the Reynal and Hitchcock edition. The many mistakes in Lowry's earlier versions of this sign justify Erskine's statement, in a letter of 8 July 1946 (UBC 1:20), that someone needed to go carefully through the manuscript and check the accuracy of Lowry's Spanish and German.

11. In a set of notes attached to an unpublished letter to Albert Erskine, Lowry says that the phrase appears in a book by Maugham whose title he cannot remember. Unlike Maugham, he says, he does not intend for the phrase to be "thematic," and if it appears so, he asks for the last instance to be cut from page 539 of the typescript, which corresponds to UV 375 (UBC 2:6, p. 3 of notes on chapter 12 attached to letter of 16 July 1946). The passage was not deleted from the published text.

12. Lowry's creative use of typography might also owe something to his memory of Carroll's experiments—for example, the presentation of the Mouse's tale in the form of a mouse's tail, in *Alice's Adventures in Wonderland*. In particular, the sign with a hand pointing the way to Parián (UV 333) recalls the signs in *Through the Looking Glass* that point to the house of Tweedledum and Tweedledee. The Lowry Archive contains another possible source for the hand: the envelope of a letter that Lowry had sent to Juan Fernando Márquez in 1940, which was returned to him because by then—as Lowry discovered in January 1946—Juan Fernando was dead (UBC 32:15; the letter itself

is in UBC 1:79). The envelope is stamped with postmarks indicating various forwardings, and both the front and the back are stamped with pointing hands that resemble the one in the novel.

13. On the contrast between the Consul and Humpty Dumpty, see also Baxter.

Chapter 4: Wrider/Espider: The Consul as Artist in Under the Volcano

1. Day says that "Lowry always insisted that the Spanish word for 'spy' was 'espider,' not 'espía'" (ML 269), but in *Under the Volcano* the term "spider" (UV 30) or "espider" (UV 371) indicates a Mexican character's attempt at an English word rather than Lowry's faulty Spanish. Whether the phrasing originated in Lowry's experience, his imagination, or a fertile combination of both areas, the allegation that he or his character was not a writer but an "espider" recurs in *Dark as the Grave* (DG 124) and the *La Mordida* manuscript (UBC 14:8, 315). The charge in *Dark as the Grave* is one Sigbjørn recalls from his arrest during his previous trip to Mexico, while in *La Mordida* both Primrose and Sigbjørn are called "espiders." In both cases, the entire section echoes the conclusion of *Under the Volcano*, suggesting that Sigbjørn's experiences are repetitive and are essentially inextricable from his fiction.

2. This passage merely describes the Consul's handwriting as "slanting," but in chapter 1, when Laruelle looks at the Consul's letter, he sees "the words themselves slanting steeply downhill" (UV 35). Thematically, this is appropriate as a description of the Consul's tendency toward self-destruction: Lowry even noted that chapter 8 begins with the word "Downhill" (SL 78). It is not, however, an accurate description of Lowry's own handwriting, which tended to slant upward, even in his pencil draft of the passage that describes the Consul's handwriting as going in the other direction (UBC 28:24, 12). The "Greek e's and odd t's" (UV 271) will be recognized by anyone who has worked with Lowry's manuscripts.

3. See Asals, "Lowry's Use of Indian Sources," for extensive discussion of the parallels between India and Mexico.

4. For a broader consideration of the relationship between *Alastor* and *Under the Volcano*, see Chapman.

5. In this sequence there are three misquotations: Geoffrey's "a star that feels," "Love as incarnate death," and "the true end" are errors for Shelley's "a slave that feels," "Lone as incarnate death," and "the true law." Since Lowry was often careless about quoting, it is perhaps unwise to read too much significance into the erroneous citations from Shelley in this draft. Misquotations that persist into the published work are another matter altogether, since Lowry and his editor, Albert Erskine, were generally conscientious about trying to eliminate unintentional errors.

6. Lowry's own copy of *Eight Famous Elizabethan Plays* contains a similar erased text of a poem, written in his hand, which the inventory to the University of British Columbia's Lowry Archive identifies as "possibly the first draft of 'Strange Type' " (Combs, p. 3 of addendum headed "Malcolm Lowry's Library"). "Strange Type" was Earle Birney's title for the poem that begins "I wrote: In the dark cavern of our birth" (CP 185; SP 79). In that poem, Lowry deals again with the ambiguity and instability of language—this time in the form of printer's errors that lend new meaning to a literary work or to the world.

7. Brian Shaffer relates the Consul's image of himself as explorer to another Faustian figure, Conrad's Kurtz (Shaffer 146).

8. The American edition has *Rechnung* (UV 330), but this seems to be an error caused by the attempt to correct Lowry's German.

9. It is worth noting that the epigraph page of the 1945 *Volcano* typescript contains four epigraphs: the three that are printed in the published book and another, inserted between the Sophocles and Bunyan quotations (but marked for deletion), from "The Hound of Heaven," lines 122–25 (UBC 27:6).

10. See also "What Is an Author?" in which Foucault observes that the original "conception of a spoken or written narrative as a protection against death has been transformed by our culture. Writing is now linked to sacrifice and to the sacrifice of life itself. . . . Where a work had the duty of creating immortality, it now attains the right to kill, to become the murderer of its author. Flaubert, Proust, and Kafka are obvious examples of this reversal" (Foucault 117). Similarly, Lawrence Lipking argues that "the mind—[Paul] Valéry's mind, at any rate—cannot bear the idea of finishing. To finish, as to know thyself, would involve a kind of immortality, or a kind of death" (Lipking 611).

11. Baxter observes that "the Consul could not have written, or imagined, *Under the Volcano*, because it contains a dialectic of opposing views toward the physical world—the Consul's and Hugh's" (Baxter 124).

Chapter 5: The Grand Scheme: The Voyage That Never Ends

1. Paul Tiessen notes that in a September 1945 letter to Lowry, Conrad Aiken "echoed [Gerald] Noxon's primary concern, indeed, what Noxon has seen as his greatest contribution to *Under the Volcano*, that of getting Lowry to overcome his fear of finishing his masterpiece, to see that the manuscript should be let go" (ML/GN 15). For the text of this letter, see Aiken, *Selected Letters* 263–64, and CA/ML 183–84; see also Aiken's letter a year later, in which he congratulated Lowry for having "at last twanged the umbilical cord and cast your Inferno off into the blue for weal or woe" (Aiken, *Selected Letters* 273; CA/ML 196). In conversation with me, Frederick Asals has suggested what is surely true: that Lowry finally decided to mail off the revised *Volcano* in 1945 only because he feared losing it altogether, as he had lost the manuscript of *In Ballast to the White Sea* during the previous year.

2. It is tempting to assume that the cyclic dream-vision structure of the *Voyage* might owe something to *Finnegans Wake* (1939), but Lowry's letters and drafts contain few references to Joyce's last book, apart from some playing with the nickname and initials of Joyce's universal protagonist—Here Comes Everybody, or HCE—in *La Mordida* (UBC 14:8, 313–15) and a passing mention of *Finnegans Wake* in relation to *Ushant* in a 1954 letter to Aiken (CA/ML 237). A more likely influence on Lowry's plans was Proust's *Remembrance of Things Past*.

3. The removal of the Mexican frame for *Eridanus* is presumably why Lowry later planned to have *October Ferry to Gabriola*—the revised *Eridanus*—follow, rather than precede, *La Mordida* (see Grace, *Voyage* 8–9).

4. Day (ML 419) says that the Catholic hospital where Lowry initially stayed was St. Paul's Hospital. After a few days there, Lowry was discharged but then entered North Vancouver Hospital.

5. In this regard it is worth recalling that Lowry often changed the

names of his characters from one draft to another. Bill Plantagenet is known as Sigbjørn Lawhill in early drafts of "The Last Address" (*Lunar Caustic*); the Consul, in *Under the Volcano*, was called William Erickson (according to CA/ML 127), William Ames, and Jeffrey Ames before being renamed Geoffrey Firmin; and the original protagonists of *Dark as the Grave* and *La Mordida* were Martin and Primrose Trumbaugh, who later became Martin and Primrose Striven, and finally Sigbjørn and Primrose Wilderness. On the other hand, the simultaneous use of more than one name fits nicely into the theme of uncertain or fabricated identity in the *Ordeal*, much as it does in "Through the Panama," where Sigbjørn Wilderness adopts the fictional identity of Martin Trumbaugh.

6. Day says that "Travers had died in a blazing tank in the Western Desert in 1942" (ML 140), a date consistent with Lowry's indication that James died seven years before the events of the *Ordeal* (UBC 22:19, 12).

7. "The Sound Machine," which Martin read in the *New Yorker*, is reprinted in Dahl's collection *Someone Like You*.

8. Grace also calls attention to a letter that Lowry wrote to Aiken in 1949, in which Lowry commented on the relevance of "Mr. Arcularis" to his hospital experience (*Voyage* 127, 143; for the letter, see CA/ML 213–15). A further possible source is Bernard DeVoto's discussion of an unfinished sequence of stories by Mark Twain, in which the protagonist awakens at the end and we realize that all of the disasters he has seen have been dreams; the protagonist, however, believes that he is *now* dreaming and that "the dream was reality" (DeVoto 223–24). DeVoto says that "some psychic block" kept Twain from completing the stories. Binns suggests this is the DeVoto article referred to in "Through the Panama" ("Lowry and the Profession" 171; HL 173; cf. SL 330).

9. Sherrill Grace has similar doubts about applying Bloom's theories to Lowry's fiction, arguing that "to do so is to risk a radical misreading of Lowry's intention and achievement." In a note, she admits that Bloom's terms may sometimes apply to Lowry with striking force, but maintains that "in psychoanalysing the author . . . one must not reduce creativity to an oedipal complex or consign the text to some pre-ordained order" ("'A strange assembly'" 189, 222).

10. In 1946 Lowry told Albert Erskine that he had once planned

to append a set of notes to *Under the Volcano* which, in addition to explaining some of the book's more esoteric symbolism, would have noted "any borrowings, echoes, design-governing postures, and so on" (SL 115). In his reply to Jacques Barzun's review of *Under the Volcano*, Lowry acknowledged that the phrase "design-governing postures" was itself borrowed from Van Gogh (SL 143).

11. Clarissa Lorenz recalls that Lowry took *Ulysses* with him on the 1933 trip with the Aikens to Spain, and read it there (Lorenz 150).

12. On the other hand, alcoholism may often be associated with writer's block, not simply because too much drinking makes writing impossible but because a writer with what Freudian psychoanalysts would recognize as a strongly oral personality substitutes drinking, and talking, for writing. Examples more or less contemporary with Lowry include Dylan Thomas, Brendan Behan, and Flann O'Brien. Behan's last books, all of them greatly inferior to such works as *Borstal Boy* and *The Quare Fellow*, were composed by dictation into a tape recorder because Behan could no longer "write" any other way; similarly, O'Brien's *Irish Times* column provided him with a kind of writing that resembled conversation during the years when he was unable to compose a more substantial work.

13. It is perhaps significant that when Lowry could write, he typically used a pencil—which would enable him to erase his words and change them—rather than a pen or typewriter. Leader observes that Coleridge might have benefited from having a word processor, which not only would have made revision easier but would have given him "the illusion of an audience," thereby lessening his solitude (Leader 229). The same might be said of Lowry, although his manner of working with Margerie, who felt free to add her comments when she typed his drafts, offered an approximation of dialogue.

14. A related phenomenon is a character's inability to sign a check, a recurrent scene in such works as the screenplay for *Tender Is the Night* (CML 209) and *La Mordida* (UBC 14:1, 288–94). See also Lowry's poem "Pity the blind and the halt but yet pity," where the greatest (self-)pity is reserved "For a man at the bank who can't sign his own name, / Though he sweat till the ultimate Manager came" (CP 128).

15. See also Mario Praz's observation that for romantic writers "the essential is the thought and the poetic image, and these are rendered

possible only in a passive state. The Romantic exalts the artist who does not give a material form to his dreams—the poet ecstatic in front of a forever blank page. . . . It is romantic to consider concrete expression as a decadence, a contamination" (Praz 14–15).

16. In their introduction to *The Cinema of Malcolm Lowry*, Miguel Mota and Paul Tiessen argue persuasively that "as metatext, in structure as in theme, Lowry's filmscript may be taken as a partial enactment" of the *Voyage* (CML 37).

Chapter 6: After the Volcano: Dark as the Grave, La Mordida, *and* October Ferry to Gabriola

1. In a 1940 letter to Lowry, Aiken wrote "Every man his own Laocoon group, complete with the serpent" (CA/ML 103). The Laocoön image reappears in chapter 8 of *Dark as the Grave*, when Sigbjørn imagines himself "wrapped in the tentacles of the past, like some gloomy Laocoön" (DG 165). He also associates the past with entrapment in chapter 4: "it was much as if by so entering the past, he had stumbled into a labyrinth, with no thread to guide him, where the minotaur threatened at every step" (DG 80). Typically, this passage presents Sigbjørn not as Theseus, who killed the minotaur and then used Ariadne's thread to guide himself out of the Cretan labyrinth— much less as Daedalus, who designed the labyrinth and later flew out of it—but as a hapless victim of the maze. On the distinction between James Joyce's use of Daedalus as a figure of the artist and Lowry's association with Laocoön, see Höfele.

2. The meaning of El Grafe's name is unclear, but for Lowry it probably evoked associations with writing (as in Spanish *grafospasmo*, "writer's cramp"). Perhaps Lowry meant to suggest a graffiti artist— a version of the artist as criminal—in contrast to a writer in the sense of a literary artist (*un escritor*).

3. On the Kilroy motif in *La Mordida*, see, e.g., UBC 13:18, 68; 13:20, 112; 13:23, 204; 13:26, 264; 14:7, 303; and 14:9, 352. The blue notebook now located in UBC 14:18, which contains notes taken by Malcolm and Margerie Lowry during the trip to Mexico, includes several mentions of Kilroy and other citations of graffiti.

4. Sigbjørn's source is apparently James's discussion, in *The Vari-*

eties of Religious Experience, of "the consciousness produced by in-
toxicants and anaesthetics, especially by alcohol":

> The sway of alcohol over mankind is undoubtedly due to its
> power to stimulate the mystical faculties of human nature, usually
> crushed to earth by the cold facts and dry criticisms of the sober
> hour. Sobriety diminishes, discriminates, and says no; drunken-
> ness expands, unites, and says yes. It is in fact the great exciter
> of the Yes function in man. . . . To the poor and the unlettered
> it stands in the place of symphony concerts and of literature. . . .
> The drunken consciousness is one bit of the mystic conscious-
> ness, and our total opinion of it must find its place in our opinion
> of that larger whole. (James 377–78)

In *The Ordeal of Sigbjørn Wilderness*, Martin refers more generally to
James's discussion of mystical experiences stimulated by anaesthesia,
in the same chapter of *The Varieties of Religious Experience:* "If you
know your William James you must be convinced that oversedation
does not necessarily destroy the validity of a supernatural experience
such as that" (UBC 22:19, 10). See also Day's citation of a later passage from the same chapter, in which James describes "delusional
insanity, paranoia, as they sometimes call it," as a species of "diabolical mysticism, a sort of religious mysticism turned upside down" (ML
335; James 417).

5. The Yeatsian principle of the union of opposites might lie behind the phrase "turning your greatest weakness into your greatest
strength," which Sigbjørn attributes to *A Vision* (DG 41).

6. The drafts of *Dark as the Grave* also contain evidence that Fernando might have become at least one of Sigbjørn's daemons: Lowry
left a note outlining a possible scene in which Sigbjørn finds "a
batch of poems" by Fernando entitled "The Lighthouse Invites the
Storm"—the name of Lowry's own unpublished collection of poems
(UBC 9:15, 541; cf. UBC 9:23). To Sigbjørn, these poems seem "like
the flowers that blossomed in Parsifal's absence," a comparison that
later drafts shift to the landscape, where the transformation anticipates the pattern of renewal that Sigbjørn associates with the work
of Fernando's Banco Ejidal (DG 68, 245). For the published text of
Sigbjørn's *Lighthouse* poems, see Appendix F of *The Collected Poetry
of Malcolm Lowry* (CP 382–90).

7. Ironically, the endings of the novel and film of *The Lost Weekend*

bear a relationship similar to that of Poe's "The Fall of the House of Usher" and Epstein's cinematic treatment: Charles Jackson's novel ends with Don Birnam having a last solitary drink and wondering why everyone made "such a fuss" over his drinking, while the movie treats him as the artist who triumphs over his problems as he settles down at the typewriter to write a novel called *The Lost Weekend*. The movie thus presents Birnam as doing what Sigbjørn and Lowry both hoped to do—breaking the cycle of drinking and redeeming his life by making it the material for his art—while the novel gives us a failed artist who will never stop drinking and write his book.

8. See also Rankin's suggestion that the later passage in which Sigbjørn compares life to a film demonstrates Lowry's recognition "that the form of *Dark as the Grave* was in some ways at odds with its themes." She believes that this realization might have contributed to Lowry's inability to finish *Dark as the Grave* ("Writer as Metaphor" 333).

9. Lowry became interested in Ortega's work around Christmas 1949, when he read "In Search of Goethe from Within" in the *Partisan Review*: in his notes on the screenplay for *Tender Is the Night*, Lowry observed that he and Margerie had already finished the part of the filmscript that involves a shipwreck when he read Ortega's essay, with its description of life as "shipwreck" and the contention that "consciousness of shipwreck, being the truth of life, constitutes salvation" (NS 78; see Ortega, "In Search of Goethe" 136–37). Three pages of typed notes on Ortega's *Toward a Philosophy of History* are included in the Malcolm Lowry Archive (UBC 2:14), and most of Lowry's letter of 23 June 1950 to Downie Kirk is devoted to a summary of ideas from the same book (SL 208–13). The brief quote from pages 107–8 of *Toward a Philosophy of History*, cited below, is included both in Lowry's notes and in the letter to Kirk, and referred to in "The Forest Path to the Spring" and in "Ghostkeeper" (HL 268, PS 223).

10. A clipping of this article is included in the Malcolm Lowry Archive (UBC 36:18). The exaggerated tone of the article continues with the remarkable claim that "during his years of wandering as a sailor, Lowry became a 'voodoo' priest of Haiti. 'It was because of my eyes,' he says, 'and I believe I went through the ceremony of becoming a priest with flying colors.'"

11. In addition to notebooks and typed transcriptions of notes on

which Lowry drew for *La Mordida*, the Malcolm Lowry Archive contains four drafts of the novel: a pencil draft in Lowry's hand (UBC 13:1–17); the 1952 typescript, which includes notes that are typed into the draft so that they will not be lost (UBC 13:18–26, 14:1–9); an incomplete carbon copy of the typescript (UBC 14:10–11); and an expanded typescript that Margerie Lowry prepared during the 1970s (UBC 14:12–15). The early chapters of the 1952 typescript contain a good deal of material that is not in the pencil draft, suggesting that Margerie used an intervening draft that has not survived; later chapters are clearly typed directly from the pencil draft except where Lowry has inserted additional notes or has had newspaper articles or other printed material typed into the draft. For a brief description of the materials in the Archive, see my article "The *La Mordida* Drafts and Notes at UBC."

12. Lowry's copy of this thirty-two-page pamphlet, *Acapulco: An Adventure in Living*, which is preserved in the Malcolm Lowry Archive (UBC 32:11), bears several annotations in his hand. Aside from passages used as marginalia in *La Mordida* and two passages that Lowry drew on for information about the history of Acapulco, the pamphlet contributed the line "It sounds like heaven, but they call it Acapulco," which Lowry uses ironically in his text.

13. See also Matthew Corrigan's observation that Lowry's aesthetic of correspondence involved him in innumerable difficulties because "a single vibration sets the whole vibrating." Thus "completion, even aesthetically, becomes a problem" (Corrigan 420).

14. On the connection between the motion picture reel and other images of wheels in Lowry's work, see Tiessen, "Malcolm Lowry and the Cinema," 139–42.

15. Lowry refers to Crane's "Purgatorio" again in *La Mordida:* "the shape of the cathedral where Hart Crane rang the sad church bells could barely be made out" (UBC 14:4, 344–45).

16. On the significance of the allusions to Mann's "Mario and the Magician" (UBC 13:19, 95–97), and their possible connection to the theme of determinism in *Under the Volcano*, see Saalmann. The references to John O'Hara's *Appointment in Samarra* are curiously limited to mechanical breakdowns (UBC 14:1, 301; 14:6, 283), although the novel's plot and its title—derived from its epigraph, a speech by Death in Somerset Maugham's play *Sheppey*—would have fitted neatly into

the idea that we create our destinies. On "a sort of good soldier Schweik scene," see Jaroslav Hašek's comic antiwar novel *The Good Soldier: Schweik.*

17. The *Selected Letters* dates this letter as "Early Summer, 1953" (SL 333), but Doyen observes that the letter's contents point to April 1953 (Doyen, "Fighting the Albatross" 290).

18. Victor Doyen quotes from an unpublished letter in which Lowry lists *October Ferry* among works that have "nothing to do with writers" (Doyen, "From Innocent Story" 174). Doyen's essay is the most thorough study to date of the composition of *October Ferry*.

19. Cf. *Dark as the Grave*, where Sigbjørn imagines that "he rather resembled the publicity photographs of Arthur Koestler" (DG 42). In "Elephant and Colosseum," Cosnahan looks at his own publicity photograph on the jacket of his novel and believes that he resembles "the young Emmanuel Swedenborg" while the tomcat he is holding in the picture looks like Theodore Roosevelt (HL 117).

20. The references to hanging in a disused elevator shaft (OF 162, 264; cf. OF 7) connect this hanging to the one Sigbjørn Wilderness imagines in *La Mordida* (UBC 13:24, 226–27) and to the case of Francis Sykes, about which Lowry wrote to David Markson in 1951: "a local injustice where a 16 year old boy was sentenced to hang (in a disused elevator shaft, painted yellow) for a rape he had not committed" (SL 269). Doyen ("From Innocent Story" 183–84, 201) discusses Lowry's interest in this case.

21. The phrase also appears in a draft of *Dark as the Grave* (UBC 9:1, 76).

Chapter 7: *Apparently Incongruous Parts:* Hear Us O Lord from Heaven Thy Dwelling Place

1. In a final twist of the Law of Series, Lowry died on 27 June 1957, thirty-five years after Sigurd launched his boat.

2. For more extensive consideration of musical theme and structure in *Hear Us O Lord*, see Grace, " 'A Sound of Singing.' "

3. Lawrence Lipking distinguishes sharply between marginal glosses and marginalia, regarding marginalia as "traces left in a book" that "spring up spontaneously around a text unaware of their

presence" while glosses tend to rationalize the text by explaining it (Lipking 612–13, 648–49). Sherrill Grace follows this distinction in "Through the Panama" and finds both genres in Lowry's text. She observes, however, that "marginal gloss and marginalia pull in opposite directions, the one back into the text, the other one into a potentially endless creation of new texts, and these contradictory impulses may well signify Lowry's own duality—his longing for perfection and completion on the one hand, with his even greater desire for the 'voyage that never ends' on the other" (" 'A strange assembly' " 218). While recognizing that aspects of the gloss and of marginalia both exist in "Through the Panama," I would argue that neither is present in its pure form, either as a gloss that exists strictly to control and direct the reader's interpretation of the "main" text or as a marginalized trace of the author's imagination that cannot be directly related to the text. Instead, Lowry's marginal notes or glosses tend to be both concentric and eccentric, simultaneously seeking perfection or completion and avoiding it. For this reason, I have used the terms "marginal gloss" and "marginalia" interchangeably.

4. The use of these names may also be related to Lowry's plan to treat "Through the Panama" as a dream sequence in *La Mordida* (see UBC 12:13 and Grace, " 'A strange assembly' " 205, 226). The published text of "Through the Panama" bears a trace of this plan: "This should occur in *La Mordida* in Trumbaugh's dream" (HL 83).

5. "In the Black Hills," another story that Lowry once intended to include in *Hear Us O Lord* (SL 267), was also left out of that collection but was published, along with "China," in a limited edition in 1974 (under the title "Kristbjorg's Story: In the Black Hills") and reprinted in *Malcolm Lowry: Psalms and Songs* (PS 250–53). The story's themes—the use of alcohol to escape consciousness and the impossibility of truly knowing another person—are handled adequately, but the story is otherwise of little interest.

6. Elsewhere Lowry writes, "He phones the second Ghostkeeper and this part is dramatised much as it happened," indicating that the search for the owner of the watch is also based on Lowry's experience (PS 215).

7. It might also be argued that "Ghostkeeper" proposes Nietzsche as a model of the writer who places the need for dynamic change and

the acceptance of ambiguity above the desire for an artificial consistency, since that is one implication of the passages from Karl Jaspers's "Nietzsche and the Present" that Lowry has Goodheart read (PS 224; see Jaspers 21, 23).

8. An earlier passage in "Present Estate," about a forest of junipers that die of fear (HL 179), recalls the fate of the Seven Sisters in "The Bravest Boat."

9. On the comic element in "Elephant and Colosseum," see Rankin, "Malcolm Lowry's Comic Vision," and Linguanti 211–15.

10. In "Strange Comfort," Sigbjørn Wilderness is an American writer, and as Lowry observed in a letter to Harold Matson, he is not identical with "the hero of the whole bolus"—presumably the dreamer/protagonist of *The Ordeal of Sigbjørn Wilderness* and *The Voyage That Never Ends* (SL 327). But *that* protagonist, Lowry said in his "Work in Progress" statement, is in turn not quite the same as the Sigbjørn Wilderness of *Dark as the Grave* (WP 77); moreover, none of these Sigbjørn Wildernesses could be identified with yet another one in *October Ferry*, a neighbor of Ethan Llewelyn who is described as "an unsuccessful Canadian composer, but an excellent jazz pianist" (OF 169–70). These Sigbjørns have much in common, however: their wives are invariably named Primrose, for example, and in "Strange Comfort," Sigbjørn's fear of being thought a spy echoes a theme of *Dark as the Grave* and *La Mordida*. Ultimately they are all versions of Malcolm Lowry, and the proliferation of Sigbjørn Wildernesses reflects Lowry's obsessive attempt to come to terms with an identity that he found increasingly unstable and fragmented.

11. Douglas Day identifies Van Bosch as Benjamin Parks, an attorney whom Lowry's father had placed in charge of his son's affairs in 1938–39 (ML 453).

12. The reference to bank clerks suggests T. S. Eliot, an identification underscored by the description of such poets' works as "hieroglyphics, masterly compressions, obscurities to be deciphered by experts" (HL 109). Other references to Eliot in "Strange Comfort" may be found in Sigbjørn's note on the "drowned Phoenician sailor" (HL 100: cf. Part 4 of *The Waste Land*) and in his speculation on a possible Roman address for the poet, one that puns on the title of Lowry's next story: "Eliot in Colosseum?" (HL 103).

13. See also *October Ferry*, where Ethan Llewelyn finds a bottle of gin that has somehow survived the burning of his house (OF 92). Recalling the legend that the ginbush had been cast out of Eden, Ethan believes that since gin is "the only liquor with a divine curse on it," nothing is "more natural than that a bottle of gin should have survived their fire" (OF 97). Ethan also associates gin with survival or natural renewal at the novel's end, when he gives a drink to Mrs. Neiman and later takes what he calls a "symbolic" drink (OF 309–10, 326).

14. For example, the narrator is a former jazz musician and presently a composer rather than a fiction writer; at the outset of World War II he tried at least twice to enlist in the army; and his father had been a musician, having played "French horn in the first performance in 1913 of Stravinsky's Sacre du Printemps" (HL 267).

Conclusion

1. For a detailed survey of links between *Under the Volcano* and *The Waste Land*, see Kums.

2. Cf. Roger Bromley's observation that Lowry's "longing for the convincing and explanatory word, the unitary and the harmonious, is constantly subverted by the fractious, the inconsequential, and the incomplete" ("Removing the Landmarks" 151). See also Suzanne Kim's description of Lowry as "a man desperately in search of a single self, groping for definition by means of an almost naïve Cratylism against the odds of a multiplicity of reeling selves" (Kim 230). On romantic and modern constructions of the self, see Taylor, especially pp. 419–93.

3. See also J. Drummond Bone's observation that "the openness of the text of *Under the Volcano*, clearly one of its strengths . . . is part of the same organic notion that drives Lowry to continual re-writing and to the metafictions of the posthumous novels. The organic paradox that life is totally organised (every part contributes to the whole) and yet never completed (the whole is in constant process) is vital both for form and theme in Lowry" (Bone 85).

4. Jakobsen links the encyclopedic inclusiveness of *Under the Volcano* to that of " 'oral', alcoholic writers whose writing as well as their

drinking represents a subconscious attempt to engulf the whole universe" ("Malcolm Lowry's *Under the Volcano*" 86). While Jakobsen notes that this "compulsively inclusive writing" served Lowry's artistic purposes in *Under the Volcano*, it is interesting that he connects this aspect of the work to the orality that I have related to Lowry's writer's block (see chapter 5, note 12). See also Schneider's description of plagiarism as "a devouring passion" associated with various eating disorders (Schneider 300–306).

5. See Dunne's *An Experiment with Time*, part 5: "Serial Time" (pp. 132–96). On Lowry's use of Dunne, see New, "Lowry's Reading" 128–29; Ackerley and Clipper, passim; Grace, *Voyage* 40–41, 65–66, 107, 140n; and Newton 71–73.

Bibliography

Except where I have indicated otherwise, page numbers refer to the most recent edition cited in this bibliography.

Primary Sources

Ultramarine. London: Jonathan Cape, 1933. Revised, Philadelphia: J. B. Lippincott, 1962.

Under the Volcano. New York: Reynal and Hitchcock, 1947. Reprint, New York: New American Library, 1971.

"Garden of Etla." *United Nations World* 4 (June 1950): 45–47.

Hear Us O Lord from Heaven Thy Dwelling Place. Philadelphia: J. B. Lippincott, 1961.

Selected Poems of Malcolm Lowry, edited by Earle Birney. San Francisco: City Lights Books, 1962.

Lunar Caustic, edited by Earle Birney and Margerie Bonner Lowry, with a preface by Conrad Knickerbocker. *Paris Review* 8 (Winter-Spring 1963), 12–72. Reprint, London: Jonathan Cape, 1968. Reprinted in *Malcolm Lowry: Psalms and Songs,* 255–306.

Selected Letters, edited by Harvey Breit and Margerie Bonner Lowry, with a preface by Harvey Breit. Philadelphia: J. B. Lippincott, 1965. Reprint, New York: Capricorn Books, 1969.

Dark as the Grave Wherein My Friend Is Laid, edited by Douglas Day and Margerie Bonner Lowry, with a preface by Douglas Day. New York: New American Library, 1968.

October Ferry to Gabriola, edited by Margerie Lowry. New York: World, 1970.

"China" and "Kristbjorg's Story: In the Black Hills." New York: Aloe Editions, 1974.

Malcolm Lowry: Psalms and Songs, edited by Margerie Lowry. New York: New American Library, 1975. [Includes early stories, reminiscences of Lowry, "The Luminous Wheel: The Evolution of Malcolm Lowry's Style" by A. C. Nyland, a short story version of chapter 8 of *Under the Volcano*, later stories, and *Lunar Caustic*.]

Notes on a Screenplay for F. Scott Fitzgerald's "Tender Is the Night." With Margerie Bonner Lowry. Bloomfield Hills, Mich.: Bruccoli Clark, 1976.

"Malcolm Lowry: Letter to Clemens ten Holder," edited with an introduction and notes by Terry Hilton. *Malcolm Lowry Review* Nos. 21 & 22 (Fall 1987 & Spring 1988): 41–71.

"Work in Progress: *The Voyage That Never Ends.*" *Malcolm Lowry Review* Nos. 21 & 22 (Fall 1987 & Spring 1988): 72–99.

The Letters of Malcolm Lowry and Gerald Noxon, 1940–1952, edited with an introduction by Paul Tiessen. Vancouver: University of British Columbia Press, 1988.

The Cinema of Malcolm Lowry: A Scholarly Edition of Lowry's "Tender Is the Night," edited by Miguel Mota and Paul Tiessen. Vancouver: University of British Columbia Press, 1990.

The Collected Poetry of Malcolm Lowry, edited and introduced by Kathleen Scherf, with explanatory annotation by Chris Ackerley. Vancouver: UBC Press, 1992.

The Letters of Conrad Aiken and Malcolm Lowry, 1929–1954, edited by Cynthia C. Sugars. Toronto: ECW Press, 1992.

The 1940 "Under the Volcano," edited by Miguel Mota and Paul Tiessen, introduction by Frederick Asals. Waterloo, Ontario: *The Malcolm Lowry Review*, 1994.

Other Works Cited

Abrams, M. H. *The Mirror and the Lamp: Romantic Theory and the Critical Tradition.* London: Oxford University Press, 1953.

Acapulco: An Adventure in Living. Departamento de Turismo de la Secretaria de Gobernación, Asociación Mexicana de Turismo, n.d.

Ackerley, Chris. " 'After Lowry's Lights': Coincidence in *Ulysses* and *Under the Volcano.*" In *The Interpretative Power: Essays on Literature in Honour of Margaret Dalziel.* Dunedin, N.Z.: University of Otago, 1980. Pp. 113–26.

——. "The Consul's Book." *Malcolm Lowry Review* Nos. 23 & 24 (Fall 1988 & Spring 1989): 78–92.

Ackerley, Chris, and Lawrence J. Clipper. *A Companion to "Under the Volcano."* Vancouver: University of British Columbia Press, 1984.

Aiken, Conrad. *The Collected Novels of Conrad Aiken.* New York: Holt, Rinehart and Winston, 1964.

——. *Ushant: An Essay.* New York: Duell, Sloan and Pearce, 1952.

——. *Selected Letters of Conrad Aiken,* edited by Joseph Killorin. New Haven: Yale University Press, 1978.

——. "The Father Surrogate and Literary Mentor." In Bowker, *Malcolm Lowry Remembered,* 38–40.

Andersen, Gladys Marie. "A Guide to *Under the Volcano.*" Ph.D. diss., University of the Pacific, 1969.

Arac, Jonathan. "The Form of Carnival in *Under the Volcano.*" *PMLA* 92 (1977): 481–89.

Asals, Frederick. "Lowry's Use of Indian Sources in *Under the Volcano.*" *Journal of Modern Literature* 16 (Summer 1989): 113–40.

——. "Revision and Illusion in *Under the Volcano.*" In Grace, *Swinging the Maelstrom,* 93–111.

Augustine, St. *Confessions,* translated by R. S. Pine-Coffin. Harmondsworth: Penguin Books, 1961.

Bareham, Tony. "Lowry and 'The Great Figure of Authority.' " In Vice, *Malcolm Lowry Eighty Years On,* 51–69.

——. *Malcolm Lowry.* New York: St. Martin's Press, 1989.

Barnes, Jim. *Fiction of Malcolm Lowry and Thomas Mann: Structural Tradition.* Kirksville, Mo.: Thomas Jefferson University Press, 1990.

Barzun, Jacques. "New Books." *Harper's Magazine,* May 1947. Excerpt in Bowker, *Malcolm Lowry, "Under the Volcano": A Casebook*, 69–70.

Baxter, Charles. "The Escape from Irony: *Under the Volcano* and the Aesthetics of Arson." *Novel* 10 (Winter 1977): 114–26.

Beckett, Samuel. *Three Novels.* New York: Grove Press, 1965.

Beebe, Maurice. *Ivory Towers and Sacred Founts: The Artist as Hero in Fiction from Goethe to Joyce.* New York: New York University Press, 1964.

Benham, David. "Lowry's Purgatory: Versions of 'Lunar Caustic.'" *Canadian Literature* No. 44 (Spring 1970): 28–37. Reprinted in Woodcock, *Malcolm Lowry: The Man and His Work*, 56–65.

Binns, Ronald. "Beckett, Lowry and the Anti-Novel." In *The Contemporary English Novel*, edited by Malcolm Bradbury and David Palmer. Stratford-upon-Avon Studies 18. New York: Holmes and Meier, 1979. Pp. 89–111.

———. "Materialism and Magic in *Under the Volcano.*" *Critical Quarterly* 23 (Spring 1981): 21–33. Reprinted in Bowker, *Malcolm Lowry, "Under the Volcano": A Casebook*, 172–76.

———. *Malcolm Lowry.* London: Methuen, 1984.

———. "Lowry and the Profession: Comfort, Discomfort, Strange Comfort." In Tiessen, *Apparently Incongruous Parts*, 164–73.

Blanchot, Maurice. *The Space of Literature*, translated by Ann Smock. Lincoln: University of Nebraska Press, 1982.

Bloom, Harold. *The Anxiety of Influence: A Theory of Poetry.* New York: Oxford University Press, 1973.

Bock, Martin. *Crossing the Shadow-Line: The Literature of Estrangement.* Columbus: Ohio State University Press, 1989.

Bone, J. Drummond. "Ron Binns' Malcolm Lowry." *Malcolm Lowry Review* Nos. 17 & 18 (Fall 1985 & Spring 1986): 82–89.

Bowker, Gordon, ed. *Malcolm Lowry Remembered.* London: Ariel Books, 1985.

———, ed. *Malcolm Lowry, "Under the Volcano": A Casebook.* Basingstoke: Macmillan Education, 1987.

———. "The Biographical Lowry: A Case of Inconsistent Ambiguity." In Vice, *Malcolm Lowry Eighty Years On*, 147–58.

Bradbrook, M. C. *Malcolm Lowry: His Art and Early Life—A Study in Transformation.* Cambridge: Cambridge University Press, 1974.

————. "Intention and Design in *October Ferry to Gabriola*." In Smith, *The Art of Malcolm Lowry*, 144–55.

Bradbury, Malcolm. " 'Design-Governing Postures': Malcolm Lowry and Modern Fiction." In *No, Not Bloomsbury*. New York: Columbia University Press, 1988. Pp. 151–72.

Bromley, Roger. "The Boundaries of Commitment: God, Lover, Comrade—*Under the Volcano* as a Reading of the 1930s." In *The Politics of Modernism*, vol. 1 of *1936: The Sociology of Literature*, edited by Francis Barker et al. Colchester: University of Essex, 1979. Pp. 273–96.

————. "Removing the Landmarks: Malcolm Lowry and the Politics of Cultural Change." In Tiessen, *Apparently Incongruous Parts*, 149–63.

Burnshaw, Stanley, ed. *The Poem Itself*. New York: Simon and Schuster, 1989.

Chapman, Marilyn. " 'Alastor': The Spirit of *Under the Volcano*." *Studies in Canadian Literature* 6 (1981): 256–72.

Combs, Judith O. "Malcolm Lowry 1909–1957: An Inventory to the Malcolm Lowry Manuscript Collections in the Library of the University of British Columbia Special Collections Division," 1973; revised by Cynthia Sugars, 1985. Photocopied typescript.

Corrigan, Matthew. "Malcolm Lowry: The Phenomenology of Failure." *Boundary* 2 3 (1975): 407–42.

Costa, Richard Hauer. *Malcolm Lowry*. New York: Twayne Publishers, 1972.

Cross, Richard K. *Malcolm Lowry: A Preface to His Fiction*. Chicago: University of Chicago Press, 1980.

Dahlie, Hallvard. "Lowry's Debt to Nordahl Grieg." *Canadian Literature* No. 64 (Spring 1975): 41–51.

————. " 'A Norwegian at Heart': Lowry and the Grieg Connection." In Grace, *Swinging the Maelstrom*, 31–42.

Day, Douglas. "Of Tragic Joy." *Prairie Schooner* 37 (Winter 1963–64): 354–62.

————. *Malcolm Lowry: A Biography*. New York: Oxford University Press, 1973.

Deck, Laura M. "An Interview with Mrs. Malcolm Lowry." *Malcolm Lowry Newsletter* No. 3 (Fall 1978): 11–22. (Part 1 of a series.)

DeVoto, Bernard. "The Threshold of Fiction." *Harper's Magazine* 180 (January 1940): 221–24.

Doyen, Victor. "Elements Towards a Spatial Reading of Malcolm Lowry's *Under the Volcano.*" *English Studies* 50 (February 1969): 65–74.

———. "Fighting the Albatross of Self: A Genetic Study of the Literary Work of Malcolm Lowry." Ph.D. diss., Katholieke Universiteit te Leuven (Belgium), 1973.

———. "From Innocent Story to Charon's Boat: Reading the 'October Ferry' Manuscripts." In Grace, *Swinging the Maelstrom*, 163–208.

Dunne, J. W. *An Experiment with Time*, 5th ed. London: Faber and Faber, 1939. Reprint, London: The Scientific Book Club, 1944.

Durrant, Geoffrey. "Death in Life: Neo-Platonic Elements in 'Through the Panama.' " *Canadian Literature* No. 44 (Spring 1970): 13–27. Reprinted in Woodcock, *Malcolm Lowry: The Man and His Work*, 42–55.

———. "Aiken and Lowry." *Canadian Literature* No. 64 (Spring 1975): 24–40.

Edmonds, Dale. "The Short Fiction of Malcolm Lowry." *Tulane Studies in English* 15 (1967): 59–80.

———. "*Under the Volcano:* A Reading of the 'Immediate Level.' " *Tulane Studies in English* 16 (1968): 63–105. Reprinted in Wood, *Malcolm Lowry: The Writer and His Critics*, 57–100.

Eliot, T. S. *Selected Prose of T. S. Eliot.* Edited by Frank Kermode. New York: Harcourt Brace Jovanovich/ Farrar, Straus and Giroux, 1975.

Ellmann, Richard. *The Identity of Yeats*, 2nd ed. New York: Oxford University Press, 1964.

Epstein, Perle S. *The Private Labyrinth of Malcolm Lowry: "Under the Volcano" and the Cabbala.* New York: Holt, Rinehart and Winston, 1969.

Falk, David. "Beyond the Volcano: The Religious Vision of Malcolm Lowry's Late Fiction." *Religion and Literature* 16 (Autumn 1984): 25–38.

———. "Lowry and the Aesthetics of Salvation." In Grace, *Swinging the Maelstrom*, 52–60.

Foucault, Michel. *Language, Counter-Memory, Practice: Selected Essays and Interviews*, edited by Donald F. Bouchard; translated by

Donald F. Bouchard and Sherry Simon. Ithaca: Cornell University Press, 1977.

Gilmore, Thomas B. *Equivocal Spirits: Alcoholism and Drinking in Twentieth-Century Literature.* Chapel Hill: University of North Carolina Press, 1987.

Goethe, Johann Wolfgang von. *Faust, Part One & Part Two,* edited and translated by Charles E. Passage. Indianapolis: Library of Liberal Arts, 1965.

Grace, Sherrill. "Malcolm Lowry and the Expressionist Vision." In Smith, *The Art of Malcolm Lowry,* 93–111.

———. *The Voyage That Never Ends: Malcolm Lowry's Fiction.* Vancouver: University of British Columbia Press, 1982.

———. " 'Consciousness of Shipwreck': Ortega y Gasset and Malcolm Lowry's Concept of the Artist." In *José Ortega y Gasset,* edited by Nora de Marval-McNair. Westport, Conn.: Greenwood Press, 1987. Pp. 137–42.

———. " 'A strange assembly of apparently incongruous parts': Intertextuality in Malcolm Lowry's 'Through the Panama.' " In Tiessen, *Apparently Incongruous Parts,* 187–228.

———. " 'A Sound of Singing': Polyphony and Narrative Decentring in Malcolm Lowry's *Hear Us O Lord.*" In *Modes of Narrative: Approaches to American, Canadian and British Fiction,* edited by Reingard M. Nischik and Barbara Korte. Würzburg: Königshausen and Neumann, 1990. Pp. 129–40.

———. "Thoughts Towards the Archaeology of Editing: 'Caravan of Silence.' " *Malcolm Lowry Review* Nos. 29 & 30 (Fall 1991 & Spring 1992): 64–77.

———, ed. *Swinging the Maelstrom: New Perspectives on Malcolm Lowry.* Montreal and Kingston: McGill-Queens University Press, 1992.

———. "Respecting Plagiarism: Tradition, Guilt, and Malcolm Lowry's 'Pelagiarist Pen.' " *English Studies in Canada* 18 (December 1992): 461–81.

Grieg, Nordahl. *The Ship Sails On,* translated by A. G. Chater. New York: Alfred A. Knopf, 1927.

Hadfield, Duncan. "Under the Tarot: A Reading of a Volcanic Sub-Level." *Malcolm Lowry Review* Nos. 23 & 24 (Fall 1988 & Spring 1989): 40–77.

Haldane, Charlotte. *I Bring Not Peace*. London: Chatto and Windus, 1932.

Harrison, Keith. "Malcolm Lowry's *Hear Us O Lord:* Visions and Revisions of the Past." *Studies in Canadian Literature* 6 (1981): 245–55.

———. "Malcolm Lowry's *October Ferry to Gabriola:* Balancing Time." *Studies in Canadian Literature* 7 (1982): 115–21.

———. "Lowry's Allusions to Melville in 'Lunar Caustic.'" *Canadian Literature* No. 94 (Autumn 1982): 180–84.

Hassam, Andrew. "Literary Exploration: The Fictive Sea Journals of William Golding, Robert Nye, B. S. Johnson, and Malcolm Lowry." *Ariel: A Review of International English Literature* 19 (July 1988): 29–46.

Heilman, Robert B. "The Possessed Artist and the Ailing Soul." *Canadian Literature* No. 8 (Spring 1961): 7–16. Reprinted in Woodcock, *Malcolm Lowry: The Man and His Work*, 16–25.

Hensley, Donald M. *Burton Rascoe*. New York: Twayne, 1970.

Hill, Art. "The Alcoholic on Alcoholism." *Canadian Literature* No. 62 (1974): 33–48. Reprinted in Wood, *Malcolm Lowry: The Man and His Critics*, 126–42.

Höfele, Andreas. "Daedalus-Laocoön: Self-Representing in Joyce and Lowry." In *Anglistentag 1989 Würzburg: Proceedings*, edited by Rüdiger Ahrens. Tübingen: Max Niemeyer Verlag, 1990. Pp. 195–206.

"The Insufficient Man." *TLS* No. 2381 (20 September 1947): 478.

Jackson, Charles. *The Lost Weekend*. New York: Farrar and Rinehart, 1944. Reprint, New York: Carroll and Graf, 1983.

Jakobsen, Arnt Lykke. *Introduction and Notes to Malcolm Lowry's "Under the Volcano."* Copenhagen: B. Stougaard Jensen, 1980.

———. "Malcolm Lowry's *Under the Volcano*." In *Papers from the First Nordic Conference for English Studies*, edited by Stig Johansson and Bjorn Tysdahl. Oslo: Institute of English Studies, University of Oslo, 1981. Pp. 83–94.

James, William. *The Varieties of Religious Experience: A Study in Human Nature*. New York: Modern Library, 1936.

Jaspers, Karl. "Nietzsche and the Present." *Partisan Review* 19 (January–February 1952): 19–30.

Jones, G. P. "Malcolm Lowry: Time and the Artist." *University of Toronto Quarterly* 51 (Winter 1981–82): 192–209.

Josipovici, Gabriel. *The World and the Book: A Study of Modern Fiction.* Stanford: Stanford University Press, 1971.

——. *Writing and the Body.* Princeton: Princeton University Press, 1982.

Kearney, Richard. *Transitions: Narratives in Modern Irish Culture.* Manchester: Manchester University Press, 1988.

Kilgallin, Anthony R. "Faust and *Under the Volcano.*" *Canadian Literature* No. 26 (Autumn 1965): 43–54. Reprinted in Woodcock, *Malcolm Lowry: The Man and His Work,* 26–37.

——. "The Long Voyage Home: *October Ferry to Gabriola.*" In Woodcock, *Malcolm Lowry: The Man and His Work,* 78–87. Reprinted in Wood, *Malcolm Lowry: The Writer and His Critics,* 215–26.

Kilgallin, Tony. *Lowry.* Erin, Ont.: Press Porcepic, 1973.

Kim, Suzanne. "The Emergence of an Authorial Figure in the Manuscripts of Lowry's Poetry." In Grace, *Swinging the Maelstrom,* 220–31.

Koestler, Arthur. *The Roots of Coincidence.* New York: Random House, 1972.

Kroetsch, Robert. "*Hear us O Lord* and the Orpheus Occasion." In Grace, *Swinging the Maelstrom,* 249–63.

Kums, Guido. "Dovetailing in Depth: *The Waste Land* and *Under the Volcano.*" *New Comparison* 5 (Summer 1988): 150–61.

Leader, Zachary. *Writer's Block.* Baltimore: Johns Hopkins University Press, 1991.

Linguanti, Elsa. "*Hear us O Lord* and Lowry's Micro/Macro Text." In Grace, *Swinging the Maelstrom,* 209–19.

Lipking, Lawrence. "The Marginal Gloss: Notes and Asides on Poe, Valéry, 'The Ancient Mariner,' the Ordeal of the Margin, *Storiella as She Is Syung,* Versions of Leonardo, and the Plight of Modern Criticism." *Critical Inquiry* 3 (Summer 1977): 609–55.

Lorenz, Clarissa M. *Lorelei Two: My Life with Conrad Aiken.* Athens: University of Georgia Press, 1983.

MacDonald, R. D. "Canada in Lowry's Fiction." *Mosaic* 14 (Spring 1981): 35–53.

Mallon, Thomas. *Stolen Words: Forays into the Origins and Ravages of Plagiarism*. New York: Ticknor and Fields, 1989.

Markson, David. *Malcolm Lowry's "Volcano": Myth, Symbol, Meaning*. New York: Times Books, 1978.

Marlowe, Christopher. *The Tragical History of Doctor Faustus*. In *Eight Famous Elizabethan Plays*, edited by Esther Cloudman Dunn, 1932. Reprint, New York: Modern Library, 1950.

Martinez, Betsy. *"Under the Volcano:* The Opening Sense of Closure." *Malcolm Lowry Review* Nos. 21 & 22 (Fall 1987 & Spring 1988): 141–53.

Maugham, W. Somerset. *Don Fernando, Or Variations on Some Spanish Themes*. Garden City: Doubleday, Doran and Co., 1935.

McCarthy, Patrick A. "The *La Mordida* Drafts and Notes at UBC." *Malcolm Lowry Review* No. 28 (Spring 1991): 6–12.

McLuhan, Marshall. *The Gutenberg Galaxy: The Making of Typographic Man*. Toronto: University of Toronto Press, 1962.

McNeill, Dr. C. G. "Malcolm Lowry Visits the Doctor." In Bowker, *Malcolm Lowry Remembered*, 158–60.

Moore, Brian. "The Albatross of Self." *Spectator* (4 May 1962): 589. Reprinted in Wood, *Malcolm Lowry: The Man and His Critics*, 155–57.

New, William H. "Lowry's Reading: An Introductory Essay." *Canadian Literature* No. 44 (Spring 1970): 5–12. Reprinted in Woodcock, *Malcolm Lowry: The Man and His Work*, 125–32.

———. *Malcolm Lowry*. Toronto: McClelland and Stewart, 1971.

———. "Gabriola: Malcolm Lowry's Floating-Island." *Literary Half-Yearly* 13 (1972): 115–25. Reprinted in Wood, *Malcolm Lowry: The Man and His Critics*, 226–34.

Newton, Norman. "Celestial Machinery: A Study of *Ultramarine*." *Malcolm Lowry Review* No. 25 (Fall 1989): 55–87. (Part 2 of a series.)

Nordgren, Joe. "Malcolm Lowry: The Destructive Search for Self." Ph.D. diss, Florida State University, 1989.

Noxon, Gerald. "In Connection with Malcolm Lowry." *Malcolm Lowry Review* Nos. 17 & 18 (Fall 1985 & Spring 1986): 10–24.

Ong, Walter J. *Orality and Literacy: The Technologizing of the Word*. London: Methuen, 1982.

Ortega y Gasset, José. *Toward a Philosophy of History*. New York: W. W. Norton, 1941.

————. "In Search of Goethe from Within." *Partisan Review* 16 (December 1949): 1163–88. Reprinted in *The Dehumanization of Art and Other Essays on Art, Culture, and Literature*. Princeton: Princeton University Press, 1968. Pp. 129–74.

Ouspensky, P. D. *Tertium Organum: The Third Canon of Thought. A Key to the Enigmas of the World*, translated by Nicholas Bessaraboff and Claude Bragdon. New York: Alfred A. Knopf, 1923.

Pagnoulle, Christine. *Malcolm Lowry: Voyage au fond de nos abîmes*. Lausanne: Editions L'Age d'Homme, 1977.

Paz, Octavio. *The Labyrinth of Solitude*, translated by Lysander Kemp. In *The Labyrinth of Solitude, The Other Mexico, and Other Essays*. New York: Grove Press, 1985.

Praz, Mario. *The Romantic Agony*, translated by Angus Davidson, 2nd ed. Cleveland: World Publishing, 1956.

Rankin, Elizabeth D. "Beyond Autobiography: Art and Life in Malcolm Lowry's *Ultramarine*." *Studies in Canadian Literature* 6 (1981): 53–64.

————. "Writer as Metaphor in Malcolm Lowry's *Dark as the Grave*." *Twentieth Century Literature* 28 (Fall 1982): 319–34.

————. "Malcolm Lowry's Comic Vision: 'Elephant and Colosseum.'" *Canadian Literature* No. 101 (Summer 1984): 167–71.

Rascoe, Burton. "What Is Love?" In *The Second American Caravan: A Yearbook of American Literature*, edited by Alfred Kreymborg, Lewis Mumford, and Paul Rosenfeld. New York: Macaulay, 1928.

————. *Titans of Literature: From Homer to the Present*. New York: G. P. Putnam's Sons, 1932.

————. *Before I Forget*. Garden City: Doubleday, Doran and Co., 1937.

Rasporich, Beverly. "The Right Side of Despair: Lowry's Comic Spirit in *Lunar Caustic* and *Dark as the Grave Wherein My Friend is Laid*." *Mosaic* 10 (Summer 1977): 55–67.

Saalmann, Dieter. "The Role of Determinism in Malcolm Lowry's Response to Thomas Mann's *Mario and the Magician*." *Malcolm Lowry Review* No. 25 (Fall 1989): 42–54.

Schaeffer, Pierre. "Notes on Dialogism and the Treatment of Time in *Under the Volcano.*" *Recherches Anglaises et Nord-Américaines* No. 21 (1988): 85–95.

Schneider, Michel. *Voleurs de mots: Essai sur le plagiat, la psychanalyse et la pensée.* Paris: Gallimard, 1985.

Shaffer, Brian W. " 'Civilization' under Western Eyes: Lowry's *Under the Volcano* as a Reading of Conrad's *Heart of Darkness.*" *Conradiana* 22 (Summer 1990): 143–56.

Shaw, Peter. "Plagiary." *American Scholar* 51 (Summer 1982): 325–37.

Shelley, Percy Bysshe. *Shelley's Poetry and Prose,* edited by Donald H. Reiman and Sharon B. Powers. New York: W. W. Norton, 1977.

Sidney, Sir Philip. *The Defense of Poesy,* edited by Lewis Soens. Lincoln: University of Nebraska Press, 1970.

Smith, Anne, ed. *The Art of Malcolm Lowry.* London: Vision Press, 1978.

Sontag, Susan. *Against Interpretation and Other Essays.* New York: Dell, 1981.

Spender, Stephen. "Introduction" to *Under the Volcano.* Philadelphia: J. B. Lippincott, 1965; New York: New American Library, 1971.

Sugars, Cynthia. "The Road to Renewal: *Dark as the Grave* and the Rite of Initiation." In Grace, *Swinging the Maelstrom,* 149–62.

Taylor, Charles. *Sources of the Self: The Making of the Modern Identity.* Cambridge: Harvard University Press, 1989.

Thomas, Mark Ellis. "Under the Shadow of the *Volcano:* Malcolm Lowry's Poetry." In Grace, *Swinging the Maelstrom,* 232–39.

Tiessen, Paul G. "Malcolm Lowry and the Cinema." *Canadian Literature* No. 44 (Spring 1970): 38–49. Reprinted in Woodcock, *Malcolm Lowry: The Man and His Work,* 133–43.

———, ed. *Apparently Incongruous Parts: The Worlds of Malcolm Lowry.* Metuchen, N.J.: Scarecrow Press, 1990.

Tifft, Stephen. "Tragedy as a Meditation on Itself: Reflexiveness in *Under the Volcano.*" In Smith, *The Art of Malcolm Lowry,* 46–71.

Vice, Sue. "The *Volcano* of a Postmodern Lowry." In Grace, *Swinging the Maelstrom,* 123–35.

———, ed. *Malcolm Lowry Eighty Years On.* New York: St. Martin's Press, 1989.

Vice, Susan. "Self-Consciousness in the Work of Malcolm Lowry:

An Examination of Narrative Voice." Ph.D. diss., Oxford University, 1988.

Wainwright, J. A. "The Book 'Being Written': Art and Life in *Dark as the Grave Wherein My Friend Is Laid.*" *Dalhousie Review* 59 (Spring 1979): 82–104.

Walker, Ronald G. " 'The Weight of the Past': Toward a Chronology of *Under the Volcano.*" *Malcolm Lowry Newsletter* No. 9 (Fall 1981): 3–23. Reprinted in Tiessen, *Apparently Incongruous Parts*, 55–70.

Walker, Ronald G., and Leigh Holt. "The Pattern of Faustian Despair: Marlowe's Hero and *Under the Volcano.*" *Malcolm Lowry Review* No. 16 (Spring 1985): 53–77. Reprinted in Tiessen, *Apparently Incongruous Parts*, 110–28.

Williams, Mark. "Muscular Aesthete: Malcolm Lowry and 1930s English Literary Culture." *Journal of Commonwealth Literature* 24 (1989): 65–87.

Wood, Barry. "The Edge of Eternity: Lowry's 'Forest Path to the Spring.' " *Canadian Literature* No. 70 (Autumn 1970): 51–58. Reprinted in Wood, *Malcolm Lowry: The Writer and His Critics*, 185–93.

———. "Malcolm Lowry's Metafiction: The Biography of a Genre." *Contemporary Literature* 19 (Winter 1978): 1–25. [References are to the original essay in *Contemporary Literature* rather than to the revised version in Wood's *Malcolm Lowry: The Writer and His Critics*, which is marred by numerous typographical errors.]

———, ed. *Malcolm Lowry: The Writer and His Critics.* Ottawa: Tecumsah Press, 1980.

Woodcock, George. "Art as the Writer's Mirror: Literary Solipsism in *Dark as the Grave.*" In Woodcock, *Malcolm Lowry: The Man and His Work*, 66–70.

———, ed. *Malcolm Lowry: The Man and His Work.* Vancouver: University of British Columbia Press, 1971.

Yeats, William Butler. *A Vision.* 1937. Reprint, New York: Collier Books, 1966.

Index